BIRNBAUM'S GLOBAL GUIDE TO WINNING THE GREAT GARMENT WAR

Third Horizon Press Ltd
7th Floor, Manulife Tower
169 Electric Road, Hong Kong

First Published March 2000

ISBN: 962-85878-1-1

Previous Titles

Importing Garments through Hong Kong
A Guide to the Perplexed

Birnbaum's Directory of Garment Factories and Agents
Hong Kong & South China

Forthcoming Titles

The Factory in the Twenty-first Century
Studies in Indirect Cost Analysis

Corruption
Studies in Macro Cost Analysis

BIRNBAUM'S GLOBAL GUIDE
TO WINNING
THE GREAT GARMENT WAR

David Birnbaum

Third Horizon Press
Hong Kong

ACKNOWLEDGMENTS

This book is the result of three years of research and conclusions based on a great number of projects carried out by Third Horizon for various clients in Asia, Latin America and the United States. Well over 100 persons located in fifteen countries have contributed the data on which this book is based. These are but a few of the people and projects who have made this book possible.

My special thanks to Ms. Josephine Bow who managed a three-year project gathering detailed information from over 10,000 garment factories and textile mills in fourteen countries. Her concentration and efforts have resulted in the largest and most complete database ever assembled in our industry. It is a unique accomplishment. Ms. Bow also edited and proofread this book.

I want to thank Ms. Jasmine Wibisono of the Indonesian Data Center who retained Third Horizon in 1996 and 1997, on behalf of the Bank of Central Asia, to carry out an exhaustive analysis of the Indonesian textile and garment industries which allowed us to examine in detail and from the inside an industry and government in a state of terminal crisis.

I want to thank Mr. Kenneth B. Clark and his colleagues at Fenwick and West who retained Third Horizon as experts in the field of transfer pricing. Their input and rigorous pursuit of detail gave us a better understanding of the problems and costs of conflicts between the governments of importing countries and companies in exporting countries.

I want to thank Mr. Frank Ying of Merrison Garment Co., Ltd., Hong Kong, and Mr. Adolfo Peniche of Merida, Yucatan State, Mexico, joint-venture partners in the first high-quality factory producing designer garments in Mexico. Much of this book is the result of what I personally learned setting up your factory.

Finally, I thank my family and friends who have put up with me during the past three years.

For Sylvia Daniels

Who supported me despite her fears.

A son can never repay the debt to his mother,

but at least this may give you a little *nachas*.

Our Company

Third Horizon Ltd. was founded in 1986 by a small group of Asian-based consultants specialized in textile and garment manufacturing. We joined together because we felt there was a serious absence of experienced and educated professionals competent to deal with the rapidly growing Asian industry. In its early stages, the company specialized in sourcing product, setting up buying offices, building factories, and assisting mills and apparel companies to reorganize to meet new challenges. At that time our clients were all garment and textile companies based in Asia.

In 1993, the company expanded its work to include research and analysis studies and created an affiliated company, Third Horizon Press Ltd., to carry out this work. Clients from outside the textile and garment industries, including major banking, accountancy, legal and consultancy firms, were added to our existing customer base. In recent years, Third Horizon has also acted as specialist advisor to several national governments investigating textile and garment industry-related problems.

Third Horizon Press Ltd. also publishes specialist papers and books for garment and textile professionals. Because of the massive amounts of sometimes complex data required for our work, the company has expanded to include its own computer-programming capabilities. Today we are able to provide our clients with sophisticated database engines geared to the specific needs of our industries.

Since 1997, the company's reach continues to lengthen. Although our client base still remains predominantly Asian, a growing part of our work now takes place in Europe and North America. As the quality of our work becomes known, we hope to add more American clients. In this regard, the company is currently involved in our first Latin-American project., a 300-machine factory located in Campeche State, Mexico for the production of high-quality ladies' lined jackets and bottoms. Phase I is scheduled to open in January 2000. Clients: Hong Kong Chinese factory group (with Mexican partners).

In spite of our growing global network, Third Horizon and Third Horizon Press remain small boutique companies concentrating solely on textile and garment manufacturing. While we are unable to assist in product design, marketing or retailing, nor do we have any intention of expanding into those areas, we believe that in our focused domain, we are one of the most innovative and competent companies anywhere in the world today.

For further information, please contact us at the following numbers:
Fax: 39.055.5978129   Fax: 852.25666401
e-mail: 113165.106@compuserve.com   e-mail: salina.cheng@ansbacher.com.hk

TABLE OF CONTENTS

Table of Contents

CHAPTER 4

CHAPTER 5

CHAPTER 6

Table of Contents

...It's a war out there. People are dropping like flies...

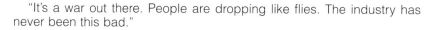

"It's a war out there. People are dropping like flies. The industry has never been this bad."

For as long as I can remember, garment people have been meeting one another on New York's Seventh Avenue, at California Mart in Los Angeles, or on the streets of Hong Kong's Tsim Sha Tsui district with the same greeting: "The garment business has never been this bad."

The garment industry has never been an easy place to make a dollar, but until recently, statements of imminent catastrophe were actually forms of reverse bragging. What people were really saying was: "My business is not doing all that well, but when compared to everybody else who is about to go into Chapter 11, I am a real success."

Today's garment industry has fundamentally and radically changed. This is in fact the worst year in its entire century-long history and next year will not be better. Importers, factories and retailers are all in trouble. There are simply too many people chasing too few customers.

For the past five years, consumers throughout the industrialized world have been spending less and less on clothing. This may be due to the rise of casual sportswear and dressing down work trends, or other major changes in consumer buying habits. Whatever the reason, the fact remains that the market is shrinking and will continue to do so for the foreseeable future.

At the same time, mass-market retailers such as Wal-Mart and Kmart have been rapidly expanding both domestically and overseas in an effort to grab ever greater market shares. Chains and department stores continue to add outlets. Even once disappearing specialty stores appear to be reviving. The glut of retail space has led to the 'perpetual sale', whereby goods put on the floor on Monday are frequently marked down on the same Monday.

The number of suppliers is rising geometrically. Virtually every developing nation looks at garmentmaking as a first step in building an export-based industrial economy. Factories in the more developed Asian countries, rather than lose their customers to the newest low-labor-cost areas, have rushed to open overseas branch factories. While in the past Korean, Taiwanese and Hong Kong factories limited their expansion to China, these same companies now operate branches located anywhere from Vietnam to the Dominican Republic. The rise of the great trading blocs—NAFTA and the EU—have dramatically altered garment sourcing chains. In five years, Mexico has emerged from nowhere to become the world's largest garment exporter to the United States. In 1998, Mexican garment exports to the U.S. exceeded the combined total of Hong Kong and China.

Factories are now willing to accept orders from legitimate customers at prices below cost just to keep their machines operating, while importers, already working on reduced markups, are giving stores markdown money, advertising money, and under-the-table money just to keep their customers. The stores themselves are doing just as badly. With the notable exception of Wal-Mart and The Gap, most major retailers are reporting diminishing garment sales with every successive quarter.

The entire industry is at war and not many survivors are expected. The great shakeout is coming. The only question is: Will you be among the winners?

Whether direct retail or import buyers, factory producers or entire national garment-export industries, the winners will be those able to provide merchandise at the lowest cost. We no longer have the luxury for error or sloppy work. Quality, delivery and price are now all matters of cost.

This book is about costs. It gives you the ultimate super-weapon—Full Value Cost Analysis—that you will need if you are to be a winner.

It is The Global Guide to Winning the Great Garment War.

INTRODUCTION

This book is a tool for buying and producing at the lowest cost. The tool is Full Value Cost Analysis (FVCA). As with any tool, you have to read the operating instructions before turning on the power.

The operating instructions for FVCA are very simple. There is only one instruction: Forget everything you ever thought you knew about garment costings. You and I, brought up in the very bowels of the international garment industry, have for years accepted certain unshakeable 'laws' of product costs. Dredge them up and throw them up.

Unshakeable Law #1: The lowest cost garments come from places with the lowest wage rates.

There exists no direct correlation between labor rates and manufacturing costs. I realize that to tell you, a professional international garment-sourcing specialist, that cheap labor does not equal cheap garments is like telling the pope that Jesus was not crucified, but pushed in front of an oncoming subway train.

However, look at this.

Case Study I—The Sri Lankan Sewer

An A-class sewer in Sri Lanka is paid $2.00 per day. An assembly line will produce about 18 shirts per day per machine, incurring a sewing cost of $0.11 per unit. The other operations, such as cutting, buttonholemaking and pressing, add a further $0.06. Total direct labor cost will therefore be less than $0.20 per shirt. Unless the importer requires Tiffany cufflinks for buttons, the total trim including packing materials will probably be under $0.25. Total of labor and trim should, therefore, be $0.45.

However, the average manufacturing or cut-make-trim (CMT) charge for a shirt in Sri Lanka is $2.10 or over four times the labor and trim cost, and about ten times the direct-labor cost. (By the way, direct labor is less than 4% of the probable $5.00/shirt FOB price).

What happened to the other $1.65?

I will return to this mystery later on. For the present, it is enough to say that the unaccounted for money does not wind up in the factory's pocket. The fact is that for most Third World factories, wage rates are not the most important component of total manufacturing costs.

If you think about it rationally, the conclusion seems almost obvious. Low labor rates do not determine garment cost. If they did, we would all be working in Somalia, North Korea, New Guinea, Cambodia, or any of the other twenty-plus countries where wage rates are six cents an hour or less. Few importers work in the truly low-cost-labor areas simply because the final costs of the products made in these countries are too high.

Unshakeable Law #2: The lowest FOB cost comes from factories with the lowest manufacturing (CMT) costs.

There exists no direct relationship between CMT and FOB costs. I know this is a little hard to swallow. It was for me. Like you, I was taught that the whole purpose of traveling to the ends of the earth to make a five-pocket jeans was to take advantage of cheap manufacturing costs. Yet the figures simply do not support this premise; in fact, sometimes they prove that the entire effort may almost be a waste of time.

Consider this example.

Case Study II—Five-Pocket Jeans

A sewer in South Korea is paid $7.50 per hour. Her counterpart in Indonesia is paid $0.20. The wage difference is 37.5 times. However, the difference in the FOB price between a 501 jeans made in Indonesia and the same jeans made in South Korea is only 15%.

The answer lies in the basic cost breakdown. The FOB price of five-pocket jeans works out to 70% for the denim fabric and 30% for everything else. This 30% has to include not only labor but trim, overhead, profit as well as quota. How much can be saved in this 30%?

If CMT in Indonesia were zero, your total maximum savings would be 30%.

But consider that overheads are at least the same in poor countries as in rich countries. In fact, telephone and electricity costs less in Seoul than in Jakarta. In a developing country, overhead can equal anywhere from 100% to 400% of direct labor. Quota costs depend on the size of the country's quota allocation, not on the state of its development. Trim costs are usually lower in developed countries than in the Third World. In the end, the only cost advantage is labor—ultimately a minor component of total FOB price. In this case, a labor cost advantage of 3750% translates into an FOB savings of merely 15%.

Unshakeable Law #3: The lowest FOB cost results in lowest actual product cost.

There exists no relationship between FOB or landed-duty-paid (LDP) costs and the actual cost of the product. I realize this is difficult to accept. I appear to be saying that costs are not costs. In fact, the real problem is that many—if not most—of the factors that determine costs are not even included in professional buyers' cost calculations. Yet all importers do use these hidden costs to make their decisions.

Here is just one example of an important cost not included in the cost sheet.

Case Study III—The One-Hundred-Twenty-Thousand-Dollar Skirt

You are a moderate-sized importer of ladies' sportswear. You have found a mill in northern China that produces beautiful wool plaid fabric at $4.00 per yard, 58 inches wide, in any pattern. The FOB price of the skirt would be under $7.00, quota included. This would be a truly great price except for two small problems—the mill has a minimum of 10,000 yards per colorway and it will provide no salesman sample fabric.

You know the styles will sell, but you must have salesman samples to sell them. Assuming that you need three colorways for your skirts, you have to commit for 30,000 yards of fabric in order to have fabric for salesman samples. Are you willing to bet $120,000? Because that is the up-front cost.

This is your dilemma. The FOB cost may be very low, but the cost of failure is very high. Do you want to take the risk? As a professional, in the end you must balance your faith in your own judgment against the facts. If the risk works out in your favor, you are a hero for about thirty minutes. If the risk does not work out, you will have to look at those racks of unsold skirts every day for five months, or however long it takes you to bite the bullet and get rid of them for less 75%.

The gamble might seem appealing, but in the end the $120,000 is too high a price to pay for a skirt. Also, don't forget this skirt is only one style of about 75 in your forthcoming line.

Most garment professionals can work out that in the case of the Sri Lankan factory, direct labor counts for only 10% of CMT. These same professionals know that as in the case of the five-pocket jeans, total CMT in a Third World factory seldom exceeds 30% of the FOB price. That means the total cost of direct labor in these factories is a negligible 3% to 4% of FOB, which in turn works out to 2% of the LDP price or about 0.75% of the retail price.

Yet despite these ratios, I and almost every other garment professional around still looks at direct labor as the prime factor in determining total garment cost. Take, for example, a senior executive for one of the world's largest manufacturers of active sportswear and footwear in April 1997 commenting on a 10.7% pay rise recently won by their Indonesian factory workers, who stated, "Indonesia could be reaching a point where it is pricing itself out of the market." [1]

At that time, an Indonesian line worker was paid about $1.80 for a ten-hour day. A 10.7% wage increase equals 1.9 cents per hour—adding a cost of a little more than a nickel on each pair of shoes retailing for about $100, or about 0.06% of its retail price. This is an amount so small that it is not even worth including in the costing. Yet the American company spokesperson stated that the problem of rising wages was so serious as to cause the company to consider relocating its production.

Decisions like this are not only illogical, they are insane—especially coming from one of the smartest management teams in the entire industry. A better solution would be to fire the man who made the statement and use his $250,000 salary to pay the wage increase. This way the buyer could increase the direct wages of 4500 workers by 10.7% and still come out saving money.

PART I

The old myths no longer work. It is past time for the entire subject of product costings to be rethought.

To be of value, the idea of costs has to be extended to incorporate all parameters for factory selection. Traditionally, importers have used three criteria for selecting producers: price, delivery, quality. The selection process involves a trade-off. Typically, you the importer can have higher quality only if you are willing to accept a higher cost, or alternatively, you could have higher quality at the same cost if you are willing to accept later delivery. It is an axiom of our industry that you cannot have the highest quality with the fastest delivery at the lowest cost. However, costs—if they are to reflect anything of value—must reduce all the determinants of factory selection to dollars and cents. Quality thus becomes a cost and so too does delivery. The problem is that what we have all been calling product costs is in fact only a small part of total costs.

Let's say you have a bag of money to pay for a 1,000-dozen jeans. That bag is labeled 'product cost'. Since the only source of income to your company is the garments you sell, all company costs are product costs. To go a step further, the bag of money can be divided between manufacturing and nonmanufacturing costs. Every step that brings physical change to those 1,000-dozen jeans—from the first designer sketch to the final pressing of the last garment in the stock order—is part of the manufacturing process. All expenses related to manufacturing are also manufacturing costs. The other expenses—such as freight, duty, your showroom and office rent, your bookkeeper's salary and your salesmen's commissions—are also product costs, but they are not manufacturing costs.

Take out all the money for the duty, the freight, the quota charge, the salesman and everything else that does not actually physically change the garment. What you have left are the manufacturing costs.

Now divide the manufacturing costs into the actual material and making charges, the direct costs; and the other, indirect costs. Your patternmaker, sample hands, the designer, the trips to Asia to correct the collection—these are all indirect costs. Take that money out.

Now look down at the bottom of the bag. What you see left is the few dollars that are the direct costs, which for the past twenty years you have been incorrectly calling *product costs*. That little bit of money is not the product costs. Most of the product costs is the money you have already taken out of the bag, which, by the way, you have not included in your costing sheet.

This book puts all the money back in the bag and sets out a system called *Full Value Cost Analysis*. FVCA takes every relevant factor in the sourcing process and includes them in the costing.

Part I

Full Value Cost Analysis presents a series of related questions and answers:

How can you as an importer buy at the lowest cost?

How can you as a factory produce at the lowest cost?

How can you as a government play a positive role to develop an industry that will compete because it operates at the lowest cost?

These are the subjects of this book.

Chapter 1
Full Value Cost Analysis

Garment importing is the only business where you can buy for one dollar, sell for two dollars, and go bankrupt in the process.

Herbie the Mouth
Notes from his lectures at the Harvard
Business School (never presented)

Every garment importer does a costing for each style. Some scribble it on the backs of envelopes, which they lose within the next hour, and call that their costing. Others use formulas so complicated that it is totally impossible to derive any information at all from their efforts.

In truth, few garment importers know why they do costings in the first place, and almost none include the important cost factors.

Take a look at one of your own costings. I am sure you have included material costs and CMT (the making cost—literally cut, make, and trim). You almost certainly have insurance, quota, freight and duty. However, have you included the cost of the samples the vendor did not make and that you had to supply from your own sample department? Did you include the cost of patternmaking and possibly grading that you did in New York? These are costs, and the fact that the vendor did not do this work adds to the cost of the garment.

Most likely, you have added a fixed amount or percentage to every style to cover the trips to Asia, Eastern Europe or Central America; after all, working in the Third World requires more personal follow-up. But have you included the cost of the styles from last season that were not shipped at all, or shipped late, or shipped with incorrect specs? These little mishaps cost you money—money that has to come out of future garments purchased from that area or from that vendor.

If you have not included all the 'costs' in your costings, it may be that you do not understand what costs are. Most importers still confuse costs with price. The price is the bottom line; the costs are the factors that make up the price.

Your supplier, whether agent or factory, takes his costs, adds them up, includes something for overhead and profit, and then will try to present you with a price. That price tells you nothing. If you allow your supplier to deal with you on a bottom-line price basis, it is time to change your profession because you will not last long in this one. A price is simply a number. The list of costs which went into that price is a tool—perhaps the most important tool the professional importer can have.

...the last of the big spenders...

Costings are tools of comparison between one time period and another, one vendor and another, or one place and another.

- What is the difference in cost between this style and a similar one last season from the same vendor?

- What is the difference in cost between this factory and that factory in the same country, or between working with a factory and an agent in the same country?

- What is the difference between producing in this country or in the other country?

The items that make up a costing must all be quantifiable:

"I get a heart attack every time I have to work in western China" has no place in a costing. Your discomfort or the inability to find a decent place to eat or even sleep cannot be reduced to dollars and cents.

However, "I *got* a heart attack working in western China" definitely is a cost factor. Your medical bills, the time lost from work, all those stupid mistakes that were made in your absence—these are all additional costs. They must be added to next season's costings. As a result, either you cannot afford to work in western China or, conversely, you have to do so much work in western China that the unit cost of your heart attack becomes sufficiently small enough that you can still save money, even though you may die in the process.

Costings must compare only like with like:

You can compare a pair of five-pocket jeans made in Indonesia with a pair made in western China, but you cannot compare five-pocket jeans with a pair of worsted flannel pants.

To be of any value, costings must be complete.

From the designer's first sketch to the arrival of your stock order in your warehouse, perhaps a hundred separate events must take place—each necessary to produce the garment. Somebody is paying for each event. If you have to pay, the item appears in your costing. If the factory includes that cost in its FOB price, the event still took place and you must still allow for that event in your costing—if only to show a cost reduction. The factory has saved you money; another factory which does not provide that service has a higher cost than the full-service factory.

Each item in the costing must relate either to the garment (direct costs), the vendor (indirect costs), or the exporting country (macro costs).

If you do business in Hong Kong, you must travel to Hong Kong. The cost of that travel must be included in the costing of every garment purchased from Hong Kong. On the other hand, it is not necessary to travel first-class, rent the Marco Polo suite at the Peninsula Hotel, or eat at Gaddi's each night. These costs are personal. You incur them, not because you are in Hong Kong, but rather because you are the last of the big spenders. These excess expenses have no more place in a garment costing than the costs of the 22-year-old playmate whom you shared your time with in Hong Kong, or the string of South Sea Island pearls you bought for your wife to assuage your conscience.

Just as some factories provide better facilities and services than others, so do countries. Some countries cost more to work in than other countries, which must also be included in the costing. Anyone with experience working in Pakistan or Nigeria knows about high country costs. Those bribes you had to pay to survive one more day must be included in the cost of the garment.

Full Value Cost Analysis (FVCA) translates delivery, price and quality—as well as everything else—into dollar-and-cent costs. Everyone knows there is a cost to late shipment or poor quality. If goods arrive late, your orders are canceled. If the quality is terrible, the customer returns the goods. Until now, these were not considered costs—they were penalties. To be of value, penalties must be reduced to costs. In FVCA, everything becomes a part of costs.

You can have fast shipment—you can airfreight your stock if you are willing to pay the added cost. That cost is quantifiable. Likewise, higher quality has its own cost. To define that cost you must not only define the factory but the buyer as well.

Finally, to fully understand FVCA you will be required to temporarily drop all your prejudices. For example, every importer from the early Pleistocene era when garment people first learned to walk erect to the present time, has insisted that the first and most important cost they consider is FOB price and, more specifically, labor rates. The less money paid to workers, the cheaper the garment. This is simply wrong. In actuality, FOB price should be the last consideration and labor rates are probably the least important cost factor of all.

With this in mind, here is how FVCA works. There are three types of cost factors: *macro costs*, relating to the country in which the products are made; *indirect costs*, relating to the mills, factories and agents making the goods; and *direct costs*, relating to the goods themselves.

MACRO COSTS

The first consideration is the country from which the garments are to be produced and exported. Each country has its own costs. In some cases, these country costs are so high that neither indirect-cost savings nor direct-cost savings are sufficient to make the product competitive. In fact, no one works in the cheapest labor-cost countries, which is precisely why labor costs in those countries stay so cheap. In North Korea, a sewer is paid perhaps $50 per year. Are you running? How would you like to put in a claim for late delivery with Mr. Kim Jong II, the Beloved Leader? Workers in Angola, Burundi, the Democratic Republic of Congo and Rwanda are paid about six cents an hour. Do you want to do your T-shirts in the middle of a civil war?

What about the second-line disaster countries? At eight cents an hour you can work in Burma and university students throughout the United States will picket the stores that sell your label.

Many importers do not consider these macro costs until it is too late. Sadly, those who assume that one country is much like another and that cheap labor equals cheap prices do not survive long in our industry.

Case Study IV—Garmentmaking in the Garden of Eden

You have discovered the ultimate Third World-producing area. The labor cost is zero. That's right—sewers work just for the pleasure that making your beautiful styles brings them. Furthermore, there are no quotas.

You rush to ship your fabric and your patterns before your competitors find out and ruin this Garden of Eden. You even send in specialty machines to ensure that the factory can make the goods. And there lies the seed of the problem.

Local import regulations do not allow the importation of machinery without a license. In the interim, until this small matter can be worked out, your container with the fabric and the patterns must be impounded, purely as an administrative procedure.

Fortunately, the owner of your factory is related to the head of customs who, for a small honorarium, will issue an import license retroactively the minute after he returns to the capital next week. It is regrettable that his schedule cannot be disturbed, but as you must understand, the head of customs is a most important person. However, this is not so terrible. Certainly you have allowed an extra seven days in your schedule.

In any case, a week goes by; the head of customs returns. You give him his honorarium; he prepares the import license. HOLD IT. Nobody mentioned that the imported machinery was of Japanese origin. How could you be so silly? Have you no regard for local sensibilities? Japanese equipment. Terrible.

You offer a compromise. "Let us take this offensive Japanese machinery and throw it in the ocean." This would have worked if only they had known that the machinery was Japanese *before* you so precipitously insisted on applying for the license. Then the machinery could have been made to disappear. Now it is too late. To throw away the Japanese equipment would offend the Japanese. You do not want to start an international incident over your little garment order.

Fortunately, there is a solution. The head of customs, the cousin of the boss of your factory, is related by marriage to the minister of education who, for a small payment, will take the machine as a

5

teaching tool for the new polytechnic school. Since teaching tools are exempt from machinery import licenses, the importation can take place at once—that is, the moment the polytechnic committee meets to approve the acceptance of your fine gift—certainly, not later than 30 days.

A month is not so terrible. You can make back at least part of the time. Finally, after two further delays, the committee meets. You provide one payment, plus five honoraria (after all, the committee members have to eat also). The gift is approved, and the head of customs can release your container with the fabric and the .... HOLD IT. Nobody mentioned ....

Is the story true? Those who have never had this experience will claim I am exaggerating. Those of us who have visited the Garden of Eden and who have tried to work there will look at this story as a model of understatement.

The Garden of Eden is not the exception. All countries have macro costs. Obviously, the country costs of working in Albania are much higher than the costs of working in Italy. But as any professional who has experienced working in Bari will tell you, Italy also has its country costs. Every country has macro costs, and these costs are, in fact, the single most important factor determining where it is cheapest for you to work.

The relative importance of macro costs over direct costs can be seen by looking at a list of the top ten textile and garment-exporting countries in the world. Nine have high direct costs but low macro costs.

LEADING TEXTILE AND GARMENT EXPORTERS 1995								
	TEXTILES		GARMENTS		TOTAL		WAGE RATE	
COUNTRY	$BIL	RANK	$BIL	RANK	$BIL	RANK	$/HR	RANK
China	13.92	2	24.05	1	37.97	1	0.34	10
Hong Kong	13.81	3	21.30	2	35.11	2	4.90	9
Italy	12.67	4	11.76	3	24.43	3	16.65	3
Germany	14.20	1	7.38	4	21.58	4	21.95	2
S. Korea	12.31	5	4.96	8	17.27	5	7.65	7
Taiwan	11.91	6	3.26	N/A	15.17	6	6.38	8
U.S.	7.37	9	6.65	5	14.02	7	12.26	5
France	7.47	8	5.62	7	13.09	8	16.45	4
Bel/Lux	7.76	7	2.56	N/A	10.32	9	25.00	1
U.K.	5.16	N/A	4.65	9	9.81	10	11.71	6

Of the ten largest textile and garment exporters, six have wages averaging between $11.70 and $25.00 per hour. Three have wages averaging between $4.90 and $7.65 per hour. Only one—China—can really be considered a low-wage country. Even here it is important to note that over 90% of Chinese garment exports come from the eastern or southern provinces where wages are the highest in the country.

Each country has its own specific cost factors completely apart from what it produces, the quality standards of its factories, or what local workers are paid. Just as macro costs in some countries can be exceptionally high, macro costs in other countries can be remarkably low. For example, shipments to the United States from Western Europe require no quota. Shipments from Mexico to the United States require no quota and are duty-free. The U.S. duty rate for garments averages 18%, while quota costs may equal 50% or more of total FOB costs. As a result, a shirt exported from China must have an FOB price 41% below the same shirt exported from Mexico, just to compensate for duty and quota. You also have to add freight costs and time. The Chinese-made shirt must be shipped by sea and can require anywhere from 30 to 45 days for freight and clearance. The Mexican shirt travels by truck and can be at any designated location in the United States within six days.

Countries like France and Germany with their solid infrastructures, stable governments and rational legal systems offer real cost advantages. On the other hand, buyers working in countries like Pakistan, Indonesia and Bangladesh where these assets do not exist have to accept higher costs. Lack of infrastructure, poor communications, bureaucratic inefficiency and corruption all add to garment cost. As a general rule, the less developed the country, the higher its macro costs. Industrialized countries have developed infrastructure, good communication and an educated population, all of which reduce macro costs. Likewise, the poorer countries tend to have more authoritarian governments, less developed commercial law and greater corruption, all of which raise macro costs.

INDIRECT COSTS

If the first and most important decision made by the importer is in which country to make the goods, the second decision is in what type of factory. The factory selected must be able to perform the tasks required by the customer.

These tasks include much more than cutting fabric and sewing panels. In a sense, the actual making is the least of the work. To manufacture a garment, over 86 separate steps are required *before* the factory can begin to cut the stock order. Someone has to make spec sheets and patterns. Then samples have to be approved. Lab dips or strikeoffs must be produced and approved. Someone has to locate, order and approve the zipper, thread and every one of the 15-25 different trim items required to produce each style.

Each of these 86 steps is a necessary element in the manufacturing process which someone must carry out if a stock order is to be produced. That someone can be either the customer or the factory. To the degree the *factory* carries out these tasks, the 'indirect costs' of this work are included in the price of the product. To the degree the *customer* carries out these tasks, the indirect costs are part of the customer's overheads. Furthermore, as anyone who runs a sample department in New York will tell you, it is cheaper to do preproduction work at the factory, provided the factory has the facilities required to carry out the tasks.

In addition, the work required by the customer includes much more than preproduction. Quality levels and standards, minimums, and production lead times are all part of indirect costs. So are worker skills, working conditions and credit facilities.

There are factories whose indirect costs are so high that even if their direct costs were zero, they would remain too expensive. In fact, there are factories whose services are so inadequate that they are only half-factories. We usually expect to find half-factories off the beaten track, somewhere in the high Himalayas or the depths of the Congo River. Sometimes, however, the half-factory still survives nearer to home.

It is widely believed that factories in industrialized countries provide greater facilities and therefore offer lower indirect costs than factories in the Third World. This is true only if you include parts of New York and Los Angeles in the Third World. Here small workshops taken straight off the streets of modern Pakistan still co-exist with other small workshops transferred directly from a nineteenth-century Polish *stetl*.

Any garment manufacturer who has ever worked with a Brooklyn contractor has learned more about operating in the Third World than the World Bank and the International Monetary Fund combined. Let's meet Louie the Lip, a typical New York specimen.

Case Study V—Louie's Last Factory

"I don't do plackets. I make the greatest T-shirts in the world, but I don't do plackets. You want plackets, you should go to China. In China they do plackets. In China they pay a sewer one bag of rice a year, but there they do plackets.

"I don't do plackets. You see a placket-making machine here? Do you want to know why there is no placket-making machine here? I'll tell you why there is no placket-making machine here. I'll tell you in one word—unions. You want plackets, you should go to Malaysia. In Malaysia if a union organizer shows up, they hang him by his thumbs, cut his head off, then they deport him. In Malaysia they have no unions, but they have plenty of plackets.

"You don't understand English good. I told you I don't do plackets. You think these lazy so-and-sos sitting here can do plackets? You should live so long. You want plackets, you should go to Turkey. In Turkey they got real workers. In Turkey they have discipline. In Turkey the worker sits at the machine fourteen hours a day—a half-hour for lunch and fifteen minutes in the afternoon to go to the toilet. The rest is work. In the United States, what do people know from work? You want plackets, go to Turkey.

"Slave wages in Asia, the unions, lazy American workers—that's why I don't do plackets.

Louie the Lip exists. He may be a stereotype, but he is not a caricature.

As a general rule, the higher the standard of the customer, the more important are indirect costs. Mass-market retailers and importers have lower requirements than importers of better goods. At the same time, they are in a position to provide for themselves what little facilities they may require. As a result, they are not interested in any facilities a factory may have. To mass-market importers only direct costs are important; they will go anywhere to save ten cents on labor.

But to any customer whose standards are above those of Kmart, indirect costs are a crucial consideration. The higher the quality standard or the more fashion-oriented, the more important become the facilities offered by the factory and the indirect-cost savings they provide. To these customers, indirect costs are more important than direct costs.

Just as the mass-market importer cannot afford the high cost of working in a factory producing designer goods, so, too, the designer label cannot work in a mass-market factory because the costs of working in a mass-market factory are too high for the designer-label customer.

Case Study VI—Kmart vs. Armani Jeans

You are the jeans buyer at Kmart.

You locate the factory that makes jeans for Giorgio Armani. The quality is truly superb. However, the CMT is $1.50 higher than at your own maker. As the Kmart customer does not require the higher quality, the cost of jeans at that factory is too high by $1.50.

Now you are Giorgio Armani. You locate the factory that makes jeans for Kmart. The quality is not quite Armani standard, but the CMT is $1.50 lower than at your own maker. But for Giorgio Armani, your customer demands a higher quality. If you ship Kmart quality to Madison Avenue, no one will buy your jeans. You may save $1.50 but will lose $75.00, the markup at retail for a pair of Armani jeans.

If Kmart works with an Armani factory, their cost rises by $1.50. However, if Giorgio Armani works with a Kmart factory, his cost rises by $73.50 per pair of jeans.

For each buyer the cost of working in the other factory is too high. Working at the Armani factory, as the Kmart buyer you face unacceptable direct costs. Working at the Kmart factory, as the Armani buyer you face unacceptable indirect costs.

DIRECT COSTS

Only after you decide upon the country where you will produce your order and what type of factory you require, can you begin to negotiate the 'costs'. This is the last choice you make. Everybody loves to argue price. Why not? Everybody loves to control, and this is the only area in the costing process where you the buyer can exercise any control whatsoever.

The buyer has no control over macro costs. If it takes two weeks for incoming material to clear customs and another five days over unpaved roads to move the material to the factory, you cannot argue with the factory. If the electricity browns out every evening at five and goes off altogether two days a week, there is nothing you can do. Those are some of the macro costs for that country.

The same applies for factory indirect costs. If the factory has only one patternmaker whose last view of fashion was the New Look of 1947, there is not too much you can do about it. If the factory lacks a decent fusing machine, there is not much you can do about that either, except change the factory or buy them a new fusing machine. Those are some of the indirect costs for that factory.

However, direct costs are something you can fight for. You cannot fight the roads or the electricity company or the corrupt customs officials whose hands are forever reaching out for a payoff. But CMT is something you can control. It doesn't matter what price the factory manager quotes—it is too high.

Unfortunately, this is not exactly the best way to source production or even to get the best price. But for those looking to get even or trying to show who's boss, direct-cost negotiations are great therapy. For those in need of therapy, the best system to follow is the Wendell Wasp Battering Ram method. Here garment buyers of the old generation can fight factories of the even older generation until both go broke.

Case Study VII—Wendell Wasp's War

The Wendell Wasp method requires no advance study of fabric cost, yields or CMTs. The beauty of Wendell's system is that it requires no information whatsoever.

Wendell's idea is that whatever price the vendor quotes, it is unacceptable. Over a period of years, through trial and error, he has been able to set the degree of unacceptability at precisely 25%. If the vendor says $1.00, Wendell offers $0.75. If the vendor says $46.39, Wendell rejects the price and immediately offers $34.7925. The beauty of the system is that it is both simple and precise. Furthermore, Wendell's strategy relies on the vendor's knowledge rather than his own. Wendell might not know anything about the cost of lambswool intarsia sweaters, but certainly the maker must know. After all, that is his business.

To succeed, the Wendell Wasp system requires stamina, persistence and a true monomaniacal compulsion. No compromise can be allowed, for to concede anything is to show the maker that you were never serious in the first place. No effort is too great because the goal is to grind the vendor down to the point where he is forced to agree. Nor can any sacrifice be considered too great. If, in the end, no maker will accept your price, you must be willing to take something out of the style. Trim can be reduced. Twelve 24-ligne ocean-pearl buttons can be pared down to ten 20-ligne polyester buttons. Long sleeves can become three-quarter sleeves, then short sleeves, or even no sleeves. Whatever the cost, Wendell Wasp must win and the maker must be made to lose. The price has to be shoved down from $1.00 to $0.75.

In practice, this strategy leaves something to be desired. For Wendell Wasp, it proved ultimately suicidal.

The first season the vendors definitely had problems. They would quote realistic prices and Wendell would beat them down 25%. Very quickly, however, they realized that the actual price was irrelevant to the negotiation. Whatever price they quoted, Wendell always pushed for his 25% reduction.

From that point on, all real negotiation ceased. The vendors quickly saw they were on to a good thing. Here was a customer who would pay anything, provided they allowed him to beat them back 25%. Wendell would agree to $1.00 if they quoted $1.33; he would also agree to $1.50 provided they quoted $2.00. And so on. In fact,

11

there was no ceiling to the price Wendell was charged—and, of course, Wendell's boss paid.

For the most part, Wendell has gone the way of the dinosaur, made extinct by the pressures of increased competition. However, every so often you will meet his counterpart in overseas factories located in out-of-the-way places. These are the suppliers who say: "We only quote prices, we give no cost breakdowns."

What they are really saying is: "Wendell Wasp, we need you—where have you gone?"

Direct costs are certainly important and importers should work to negotiate the lowest direct costs possible. However, direct costs are not a substitute for low macro costs or low indirect costs.

To be complete, the costing must include macro costs (the costs of doing business in that country), indirect costs (the costs of working with that agent and in that factory), and the direct costs (the costs of the goods themselves). Together, these three factors define the cost of manufacturing. Each operation or material in the manufacturing process can be part of direct, indirect, or macro costs, or simultaneously part of all three.

Case Study VIII —The Button

Everybody's costings include buttons.

1.   Buttons are direct costs. CMT stands for cut-make-trim and buttons are part of trim. Buying of buttons is a factor of direct cost.

2.   Buttons are indirect costs. Someone had to choose the button. Someone else has to ensure the stock button arrives as ordered, on time, and in the right color—because if the buttons received are not the same as the buttons ordered, or if they arrive late, or in the wrong color, the goods cannot be manufactured. Ensuring the button arrives as it should is an indirect-cost factor.

3.   Buttons are macro costs. If the button is imported, someone must organize the importation, obtain licenses, clear customs, and pay whatever bribes are necessary to expedite the procedures. Even if the button is produced domestically, the raw materials had to be imported, requiring the same work. Expediting logistics and importation is a macro-cost factor.

Without the actual purchase, follow-up and logistics, the buttons would not arrive. All three are required.

FVCA AND THE GLOBAL ECONOMY

Imagine a company where raw material is purchased and moved 10,000 miles for processing, and where that processed material is then moved another 7,000 miles to be turned into a finished product, which, in turn, is then moved 12,000 miles further to be sold.

Imagine a company where 50-200 separate and distinct models go through this schedule each selling period, three to five periods a year.

Finally, imagine a schedule so strict that one-day-late delivery on any order means an automatic cancellation.

Where is this cutting edge of management skill and system to be found? What type of company can maintain a manufacturing schedule involving so many models and a logistic system spanning 29,000 miles? Neither computers nor automobiles can approach this level of efficiency.

In fact, this process describes neither the computer industry, nor the automobile industry, but the normal pattern of any American sweater importer.

Raw wool is exported from Australia to Italy where it is spun into yarn and dyed. The dyed yarn is shipped to China to be knitted into sweater panels, then moved to Hong Kong where the panels are linked into finished sweaters which are then exported to the United States. An average sweater importer runs anywhere between 50-200 styles a season.

I have never heard any economist or management expert refer to Broadway sweater importers as high-tech or at the leading edge of the global economy. These terms are usually reserved for automobile companies that design two models a year, or computer companies that periodically rush new styles to the marketplace and are only six months late.

Yet any importer hoping to survive the next season must deal globally. To do this, he must cost globally. All product costs are a part of each style costing. An advantage provided by the factory in Asia may save money from work normally done in New York. It is of the utmost importance in working on a global basis that each supplier become part of a sourcing chain.

A supplier who cannot operate as an efficient link in that chain raises the costs of every other supplier in that chain. The fabric supplier who ships late, the fabric dyer whose lab dips are wrong, the button supplier who ships the wrong style or the incorrect size, the agent who fails to provide proper follow-up—each raises the cost of every supplier downstream. Each may quote the lowest price for their products or services, but their costs become too high when you consider the effects of their mistakes on the other links in the sourcing chain.

Full Value Cost Analysis

If you cannot cost your product to include these factors, you have no idea just what you are paying your suppliers. FVCA provides a method to work out the full value costs of each product.

Chapter 2
Macro Costs: Exporters

Buying garments at the best price is the easiest thing in the world. Any putz can do it. You find a country where the wages are good and low, get a decent agent, and in three months you are shipping garments. You put all your work there until the unions come and push wages up. Then you run like hell to the next country. For me, I draw the line at twenty-five cents. When a sewing girl gets a quarter an hour, it's time to get out.

Herbie the Mouth
at his latest Chapter 7 hearing

The days when importers could decide where to buy on the sole basis of labor rates, or even making costs, are over. In an earlier and perhaps easier age, importers could prosper despite late delivery, poor quality, and an infinite series of last-minute crises. The conditions characterized an industry which worked in countries where there were no proper facilities and factories without proper structure. That industry is now too competitive to allow Herbie and his kind to survive.

For the contemporary importer, making costs is the last factor to be considered. The first and most important cost decision is: Which country should you work in? This is a question of macro costs. If you want to survive for another season, look at the macro costs.

Macro costs are the measure of relevant facilities offered by the country. The greater the facilities, the lower the cost. These facilities may be the result of government—e.g., Singapore has an efficient bureaucracy. They may be the result of cultural norms—e.g., in Germany, quality standards are very high. They may simply exist because of geography—e.g., gas is cheap in Saudi Arabia. Whatever the case, macro costs are fixed. The buyer cannot change them and neither can the factory. Macro costs, high or low, are simply the reality of working in a particular country. Any possible change lies in the hands of the government. As a result, you the importer must decide in advance: "Can I afford to work in this country?"

Macro costs include such items as bureaucratic efficiency, the legal system, customs clearance times, import duty rates, tax systems, level of education, infrastructure, and quota. Other items such as political freedoms are also entering the list.

Macro costs change not only from one exporting country to another, but also from one customer's country to another. Macro costs are not only a question of what does your country offer, but also what do I, the customer, need.

To U.S. importers, the macro costs of doing business in Hong Kong are among the lowest in the world. This is true despite certain conditions that raise macro costs considerably. Hong Kong rents are the highest in the world and salaries are commensurate with the high cost of living. Hong Kong is the single most overcrowded place on this planet. Yet these macro costs are greatly outweighed by other more important macro-cost savings. Communications and logistics are superb; the population, hardworking and educated. Hong Kong's commercial legal system, even under Chinese sovereignty, is excellent and levels of corruption are low. Finally, its geographic location works very much in its favor. As a result, despite the high rentals and salaries, international companies continue to set up in Hong Kong because, after all is said and done, Hong Kong offers very low macro costs.

To European buyers, however, Hong Kong—while attractive by Asian standards—does not have the same macro-cost advantages as seen by Americans. U.S. importers look to Asia as a key area for production. Therefore, the place with the lowest macro costs in Asia is the place American importers want to be. Europeans, meanwhile, have access to high-quality factories closer to home.

To an Italian importer, a trip to Hong Kong is a major effort. He must be prepared to spend at least ten days away from his business. He must travel to a place where all communication is carried on through translators and the simplest instructions are sometimes garbled.

The Italian importer has the alternative to go to Central Europe where high-quality factories are in production. He can fly from Milan to Budapest in the morning, conduct all his business in German—a common second language—and return home in time for late dinner. For the Italian, working in Hungary, Poland or the Czech Republic is easier than working in the southern parts of his own country. Hong Kong may have low macro costs, but they do not compare to those in Central Europe.

Such advantages—whether they be an educated population, solid legal structure, or a society relatively free of corruption—are clearly cost advantages. Let us note, however, that issues of morality do not enter into macro costs. In any case, these issues are seldom clear-cut. Take, for example, the fact that Hong Kong has very little corruption, although bribery is endemic to China. Companies working in China must therefore factor cost of bribes into their total costings, while those working in Hong Kong do not. The cost factor is clear; the moral factor is not. Consider that it is Hong Kong business people and companies doing most of the bribing in China. It would therefore be a little ingenuous for Hong Kong to claim the moral high ground.

Discussed from a moral stance, the debate has no obvious answers. What is important for our purposes is that corruption, like low levels of education and lack of infrastructure, raises macro costs, and these costs are far higher than any direct-cost advantages.

Countries like Hong Kong, Singapore, Germany and Italy have low macro costs. At the other end are countries where macro costs are enormous by any standards. For example, North Korea has some of the lowest salary and wage rates in the world. Rentals in Pyongyang approach zero. However, there is no infrastructure. Road and rail networks are poor and there is little rolling stock. The country has the lowest rates of electrification and the lowest number of telephones per thousand people in Asia. Importation of raw material is not possible and almost no materials are produced locally. The government is authoritarian and its policy inconsistent. In short, the macro costs of doing business in the Democratic People's Republic of Korea are so high that it would be too expensive to work there, even if the workers were paid nothing at all.

Macro costs are the single most important product cost. This is particularly true in an industry such as garment manufacturing, in which setting up factories is relatively easy, capital costs are low, and in most cases, the origin of the basic raw materials is of secondary importance.

Oil companies have no choice—if they want the oil, they have to work in those countries where oil can be found. They must accept the governments in those countries as they find them. Mining companies are in the same position. If you want Burmese rubies, you have to go to Burma. If you want cobalt, you have to go to Zaire or what is now called the Democratic Republic of the Congo. The government of Marshal Ne Win might be composed of a bunch of thugs and the gang presently governing Zaire may be even worse, but if you want the rubies or the cobalt, these are the people you have to deal with.

Garments are different. For the importer, it is with few exceptions strictly a buyer's market. No one has ever claimed that a well-made pair of pants is as precious as rubies. The buyer can go anywhere in the world and find a supplier. If working in one country becomes too difficult, there are to date some 195 other countries equipped to make his product. With choices like that, it does not take much for a customer to pack his bags and take off for the next place. To keep the customer, the country itself must offer low macro costs.

All macro-cost factors are political. Some, like bureaucratic inefficiency and high interest rates, are more political than others. However, even 'nonpolitical' macro costs like infrastructure are in fact largely affected by political considerations. This means that obvious solutions to a buyer's problems seldom work because many obstructions have a political purpose.

Of all the macro-cost factors affecting the importer, the most important is, surprisingly, education. This is not some theoretical conclusion—this is the simple truth. You can overcome anything, but if the people with whom you must work cannot understand what you are saying, cannot understand what you need, or lack the technical skills to translate those needs into actual production, do not bother unpacking your bags. Any effort spent in that place will be a very costly waste of time.

17

EDUCATION

If the merchandiser does not understand you, if the patternmaker is not well trained, if the management cannot get it together, you simply stand no chance of receiving what you asked for when you need it.

Experience is the best teacher may have been the motto of Herbie the Mouth's generation. But that type of education is too expensive today. When someone tells you, "I learn from experience," what they are really saying is, "My customers pay for my education. You can pay for my mistakes."

We live in an information age which impacts the garment industry as much if not more than the computer industry. Logistics, communications and system are probably more sophisticated in the garment industry than in any other. They have to be—because the international garment industry *is the only truly global industry in the world.*

Try working with a poorly trained, poorly educated factory merchandiser. Where educated merchandisers do not exist, the probability of catastrophe rises. For a merchandiser to be of value, his education must encompass three areas: language skills, technical knowledge and an understanding of the customer's home market.

- Language skills: This involves far more than knowledge of English or whatever language is native to the customer. In a real sense, the merchandiser must re-learn his own language. Every language has its own technical vernacular.

  The customer requires 'aubergine color'.
  The customer requires a 'drop shoulder'.
  The customer is concerned about 'dry crocking'.

  The merchandiser must communicate these requirements to non-English-speaking technicians, using the idiom of the local industry. Unless the merchandiser knows what a 'drop shoulder' is and knows the Chinese, Korean or Indonesian term for 'drop shoulder', there's no telling what your duplicate will look like.

- Technical knowledge: To communicate, the merchandiser must understand what the customer is saying. This is more than language. If the customer requires 'double mercerized', 'open-end warps', or 'sublistatic print', the merchandiser must not only understand the terms—he or she must also have knowledge of the underlying technology. Often the customer's directions are unclear, and the merchandiser must communicate further with the customer before taking action. Sometimes the customer does not know himself what he wants or means. Sometimes the customer's instructions may make no sense at all. A merchandiser without technical knowledge will take nonsense instructions, translate them, and instruct operations departments to take action. This leads to confusion, errors, loss of time and added expense.

I require black silk fuji with dry crocking AATCC level 5.
I can't raise my arm, drop the armhole 1 inch.

The first instruction is technically impossible, while the second makes no sense whatsoever. When a skilled merchandiser receives instructions such as these, he must query his customer and explain the underlying problem. "We cannot achieve level 5 for black silk fuji. Please change your requirements or the color." "Dropping the armhole will only make raising the arm more difficult. Perhaps we should raise the armhole instead."

- Understanding the customer's market: This is the most difficult skill to learn. Buyers often prefer to work with factories located in their home market or adjacent areas because the staff understand what their market requires. Every market is different and each season brings change to each market.

As you move from one market to another or one season to another, fit changes, look changes, and what is 'right' changes. In a successful factory, the merchandiser knows his customer's market. When the customer comes with the latest look, the merchandiser already knows what the customer is talking about. The merchandiser is aware that the difference between a 'cheap' product and a 'fine' product is not money— it is the look. The factory that can provide that look is paid accordingly because they have low indirect costs. The factory that provides a cheap product is also paid accordingly because working with them entails high indirect costs.

If the merchandiser cannot understand you or explain your requirements to the production people, you have no chance of receiving a decent product. This requires both technical and language education.

Today's importers are no longer buyers of finished product just as factories are no longer suppliers of finished product. In fact, the entire buying process has been replaced by the sourcing process.

Customers no longer go to factories with a sample garment and ask them to produce a finished garment. A garment is looked at as a product of a series of materials and processes, and it is broken down accordingly. The sweater in the sourcing chain described on page 13 was neither purchased from nor manufactured by any one factory. It has no single country of origin. It was manufactured by a series of companies, starting at a sheep station in the Australian outback and completed in a Hong Kong factory where panels previously knitted in China were linked together into a finished sweater.

To compete in this industry, buyers must have staff with the knowledge and training to organize and control a global sourcing chain. Suppliers must give up their role as sole manufacturer and become part of this chain.

Without an educated staff, this is simply not possible. If tomorrow Hutus and Tutsis stopped killing each other in Rwanda, the Democratic Republic of Congo and Burundi, if tomorrow a miracle occurred and the governments of these three countries suddenly transmogrified from a bunch of hoodlums into responsible leaders—a viable export-garment industry would still not be possible because there are not sufficient numbers of educated people in those countries to become part of a sourcing chain.

Where you cannot find educated management and technical staff, you cannot work—not in today's world.

A modern textile and garment industry requires university graduates with advanced degrees in management and engineering. Not surprisingly, all the top ten textile and garment-exporting countries, including China, have well-established technical universities with either departments or institutes devoted entirely to textile and garment design and production.

INFRASTRUCTURE

All factories are dependent on electricity to operate, telephone systems to communicate with their customers, and road and rail networks to move material in and finished goods out. Neither customers nor producers have any control over infrastructure. These are all macro costs.

Electricity

This is a problem that concerns all industries in developing countries. The expenditures required for plants to generate power and the lines to carry the power to the end users have grown enormously in the past decade. Today most countries lack sufficient electrical power for their present needs. It is difficult to keep to a production schedule when the electricity stops working twice a week, or where brownouts occur every afternoon at four o'clock.

When the factory manager tells you, "I am sorry your order is late because we did not have sufficient electricity this month," there is not much you can do. It is too late to do anything. Yelling certainly will not help. The time to do something is when you first arrived in the country, before you placed your order. That was the time when you should have turned around and gone elsewhere.

Communications

Ours is an industry of details, thousands of details. You are about 10,000 miles away from your supplier. Your only connection is a telephone wire. We in the international garment industry measure daily receipt and output of faxes and e-mail by the yard. The factory fax machine had better work. If it takes two days to send a fax (Bangladesh), if the machine breaks down every week and it requires a week for the repairman to show up (Indonesia), you are going to have problems. If the lines are open but no one is communicating, you have problems. In a well-managed company, faxes and e-mail queries are answered every day. Even if information is not yet available, you should receive a reply telling you when the requested information will be faxed. This is not true of all societies. India, Indonesia, Pakistan and Sri Lanka are all *mañana* societies. You work there, you have to pay for that.

Transport

Roads, ports, rails and airfreight are all necessary components of our industry. We have to move material and trim to the factory and take finished goods out. Logistics, the movement of goods, can take more time than actual production. For example, for many years Mauritius was a center for T-shirt production. The main problem with working in Mauritius was that materials had to come from Hong Kong. T-shirt production time from receipt of order should be approximately 30 days—including knitting, dyeing and sewing. But for Mauritius, an additional 45 days were required just for sea shipment of raw materials alone.

Countries that have limited port facilities can require turnaround times measured in weeks. Until recently, it was cheaper and faster to move goods from Shanghai to Hong Kong by rail and then ship to the United States than to use Shanghai port facilities, where turnaround times could exceed three weeks. If it takes four hours just to travel from the Bangkok airport to the city, how long does it take to move goods from the Thai factory to the port?

The problems of infrastructure do not concern only its availability—they also involve the costs of that infrastructure. It is cheaper to telephone from New York to Hong Kong than from Jakarta to Jogyakarta, a distance of a few hundred miles. India has the highest electrical power cost in the world. A moderate-sized factory can easily have a monthly electricity bill ranging from $12,000 to $14,000.

These expenses have to be added to garment costs. So-called 'low-cost' producers have extremely high overhead costs. Case Study I, in the Introduction, is an excellent example. Labor and trim for the shirt might only be $0.45, but somewhere along the way another $1.65 is spent. To a large degree, it was eaten up by the electricity and telephone companies. Logistics, communication and infrastructure are factors you should check before placing orders.

Education and infrastructure are factors determined primarily by political considerations. The remaining macro costs are *entirely* political costs.

BUREAUCRACY & GOVERNMENT

In almost all of the cheap-labor countries, government is the biggest business. Sometimes, as in the old communist states, government is the only business; in other cases, government is a family business. In every case, governments cost you money completely apart from legitimate taxes and fees. Government trade, as well as monetary and investment policies, are part of the costs of doing business in a country. As a professional garment importer, you can no longer stand apart from the politics of your suppliers' countries. Even if these policies are beyond your control, the expenses they incur are real. Government policies need not be rational. You must know what type of government you will be dealing with before you place your orders—because you will be dealing with government.

Every year a group of specialists led by the Heritage Foundation sits down to calculate the economic freedom of each country in the world.[2] They include ten factors: trade policy, taxation policy, government intervention, monetary policy, capital flows and foreign investment, banking policy, wage and price controls, property rights, regulation policy and 'black market' conditions.

The contention is that the easier it is to do business in a country, the more business people will do and the higher will be the income of its citizens. The authors' conclusions are not perfect, but the results seem to be fairly compelling. An importer looking for a country where he will buy sweaters would do well to check the 1997 *Index of Economic Freedom*. For example, you might be surprised to discover how much higher Sri Lanka (rank 27) fares over Pakistan (rank 78) or India (rank 118). You probably don't need to be warned about the dangers of working in Cuba, Laos or North Korea (equally tied, at rank 148).

The argument is not that the governments of Laos and North Korea are terrible or that they oppress their people—it is simply that the cost of working in these countries is too high, despite the fact that these and the other lowest-ranking 20 countries offer some of the lowest wages in the world.

Naturally, your requirements as a garment importer do not entirely coincide with those of a Ford Motor Company or DuPont Nemours. You will therefore be more interested in some factors than others. For a garment importer, local regulations governing banking, capital flows and monetary policy would be of less importance to you than bureaucratic regulation and the black market.

Bureaucratic Regulation and Obstruction

All governments place limits on doing business and all bureaucracies have regulations. To a great degree, these limitations and regulations are reasonable and justifiable. Laws governing employment of women and young persons are important. Building and operating safety regulations are necessary for everyone's protection. Likewise, social legislation such as compulsory education is an excellent investment in the future.

However, as the level of government and bureaucratic regulation increases, it often becomes more difficult to do business. The justification for increased regulation may often sound reasonable, but the results can be very costly indeed. Well-meaning but poorly conceived policy often harms those it sets out to protect the most. Policies to protect jobs may result in increased unemployment. Regulations to increase minimum standards for working conditions may result in companies going underground where workers have no protection whatsoever. Obstructive bureaucracy can suffocate an industry, its workers, and in some instances, the entire economy.

Beyond bad policy there is intentional bureaucratic delay and obstruction. Here parts of the government rely on their ability to slow the system down or stop it altogether. Regretfully, a situation can arise when certain persons in the bureaucracy have a vested interest in heightening levels of obstruction. In this case, not only are there increased delays and expense, but some favored individuals are able to circumvent the system altogether.

Delays for any reason add to costs, even when unaccompanied by a suggestion that a small payment can solve all problems. In countries where the role of bureaucracy is to obstruct, you must include provisions for these added expenses in your costs.

Two areas that are always affected are customs clearance and required permits. While tariff levels are part of government legislation, collection of customs duties is in the hands of the bureaucracy. In many countries, individuals are able to make special arrangements to avoid paying duty. The result is not only loss of revenue to the government, but also inequities which give some companies a marked cost advantage over their competitors.

Unnecessary custom clearance delays are equally serious. Any mill or factory must deliver each order within a specified period of time. Clearance delays of raw materials reduce the time the supplier has to complete production. In an industry known for tight deliveries, having material stuck in customs can be the difference between on-time or costly late shipments.

In any country, the need to have licenses and permits is a normal part of doing business, ensuring that companies have conformed to safety and other regulations. However, in many cases, permits may be delayed or conversely issued prematurely, depending on the relationship that exists between the company and the bureaucracy.

The most common area where licensing obstruction occurs is in labor regulations. Most countries, including developed ones, have regulations to protect workers' jobs. There are others which believe that job protection ultimately stifles job creation. After all, why hire someone in good times if you cannot fire them in bad times? Clearly, the American experience where the economy appears to be booming despite minimal job protection would support this stand. Whatever your personal opinion, there are valid arguments for both views—within limits.

Take, for example, India. Here regulations have reached a point where job protection means no new jobs at all.[3]

Case Study IX—Job Protection Indian-Style

Imagine you own a company in India employing 25 workers. This is not a large number. However, it is large enough for you to be required to conform to the 45 separate laws governing employment. These are 'concurrent laws', meaning that there are both central and state government laws which frequently contradict each other.

As a large employer—since only 3% of the entire working population is employed by companies with more than ten workers, employing 25 workers definitely puts you in the upper reaches—you have special responsibilities.

For example, in the event of any vacancies, you have to notify the official labor exchange and accept whomever they send over to fill the place. In many cases, not only are you prohibited from firing this worker for any reason, but even after he dies, his job automatically goes to his son or other nominee.

All job specifications are registered with the government, and since you are a large employer you must obtain state permission to change the job specifications. You might also have to arrange for a plebiscite among your 25 workers, who must vote unanimously for any change to take place.

Consider yourself lucky that you do not employ a hundred workers. With a hundred workers, to fire someone you need permission from the state government. You can imagine how often the state gives permission.

Okay, the nightmare is over. You no longer own a company in India. However, next time, you become angry with the union or local employment laws, remember, you could be worse off.

Imagine—you own a company in India.

The problem of bureaucratic inefficiency is not unique to developing countries—it occurs to some degree almost everywhere. However, truly intentional bureaucratic obstruction is a primarily Third World phenomenon, an inevitable by-product of corruption. In an environment of bureaucratic obstruction, there are those who face constant delays and overcharges while others appear to sail through untouched. In general, the latter have special relationships.

INTEREST RATES

Why should you as a buyer be interested in local interest rates in Dhaka, Jakarta or Colombo? You have enough problems with your factor in New York. You are not planning to borrow money in Bangladesh, Indonesia or Sri Lanka.

The answer is that while you may not borrow money in these countries, your suppliers do—and the cost of those loans is certainly a part of the price you pay for the garment. Just as the high cost of telephone and electricity is included in the price of the Sri Lankan shirt, so is the cost of borrowing money in Sri Lanka.

Interest rate can be defined as a premium paid for risk. It reflects the perceived risk of leaving money in a particular country. This is the reason that interest rates in the industrialized nations tend to be lower than those in the less developed areas.

Interest rates are determined by the market. This is particularly true when a country wishes to attract foreign funds. If the rates offered are too low, people will not put their funds in that country and may well withdraw the funds already there. Conversely, if interest rates are too high, local industrial borrowers are squeezed out of the market, particularly when borrowing long term for purchases of plant and capital equipment.

Finally, when rates are unusually high, they reflect a high perceived risk. In this situation, foreigners may still put their money in the country; however, they will do so only on a short-term basis. The result is a great deal of hot money, which can leave at any time when interest rates fall or risks are perceived to rise.

25

Macro Costs: Exporters

Country	Short Term Rate (as of Oct 1998)[4]
Turkey	80.00%
Indonesia	56.65%
Thailand	10.00%
S. Korea	23.28%
Mexico	31.20%
Philippines	11.37%
Malaysia	7.52%
China	8.10%
United States	5.08%
Hong Kong	8.16%
Taiwan	6.65%
Germany	3.56%
Singapore	4.25%
Japan	0.38%

All investment involves risk. When the risk is known and understood, prudent investors factor that risk into their costs and the expected return on that investment must rise or fall accordingly. However, when that risk is the result of uncertainty of government policy or when the investor has reason to believe that government policy may at any time place additional risk on his investment, the prudent investor must factor the worst-case scenario into each investment and demand a commensurate return to the increased risk.

CORRUPTION

Bribery and corruption are very much a way of life in textile and garment-exporting nations. In many of these places, you—or more likely your supplier—have to make regular payoffs if you expect the manufacturing process to work. Before you gasp, remember that corruption is a worldwide phenomenon. Anyone who believes that bribery is unique to Asia has never tried to arrange garbage collection in almost any major American city, or for a shipment of garments to be trucked out of almost any U.S. airport.

There are some 'Asian specialists' who write knowingly that corruption is part of an Asian heritage and plays a positive role in Eastern cultures. This is nonsense. There is no Asian experience or gene that makes Chinese, Koreans or Indians congenital crooks. You pay off in Asia. You also pay off in Central America, South America and the Middle East. Corruption is pervasive when countries are poor, the population uneducated, and often where there is one-party government. As countries develop and as the level of education rises, the level of corruption falls. Contrast the low level of corruption in Japan, Singapore and Malaysia with the high levels in India, Pakistan and Bangladesh. Better yet, contrast the low levels of corruption in Hong Kong, Taiwan and S. Korea in 1999 with corruption in those same countries in 1969. As countries develop, corruption ceases to be a way of life and becomes a criminal act.

However, in countries where bribery is endemic, either you pay or you get out. As with any macro cost, you had better decide if you are willing to play before you join the game.

Bribery is a cost. Like every cost, it is included in the price of every garment you buy in that country. Whether you pay or the factory pays, the truth is you pay. In some countries, it begins even before you get into the country as you go through immigration. In these places, a small bill folded in your passport will see you safely through. The alternative is a ten-hour wait on a hard bench while the officer verifies that your grandmother's maiden name was Schmendrich.

In a well-organized system of corruption, almost every operation requires its own payoff. What is important to remember here is that it is still possible to produce your garments—provided you are working in a place where corruption operates efficiently.

The difference between efficient and inefficient corruption was once described as follows: *Putting up a hospital in either Lagos, Nigeria, or Bangkok, Thailand, requires payoffs. The difference is that in Bangkok, they actually build the hospital.* In this sense, there is some difference between a corrupt bureaucrat and a thief. With the corrupt bureaucrat, if you want the permit, you pay; with the thief, whether you pay or not, you still don't get the permit.

There is a second set of costs beyond the actual bribe—the costs of delay. Bribery usually begins as an effort to expedite an inefficient process. You pay your money to get to the head of the line. However, very quickly the payoffs produce additional delays as bureaucrats invent new procedures and permits to increase the number of people in their line. There was a time in Beijing when the government, having run out of ideas for additional permits, simply increased the number of departments that had to sign the permit—a combination of Karl Marx and P.T. Barnum: *From each according to his need, to each according to his greed.*

Eventually, the number of open palms and required licenses, forms and permits increases to a point where the whole system collapses and nothing moves. At that point the system reforms. This may result in a real effort to stamp out corruption, as the Chinese are now trying to do. On the other hand, the crooks can also take over altogether and rationalize payoffs by adding an additional management layer. This is what has happened in Russia and Pakistan.

All societies are to some degree corrupt. You have to play the game wherever you go. Those looking to take advantage of local assets, whether materials or markets, have little choice. However, for any garment importer, there is little incentive to work in the low end of the ethical marketplace. The ultimate costs are just too high.

All corruption may be dishonest, and clearly all corruption raises macro costs. This doesn't mean, however, that all corruption involves people putting their own interests above those of their employers. Not all corruption involves payoffs. A government or a society may become corrupt even though its members act in what they perceive to be the best interests of their country or company. Nowhere was this more manifest than in Hong Kong in the period leading up to the Chinese resumption of sovereignty in July 1997.

Case Study X—Corruption in Hong Kong: Macro Costs

Hong Kong is a physical pygmy. It has a population of 6.3 million and a land mass of 320 square miles. In comparison, China has a population that is 185 times larger and is over 6,000 times bigger geographically.

Hong Kong is an economic colossus. Its gross domestic product (GDP) is $160 billion—20% of China's; its per capita GDP is $23,500 per annum. China's per capita is $577—1/40 of Hong Kong's. Hong Kong is the tenth largest trading nation in the world; China, the eleventh. Hong Kong's bank assets are 1.3 times those of China.[5]

These numbers explain the widely held belief that Hong Kong is too important for China to play around with. China needs a prosperous Hong Kong and, while Hong Kong might not care about human rights and personal freedoms, it will fight to retain its prosperity. As the transition to Chinese sovereignty approached, what happened in Hong Kong was that macro costs began to rise. The system began to corrupt.

In February 1997, Next Publications, which was scheduled to go public in April, suddenly found that their underwriter Sun Hung Kai, a leading local merchant banker, had decided to opt out. When asked why, the voice on the phone said: "You know why."[6]

Unfortunately, everyone knew why. The problem was not the profitability of the company. Its newspapers and magazines enjoyed high readership and the company was making money. The problem was not management. Its founder and chairman, Jimmy Lai, had an excellent track record. The problem was that Mr. Lai had upset China's leaders. He was no longer politically correct.

It can be argued that as Hong Kong was about to revert to Chinese sovereignty, politically correct views of a news publishing company might be important to its profitability. However, that argument is substantially shakier when used to justify a second incident which occurred about the same time.

An analyst for a Hong Kong brokerage house wrote a negative report about a Chinese listed company. The analyst was fired.[7] The message was clear: Don't write bad reports if you want to keep your job. Unfortunately, annual reports issued by most mainland Chinese companies aren't factual according to Western standards and require specialist analysis and interpretation for non-Chinese investors.

Firing the analysts because you don't like what they say is something that future investors will have to take into consideration. If Hong Kong's status shrank to the point where it became just an important city in southern China, this type of corruption would be quite acceptable. People know the added macro costs of dealing in China. However, for companies who deal internationally, the actions of Sun Hung Kai and the brokerage house were unacceptable. They were the acts of small-time people and they make Hong Kong small-

HUMAN RIGHTS

For the garment professional, the human rights issue is not a matter of morality but a question of macro cost. Importers and suppliers must accept that human rights conditions in the exporting countries they deal with can no longer be divorced from retail sales. At least in the United States and Europe, people buy what they like, and increasingly their considerations are based on more than the traditional product quality, look or price.

In the past two years, export-garment volumes produced by Burmese factories have fallen by two-thirds. Companies like Eddie Bauer, Liz Claiborne and Federated Department Stores who previously found some of their best bargains in Burma, now find they simply cannot afford to work there. This is not a matter of direct-cost or quality considerations. There is only one factor involved here—Aung San Suu Kyi.

You may ask: "What does Aung San Suu Kyi have to do with fashion?" The latest answer is: "A lot." People will no longer buy garments from a country where that woman is 'oppressed'.

She and people like the Dalai Lama are becoming important arbiters of fashion, particularly when deciding just which factories produce the most acceptable fashion.

It is only natural that garment people, and particularly importers of younger fashion, would lead this trend. Your customers are not only more aware but sufficiently fickle to permit human rights in Tibet to influence the decision about which brand of blue jeans to buy. Furthermore, the international garment industry is very flexible. Lost production from one area can be replaced from elsewhere in a matter of weeks.

I am not making a moral statement about political events in China or Burma. However, I am suggesting that consumers are influenced by individuals who are perceived as heroes fighting against *evil and corrupt* government. When such an individual becomes newsworthy, buyers must consider the macro costs.

Chapter 3
Macro Costs: Importers

An exporting country cannot control all factors affecting macro costs. Education, infrastructure, bureaucratic inefficiency and human rights are all in the hands of the exporting country. However, other factors such as trade disputes (both real and imagined), tariff rates, quota restrictions and country-of-origin regulations are controlled by the importing countries. These can affect macro costs as much or even more than exporter-controlled factors.

Unfortunately, those factors associated with importing countries tend to be negative, leading to inflated macro costs. There is real cost benefit to any system which rewards those that provide products at lower costs, higher quality, and with better delivery. More education, superior logistics, better government and less corruption all bring benefits to those individuals, companies and societies that operate efficiently.

However, tariff and quota restrictions, country-of-origin regulations and trade disputes—all of which are controlled by the importing countries—tend to reward some groups over others, and those rewards have nothing to do with the ability of individuals or groups to produce a better product more efficiently. In most cases, it is the individuals and companies least able to compete who receive the greatest rewards. Furthermore, these benefits do not necessarily improve results. The U.S. garment industry is a good example. Despite receiving every form of macro-cost advantage that the American government can provide, today it is less competitive than 35 years ago when imports were first restricted by quota.

QUOTA

Quota is a quantitative limitation. In the context of the garment industry, quota is the maximum number of garments that can be exported legally by a particular country to another country on an annual basis.

In theory, quotas are negotiated voluntarily on a bilateral basis between importer and exporter countries. In practice, they are imposed by the exporting country. Let's face it—no country really volunteers to restrict its own exports. At the present time, quotas exist on garments and textiles exported to the United States, the countries of the European Union, Canada and Norway. All bilateral quota agreements are brought together under the Multi-Fiber Agreement (MFA), under the jurisdiction of the World Trade Organization (WTO).

Quotas are divided into categories. The United States in particular tries to divide garment quotas into as many categories as possible in order to further limit imports. The greater the quantity imported from a particular country, the more categories a specific product is divided into. For example, *Trousers and Shorts* is Category -47/-48. For major exporting

...Quota is the single highest of all macro costs...

countries, the category is subdivided into *Trousers and Shorts, Men's and Boys'*, Cat. -47, and Trousers and Shorts, Women's and Girls', Cat. -48. For the really large exporting countries, this is further subdivided into *Trousers and Shorts, Women's and Girls'*, Knit, Cat. -48K, and *Trousers and Shorts, Women's and Girls', Woven*, Cat. -48W.

Finally, the United States divides all garment quotas into groups by fabric so that *Trousers and Shorts, Women's and Girls', Knit, Cotton*, Cat. 348K, could not be used to ship *Trousers and Shorts, Women's and Girls', Knit, Synthetic*, Cat. 648K. As a result, a pants factory in Hong Kong could be required to hold quota in twelve separate categories just to ship its pants to the United States. The permutations are almost infinite. For example, Cat. 340-T is defined as *Shirts, Men's and Boys', Woven, Cotton, Yarn-Dyed, Not Flannel*.

Quota is the single highest of all macro costs. First, there is an immediate cost. Because quota is actually a license to export, it has real value. As a result, the quota holder charges a premium for the quota. This can be a separate charge as occurs in China and Hong Kong, or an indirect charge where the premium is added to the FOB price as in Indonesia. The premium can be quite substantial. In some cases, the quota premium can be larger than the cost of making the garment, and in a few cases larger than the entire FOB cost.[8] In the past, any country which began exporting garments to the United States was soon required to enter into a bilateral quota agreement.

Case Study XI—Pants: Quota Cost

You are a buyer for Wrangler jeans in the United States. You have two choices: you can buy your jeans in China or you can buy them in the Dominican Republic.

If you buy Chinese jeans, you use Chinese denim. If you buy the jeans in the Dominican Republic, you use American denim which is somewhat superior. The cost of the quota for Cat. 347/348 (cotton pants) in China is $2.20 per pair. There is no quota cost for pants shipped from the Dominican Republic.

The FOB price of a five-pocket jeans made in the Dominican Republic is $7.25. To be competitive, the Chinese jeans would have to cost $5.05, about 30% cheaper.

Now, you are a buyer for Diesel (an Italian jeansmaker). You have approximately the same choices. You, too, can buy your jeans in China, again using Chinese denim, or you can buy your jeans in Hungary, using Italian denim which is far superior to Chinese denim, with no quota cost. The cost of the quota in China for Cat. 5 (pants) is $2.58 per pair.

A five-pocket jeans made in Hungary costs approximately $7.50. To be competitive, the Chinese jeans would have to cost $4.92— about 34% cheaper.

IMPORTER	SUPPLIER OPTIONS				CHINA DISADVANTAGE
U.S. Wrangler	1. Dominican Republic	FOB $7.25			
	2. China	FOB (incl. Q) $7.25	Quota $2.20	FOB $5.05	-30.3%
Italy Diesel	1. Hungary	FOB $7.50			
	2. China	FOB (incl. Q) $7.50	Quota $2.58	FOB $4.92	-34.4%

In addition to the initial premium payments, the existence of quota raises macro costs in many other—more serious—areas:

Quota makes efficient producers less competitive and stops new producers from entering the industry. In countries such as China and Hong Kong, quota is seldom held by the actual producers. In China, the quota is owned by state trading companies. In Hong Kong, while quota was originally allocated to those who actually produced and exported garments, today it is mostly held by companies whose interest in the industry is purely tangential. In both countries, the true producers and exporters must pay the quota owners a fee to rent the quota. The quota holders themselves contribute nothing to the industry; they simply make the product more expensive and, therefore, less competitive.

Quota allows inefficient producers to stay in business without making any effort to become more efficient. Companies and countries that have quota can continue to sell, even though their products are not competitive, because quota bars efficient manufacturers from increasing market share. The very existence of garment-export industries in several countries is based on this reality. For example, there are many jeans manufacturers in Indonesia even though they cannot compete with China. Indonesian denim is more expensive than Chinese and of generally poorer quality. Making costs are higher than jeans produced in China. But Indonesia has substantial pants quota and can therefore ship pants long after the Chinese quota has been exhausted.

Because Indonesian jeansmakers have this license to ship, they need not make any effort to produce a better garment or increase efficiency. Why make the effort when the customer has no choice?

Quota prevents producers in importing countries from investing the necessary capital to make their companies more competitive. In a normal situation, a company that has a problem competing invests capital to increase efficiency. Increased efficiency lowers costs and everyone assumes that lower costs will bring more customers. In a normal situation this would be true; however, in a market distorted by quota this does not occur. Quota, first introduced to give U.S. manufacturers a temporary respite while making necessary investments and improvements, has in fact caused the industry to deteriorate even further.

Take the following example.

Case Study XII—Investment Overhang

The year is 1992. You manufacture jeans in Milwaukee. You have a problem competing with jeans from Hong Kong. They can land jeans for $8.15, and the best you can do is $9.00. You must do something to compete. You have a plan. You are going to buy new state-of-the-art machinery. You are confident that with the right investment you can reduce your costs sufficiently to sell your jeans for under $8.00, a savings of over 12%. This will surely bring in more customers and more orders, allowing you to compete as well as amortize this expensive investment. You go to your bank and explain your plans. The bank agrees. You buy the machinery, upgrade your efficiencies at considerable effort, and are now in a position to sell for $7.90 and make a profit. All you have to do is get back your customers.

You approach your former best customer. "Sam, forget about those Hong Kong people with their $8.15 price. I can sell you at $7.90."

"Sorry, Fred," he replies. "The Hong Kong factory is now quoting $7.07."

This is definitely not good news. Obviously, the Hong Kong factory has also been making large investments to cut their costs. However, you are a resourceful fellow. You have read somewhere that worker training can cut costs considerably. You contact the consultants and they guarantee a 15% reduction in costs. The investment costs are more than you can afford but, if you save 15%, you can sell for $6.75 and still make a profit.

You go back to the bank. They are not too happy, but they admire your grit and they lend you the money. One year later you're back in Sam's office. "I did it. I can sell you for $6.75 and the Hong Kong factory can drop dead."

"Sorry, Fred," replies Sam. "The Hong Kong factory is still alive, you are the one with problems. They are now quoting $6.40."

"This is not possible," you protest. "They have to be losing money. They cut their prices 21%. It is just a matter of time before they go broke."

In the event, you are the one who goes broke. In Milwaukee, each cost savings required an additional investment. In Hong Kong, the manufacturer made no additional investment at all. His entire cost reduction came out of the quota premium. From 1992 to 1996, the premium for quota Cat. 348 fell from $2.33 a unit to $0.58. Without any change in raw material or manufacturing costs, his total product cost fell 21%. In fact, compared to you, the Hong Kong manufacturer's cost could have fallen another 7% before he would have had to begin thinking about reducing costs elsewhere.

On December 31, 2004, as a result of the Uruguay Round of Negotiations which culminated at the end of 1994, the MFA is scheduled to come to an end, and all textile and garment exports will be free of quota. However, there is a growing belief that this lifting will be delayed indefinitely. Interest groups in both importing and exporting countries simply see quota restrictions as the only way for their constituents to survive.

Domestic U.S. and Western European garment producers fear an influx of made-in-China apparel whose high quality and low prices would completely take over the market of the entire developed world. This same fear is held by the major exporters in Asia and elsewhere. They, too, are concerned that China will dominate the entire international garment industry. Together, they may agree to shelve trade reform temporarily for perhaps as much as another 35 years.

Like most fears, however, this sentiment is irrational. China will no doubt be a major player in a new, more open trading environment. However, in order to participate, the Chinese will have to open their own market to imports. Given the size of their domestic market, any increase in Chinese exports would be more than offset by increases in imports.

Secondly, China's present advantage is not unique. The success of China as a textile and garment exporter is not due to any innate advantage. For example, labor rates for workers in China's export-garment industry are higher than those for similar workers in Indonesia, Bangladesh or Sri Lanka. China certainly has some valuable resources. Since 1997, it has been the world's largest cotton grower. However, the quality of Chinese cotton is poor, and more importantly, despite the size of its crop, China is also the world's largest importer of raw cotton

China's advantage, in fact, stems from its low indirect costs (see Chapter 15), which manufacturers in other countries could emulate—if they were willing to create the facilities to reduce their indirect costs.

However, the greatest argument against this fear is that China—as well as all other Asian garment-exporting countries—faces common competitors who enjoy macro-cost advantages far greater than anything existing in anywhere in Asia. These are the international trading blocs that will inevitably dominate the global textile and garment industries in the coming decades.

TARIFFS

After quota, duty is the single greatest immediately quantifiable macro cost. Although the duty rates imposed on each country are assumed to be uniform for all exporters, this is in fact not the case. In practice, the United States has four separate tariff schedules.

A. Non-MFN: The worst off are those countries without most-favored-nation status. At present, the list includes Afghanistan, Cuba, Iran,

Libya, North Korea and, for the moment, Vietnam. With the exception of Vietnam, none are major textile or garment producers.

The duty rate differences between MFN and non-MFN are substantial.

PRODUCT	IMPORT TARIFF	
	MFN	Non-MFN
Shirts (M&B) wool	$0.529/kg + 21%	$0.529/kg + 45%
Shirts (M&B) cotton	21.0%	45.0%
Shirts (M&B) MMF	$0.309/kg + 27.5%	$0.309/kg + 76%
Blouse silk	7.5%	65%
Blouse cotton	16.4%	90%
Blouse linen	3.7%	90%
Blouse MMF	28.6%	90%

B. MFN—Most-Favored Nation: To the United States, almost every country in the world is a most-favored nation. Countries so favored are permitted to ship goods to the United States with what is in effect the standard duty rate. The average MFN rate for products from all manufacturing sectors is about 4%. For garments, it is 18%—the highest of all major categories.

C. CBI—Caribbean Basin Initiative: Alone of all the major trading nations, the United States provides no duty relief for imported garments made of domestically-produced textiles. Anyone buying U.S. fabric, shipping it overseas, and using it to produce garments has to pay duty on the value of the U.S. fabric when importing the finished garments to the United States. In truth, for many years the U.S. textile industry had little interest in exports and, therefore, never pushed Congress to pass a law providing relief.

However, since the promulgation of the Monroe Doctrine in 1822, the United States has taken a proprietary interest in the countries of the western hemisphere. In the past 35 years, this interest was demonstrated in various initiatives, including the Partners for Progress program and the Organization of American States (OAS). More recently, American policy toward Cuba has resulted in greater efforts to assist the 'noncommunist' countries of Central America.

In 1963, an exception to the no-duty-drawback policy was made for Central American countries in the CBI. Item 807.00 was added to the tariff schedule, allowing for outward assembly of U.S.-made components sent to CBI countries to be returned to the United States duty-free except for the cost of the actual assembly work. Furthermore, where garments are under quota, special quota categories were created for goods shipped under 807. As a result, the size of the quota for 807 garments is, in practice, unlimited.

D. NAFTA—North American Free Trade Agreement: Under the terms of NAFTA, all merchandise produced in Canada, the United States and Mexico can be imported to member countries free of duty and quota. For textiles and garments, free trade is scheduled to gradually take complete effect over a period of time.

This apparent equal advantage to all NAFTA members is in fact offset by strict country-of-origin regulations prescribed in NAFTA. Unlike normal international standards that define country of origin at the product level, NAFTA defines country of origin at the yarn level. As a result, for a garment to be considered of NAFTA origin, it must be produced in a NAFTA country, of fabric woven and finished in a NAFTA country, and made from yarn spun in a NAFTA country.

In practice, NAFTA country-of-origin regulations protect the American (and to a lesser degree the Canadian) textile industry against foreign competition. As a result, Asian producers must not only compete against a very efficient U.S. textile industry, but also against a U.S. industry which now has the capacity to produce garments in a low-labor-cost area.

The same series of relationships that the United States has between MFN, CBI and NAFTA countries is mirrored in Western Europe. The members of the EU, like NAFTA, trade between themselves without quotas or tariffs. The Western European countries have their own preferred exporters, similar to the CBI, namely the countries of Eastern Europe, North Africa (particularly the French-speaking countries), and Turkey, who receive tariff advantages. The rest of the world is given the European equivalent of MFN, which carries duty rates for garments averaging 20%. The countries of the EU are far less reliant on Asian textile and garment imports than the United States

The total macro-cost advantage for preferred exporters is overwhelming. Unless Asian producers can compensate for the lower duty rates given to these countries, neither China nor the other major Asian exporters will be able to maintain their positions. The seriousness of the situation is obvious when you look further at the example of the jeans in Case Study XIII.

Case Study XIII—Pants: Duty Cost

Once again you are working for Wrangler.

You still have two choices. You can buy your jeans in China or you can buy them in the Dominican Republic. If you buy your jeans in the Dominican Republic, you pay duty on only the processing work carried out in the Dominican Republic. The fabric and trim, which are of U.S. origin and account for 70% of the FOB cost, are duty-free. Under CBI regulations, such work as cutting must be done in the United States and its cost is, therefore, duty-free. As a result, only 20% of the Dominican Republic jeans is dutiable. At 17.7% duty for cotton pants, total duty comes to $0.26. Assuming another $0.25 for freight, the Dominican jeans arrive in the United States, landed-duty-paid (LDP) for $7.76.

Complete duty must be paid on the Chinese-made jeans. As a result, they cannot cost more than $4.51 if they are to compete with the Dominican jeans. China must sell at a price 38% lower in order to compete.

As the buyer for Diesel, you are in a similar position with the same result.

The jeans from Hungary are also 80% duty-free. As a result, total duty is only $0.30. The Hungarians have an even greater freight advantage—they can ship from Budapest to Italy by truck at a cost of $0.15.

The Chinese jeans, on the other hand, are subject to 20% duty on the full FOB price, plus $0.30 freight. To compete, the Chinese would have to ship FOB $4.23—44% lower than the Hungarian FOB price.

BUYER	LDP	Freight	Duty	Quota	FOB
U.S. – Wrangler					
China	$7.76	$0.25	$0.80	$2.20	$4.51
Dominican Republic	$7.76	$0.25	$0.26	0	$7.25
Italy – Diesel					
China	$7.95	$0.30	$0.84	$2.58	$4.23
Hungary	$7.95	$0.15	$0.30	0	$7.50

COUNTRY OF ORIGIN

All garments exported to the United States or Western Europe are labeled with the country of origin. The consumer has a right to know where a product is made. Producing in some countries increases the value of the garment to the customer, while garments produced in others are considered to be worth less. To some degree these perceptions are correct. A blouse made in France or Italy is almost certainly of superior fabrication and better design than a blouse from Bangladesh. In any case, whether or not these perceptions are borne out by reality, country of origin is an important determinant of macro costs.

However, apart from any practical considerations, country of origin has a legal definition used for quota determinations, and that legal country of origin has little to do with where the garment is actually manufactured. Previously, when the international garment industry operated more simply, each garment was produced in one factory located in a single country. Today, this is no longer possible. The garment industry has gone global, and the manufacturing process for a single piece may extend to several factories or branches of a single factory located in several different countries.

Given the nature of the industry and the state of current U.S. Customs regulations, the legal definition of country of origin makes little sense, resulting in a continuous state of confusion. In theory, U.S. Customs contends that a garment is manufactured at the location where the major work takes place. This may not be too clear, but it is at least logical. However, specific regulations make nonsense of this definition. Here are some examples:

- The country of origin for a sweater is the place where the panels were knitted—except in the case of silk blend or linen sweaters knit in China, which may be listed as made in Hong Kong.

- The country of origin for silk scarves dyed, printed and sewn in Western Europe is China if the raw fabric was produced in China.

- Garments totally produced in Sweden are of Swedish origin regardless of where the fabric was woven. On the other hand, garments produced in Mexico are not of Mexican origin for NAFTA purposes if the original yarn used to weave the fabric was not produced in North America, even if the fabric was woven in Mexico.

This confusion means that you often do not know what the legal country of origin is until the U.S. Customs Department steps in and tells you that you have in fact acted illegally and slaps a fine on you.

In an effort to follow each subsequent twist in the country-of-origin regulations, manufacturers make investment decisions that often have little to do with their efforts to produce a better or less costly garment. Like quota, country-of-origin regulations simply distort the market without ever really informing the customer just where the garment was made.

Here is a case of a factory owner who started with the idea of expanding his production base to increase quality and reduce costs. In the end, his investment decisions were determined by regulations, not sense.

Case Study XIV—Brassiere

You are a Hong Kong brassiere manufacturer. Originally, all making was done in your Hong Kong factory. Your workflow was very simple. Everything was done in your one factory.

PCT OF WORK	OPERATION	LOCATION	STAGE
15% - 25%	Cutting	Hong Kong	Stage 0
5% - 15%	Laminating	Hong Kong	Stage 0
15% - 25%	Molding	Hong Kong	Stage 0
40% - 60%	Sewing	Hong Kong	Stage 0

To take advantage of production-cost differentials, you decide to globalize your production. The actual making of a brassiere involves four major steps. The location of operations is first based on quality requirements and direct-cost benefits. Currently your main customers are mass-market retailers, so quality considerations are not of the highest priority. However, you are planning to start work for more upmarket customers.

Your first step is to relocate molding offshore to China. Molding is labor-intensive but requires little skill. You next relocate cutting and laminating to the Chinese factory. The sewing and finishing are retained in Hong Kong where you can control quality.

PCT OF WORK	OPERATION	LOCATION	STAGE
15% - 25%	Cutting	China	Stage 2
5% - 15%	Laminating	China	Stage 2
15% - 25%	Molding	China	Stage 1
40% - 60%	Sewing	Hong Kong	Stage 1

Now enter the macro-costs problems of quota and country of origin.

In 1988, the U.S. rules of origin changed. Origin is now based on cutting. Therefore, in Stage 3, you return your cutting to Hong Kong. All goes well until 1994 when the quota situation changes. Where previously synthetic brassieres were listed under a nonspecific quota category readily available at zero cost, the new regulation places the same synthetic brassieres under Cat. 649 at a cost of $3.80-$5.20 per dozen, a considerable figure when compared to your FOB price.

To cope with this situation, you now expand production to Macau which has no quota. You now have three links in your chain, Hong Kong-Macau-China. While the Macau factory improves neither production efficiency nor quality, it does have real macro-cost advantage because of the free quota.

41

PCT OF WORK	OPERATION	LOCATION	STAGE
15% - 25%	Cutting	Macau	Stage 3
5% - 15%	Laminating	China	
15% - 25%	Molding	China	
40% - 60%	Sewing	Hong Kong	

All goes well until 1996 when the U.S. government once again changes the rules of origin to the country of major work. In Hong Kong-Macau-China, you face a dilemma. You have to relocate sewing from Hong Kong to Macau, which will bring the Macau portion of the work to almost 50% of total work. However, this may not be enough and you have no guarantee that U.S. Customs will accept your breakdowns. More importantly, your customers have concerns over the situation. In the end, you regretfully decide to move your molding back from China to Hong Kong.

These changes make life difficult. Macau sewing is not as good as the work done in Hong Kong. Molding in Hong Kong is also a problem: costs are higher. You will recall that you originally moved your molding work to China to save on labor costs, just like many of your competitors over the past decade. The number of people doing this work in Hong Kong has been greatly reduced. Now there are only a few small molding factories left and bottlenecks occur as you wait your turn in line.

PCT OF WORK	OPERATION	LOCATION	STAGE
15% - 25%	Cutting	Macau	
5% - 15%	Laminating	China	
15% - 25%	Molding	Hong Kong	Stage 4
40% - 60%	Sewing	Macau	Stage 4

TRADE DISPUTES

No one wants their orders caught up in a trade dispute. From first design to final stock shipment, the complete manufacturing process may take up to a year. If, during that time, the government of the country where you are placing your orders gets into a fight with U.S. Customs, there is a possibility that your supplier will not be able to ship—or ship so late that all your orders are canceled. When disputes with the same exporting country continually occur, as has happened between the United States and China over MFN or the United States and Hong Kong over illegal transshipments, as a prudent importer you had better begin looking elsewhere for suppliers simply to cover yourself.

In recent years, the number of trade disputes between the major importing nations and their principal Asian trade partners has escalated dramatically. As a result, many importers now find themselves looking ever further for new suppliers.

A. Antidumping Suits: Under WTO regulations, exporters are expected to sell their products at *fair market value*—at a price above cost and without imposing higher domestic prices for the same product that would in effect subsidize their lower export prices. In the event of predatory pricing from a particular company or country, the importing country is allowed to impose a duty surcharge on the imported product to bring the final price up to fair market value.

Antidumping regulations and the whole concept of fair market value began with anti-trust fears in the United States and Europe, where governments believed that free competition would not work unless protected by law. In actuality, these regulations have been ineffective. Countries that routinely engage in predatory pricing are not deterred. For example, in Japan the difference between domestic and export prices for some products such as cameras and electronic goods are so great that independent wholesalers are able to reimport made-in-Japan goods from other countries for resale in Japan—and still price their merchandise below domestic market price. Yet these practices remain unchallenged while legitimate exporters from Third World countries are continually subjected to nuisance lawsuits often based on little merit.

The idea that an unscrupulous band of dumpers will drive competitors out of business, leaving the remaining producers with a monopoly where they can feel free to raise prices, makes little sense to light industry. For extremely capital-intensive goods such as sheet steel, automobiles or semiconductors, there may be an argument for antidumping regulations. World production of these products is in the hands of relatively few companies, each of which has invested hundreds of millions, if not billions, of dollars in production facilities. In some countries such as China and Japan, these companies have joined together into cartels that set prices and control costly competition. These cartels could conceivably export to the United States at below-cost price to increase their market share and drive indigenous producers out of business, at which point they could use their monopolistic position to jack up prices.

For garment producers, however, this scenario is strictly science fiction. Garment manufacturing is not like semiconductor production. A modern semiconductor factory can cost over a billion dollars to set up, and worldwide there are a limited number of such facilities in existence. You can set up a garment factory for under $100,000. There are places where you can set up a garment factory for under $10,000, and there aren't hundreds of garment factories worldwide—*there are hundreds of thousands, if not millions, of factories*. A T-shirt cartel stands about as much chance of achieving a monopoly as a scheme to corner the market on tap water.

The reality is that interest groups in the United States and Western Europe use antidumping regulations to limit legitimate imports. Any

43

American manufacturer, no matter how incompetent, can blame his failures on cheap labor imports. Once the manufacturer provides evidence, however scanty, that he has been harmed, the 'offending' overseas manufacturers are required to defend themselves against every accusation. Defense against dumping can cost a factory over a half-million dollars and few Asian garment manufacturers have the necessary capital. For many years, an unsubstantiated charge was all that was necessary to drive a foreign factory out of business.

More recently, governments and trade groups in exporting countries have started to assist factories in defending themselves against spurious antidumping suits. Hopefully, this will reduce the number of such suits in the future.

B. Country-of-Origin Disputes: Ill-conceived definitions cause serious problems to importers and exporters alike in their attempts to conform to ever-changing country-of-origin regulations. Ambiguity notwithstanding, country-of-origin regulations brought on the rise of massive illegal transshipments. For years, garments produced in China have been routinely shipped elsewhere—notably Hong Kong, Macau and Mongolia—where they are relabeled and subsequently reshipped to the United States using the quota of the transshipping country. This is not an open secret. This is no secret at all.

For many years U.S. Customs closed their eyes to what was going on. Suddenly in 1996, they decided to open them, imposing special restrictions on four categories of garments shipped from Hong Kong. The most serious stipulation required importers to post a cash bond for each shipment imported from Hong Kong as surety that the goods were, in fact, produced there. The cost of the bond could be as much as three times the FOB value of the shipment, vastly inflating macro costs. Importers literally fled Hong Kong to find other producers for these four categories.The dispute, which began in June 1996, is a case study of how government trade disputes can decimate an established industry.

Because quota distorts trade patterns, normal trade statistics are of little value when exports are restricted by quota. Values listed on export invoices and licenses seldom include the full quota premium. Statistics drawn from these sources may be off by as much as 50%. Furthermore, since quota imposes an artificial ceiling on exports, it is difficult to gauge changes in demand by examining export statistics. Demand may rise with no discernible effect on exports since quota has limited manufacturers' ability to meet that demand. Similarly, demand may fall appreciably with no discernible effect on exports. A situation may occur in which previously two customers existed for every item under quota, whereas now there is only one. Demand has halved but export volumes remain unchanged.

A record of garment quantities licensed for each quota category, using 1992 as a base year and compared with 1995 and 1996, is interesting only in that it shows no major changes occurring in export volumes shipped to the United States after the U.S. imposed the severe restrictions in June 1996. Since prices are negotiated long before shipment is made, it is reasonable to assume there would be little change in the period immediately following the imposition of restrictions.

However, further investigation reveals other developments. Hong Kong has its own special informal statistics which, in this case, are more accurate than anything available to the Hong Kong Trade Department. In Hong Kong, quota is traded openly. Specialist quota brokers quote prices daily. These quota prices provide precise information about immediate changes in demand for Hong Kong-made garments. In 1996 while there was no change in the quantity of garments shipped, the change in the value of quota was immediate and catastrophic. It was as if Hong Kong's major customers had all decided in one breath that it was time to begin working elsewhere.

The table on the following page lists price changes in selected U.S. quota categories from 1992-97. Categories are listed by garment type. For example, dresses are -36. Listed are 336 (cotton dresses), 436 (wool dresses), and 636 (synthetic dresses).

First, we need to draw a distinction between long-term trends and those that occurred as an immediate result of the June 1996 dispute. The table shows average prices and indices of prices for 1992, 1995 and 1997. There are two listings for 1996: pre-dispute and post-dispute. The items listed that were affected by the dispute are Cat. 636 (synthetic dresses) and Cat. 642 (synthetic skirts).

U.S. QUOTA PRICES 1992-97*

		PRICES						INDEX (1992 = 100)					
		'92	'95	'96		'97	5/97	'92	'95	'96		'97	5/97
CAT	DESCRIPTION			PRE	POST					PRE	POST		
335	Coat	18	23	33	9	8	2	100	128	183	50	44	11
435	Coat	111	19	46	45	43	41	100	17	41	41	39	37
635	Coat	20	4	4	2	2	1	100	20	20	10	10	5
336	Dress	37	49	33	26	10	6	100	132	89	70	27	16
436	Dress	21	16	18	8	10	6	100	76	86	38	48	29
636	Dress	12	27	22	7	7	4	100	225	183	58	58	32
340	Shirt	25	8	6	2	4	3	100	32	24	8	16	12
640	Shirt	7	2	1	1	1	1	100	29	14	14	14	9
341	Blouse	13	3	2	1	2	1	100	23	15	8	15	5
641	Blouse	11	2	1	0	1	1	100	18	9	0	9	6
342	Skirt	18	23	33	9	8	5	100	128	183	50	44	28
442	Skirt	54	16	24	7	14	9	100	30	44	13	26	17
642	Skirt	23	39	26	7	8	4	100	170	113	30	35	19
345	Sweater	41	23	24	65	40	40	100	56	59	159	98	98
445/6	Sweater	16	24	27	9	29	26	100	150	169	56	181	161
645/6	Sweater	4	3	8	13	16	16	100	75	200	325	400	388

* Figures in U.S. dollars per dozen

In the four years from 1992 to 1995, Hong Kong quota prices generally fell due to the overall drop in demand as more customers and factories moved from Hong Kong to China; yet during this period, quota in almost every category remained fully utilized. Whether this was the result of massive illegal transshipments, as alleged by the U.S. Customs Department, or simply the previous existence of demand in excess of supply is irrelevant. What is important is that while all coat quota was utilized every year, the quota premium for Cat. 435 (wool coats) fell 83% and Cat. 635 (synthetic coats) 80% during that period.

Furthermore, not every category fell equally. Quota prices for Cat. 345, 445/6 and 645/6, after generally falling, actually rose in value from 1992-97 due both to substantial increases in worldwide sweater demand and Hong Kong's excellent reputation for producing quality sweaters.

In the case of the categories involved in the dispute, however, a more clear-cut story emerged. In both cases (Cat. 636 and 642), demand had actually increased from 1992-95—contrary to the general trend. Demand remained relatively strong in 1996 up to the dispute, at which point the quota price crashed. In the case of Cat. 636, the index fell by more than two-thirds from 183 to 58—and by almost three-quarters—from 113 to 30—in the case of Cat. 642. Neither price recovered in 1997 even though the U.S. government subsequently voided the individual bond requirement. The quota premiums for May 1997 fell still further.

In a knock-on effect, the premiums for other skirt and dress categories—Cat. 342, 442, 336 and 436—fell to the same extent as the two categories specifically singled out by the U.S. government, and these have also remained extremely low.

The data underscores a trend that bodes ill for Hong Kong's garment industry: the trade dispute clearly caused customers for these items to go elsewhere. As long as the Hong Kong government ensures that local factories conform to U.S. regulations, Hong Kong industry cannot utilize its own quota. As a result, Hong Kong producers not only lost a large portion of their market for the penalized items, but for related items as well. What's worse, a year later, far from returning to their Hong Kong suppliers, even more customers were leaving.

This trade war hurt not only Hong Kong but Chinese industry as well. Stricter supervision by the Hong Kong Trade Department virtually eliminated most illegal transshipments; Hong Kong companies must now use Chinese quota to ship their made-in-China garments. For proof, you have only to look at the prices of Chinese quota which reached unprecedented highs just as the price of Hong Kong quota plummeted to all-time lows. Strangely, while U.S. Department of Commerce statistics showed a single-digit rise in China apparel imports for 1997, according to anecdotal evidence and industry estimates, overall real volumes from China to the U.S. actually fell by as much as half.

No country can afford a trade war. However, Hong Kong—where foreign trade accounts for 180% of GNP—is singularly vulnerable.

C. General Disputes: Having your orders held up indefinitely by U.S. Customs because of illegal dumping can be costly and upsetting. So too can having your merchandise held up because of incorrect country-of-origin labels. In these cases, you are at least to some degree responsible. You might have taken the time to consider that undamaged jackets at less than half-price was simply too good to be true. You should have known that Zimbabwe does not have a silk industry and that the blouses being shipped were more than likely produced someplace else.

But imagine how you would feel if your order of cotton shorts was trapped in customs due to a dispute over oranges—or if every time the United States had a dispute with China over its policy in Tibet or rules governing computer software you received a letter from your government saying:

Greetings from the President:

The Chinese government has irresponsibly refused entry to three boatloads of Sunkist oranges into their country. Their high-handed action has caused great concern to farmers in Florida.

Your government has decided that this situation is unacceptable. We have, therefore, nominated you and your fellow partners at Schmidlap Sleepwear to take positive action. Until further notice, we ask you not to import any more pajamas from China. To assist you, we have instructed U.S. Customs not to release any new shipments of Chinese sleepwear and pajamas until the Chinese accept our Sunkist oranges, which you will be happy to know are fortified with vitamin C.

Mrs. Clinton and I want you to know that we support your courageous action. We stand behind you 1000% percent.

Thank you and bless you.

D. 301 and Super-301: The U. S. government can by law restrict the imports of any commodity from any country that restricts imports of U.S. merchandise into theirs. This position translates into the creation of potential sources of additional import duties and other restrictions on imports from Asia.

Under the 1988 Omnibus Trade Law, the administration must identify to Congress any trade partner who engages in unfair competition. If the situation cannot be remedied, the administration is required to place additional duties on the products of the offending nation to equal the estimated loss of revenue to U.S. producers. India, Japan, Taiwan and Thailand have been among the Asian nations previously identified under 301. China—the largest exporter of garments and textiles to the U.S. and a prime target for retaliation—has often been singled out, for reasons including:

- Failure to publish regulations, laws, judicial decisions and administrative rulings showing customs requirements, restrictions or prohibitions of imports;

- Selected product and sector-specific import prohibitions or quantitative restrictions;

- Restrictions on import licensing;

- Technical barriers to trade, including unreasonable inspection rules;

- Import tariffs ranging from 120%-170%.

By heightening uncertainty which, in turn, increases macro costs, trade disputes inevitably hinder the ability of importers to work freely with certain countries. Prudent importers must consider the risks and consequences of these disputes when deciding where to buy goods.

Buying quality merchandise from reliable factories at reasonable prices does not help your company unless you can bring the goods into the United States.

TRADING BLOCS: THE POLITICS OF TRADE

All macro costs involve politics, but the most political macro costs of all are trading blocs. NAFTA, the EU and APEC (Asia-Pacific Exporting Countries) were created solely for political purposes. Trading blocs as a macro-cost factor will completely change the patterns of international trade in this century. Exporting countries that were previously the most competitive will become increasingly less so, while countries inside the various blocs will have unbeatable cost advantages.

The trend is so strong that it is conceivable that outsiders will simply not be able to compete. The figures are irrefutable (see chart on following page). During the twelve-month period from July 1995 to July 1996, imports to the U.S. from NAFTA members Mexico and Canada soared 40.94% and 21.95% respectively. For the same period, those from the leading Asian suppliers fell—Hong Kong by 9.31% and China by 21.39%.

The purpose of all trade blocs is to maintain a captive market for the goods produced inside the bloc by excluding, at least to some degree, everyone outside from competing within the market. Exclusion can be measured by the magnitude of the advantage members of the bloc enjoy over the rest of the world.

Where normal tariffs are low, advantages to producers within the bloc are also low. For the duty rate on automobiles at 4%, producers in NAFTA countries have little advantage over their competitors in Japan. However, where duties average 18%, as in the case of garments, the advantage is considerable. Furthermore, when there is also quota, the cost differences can be overwhelming. Look at the calculations below.

Case Study XV—Polo Shirt

You are now buying polo shirts for Target Stores. You have a choice—you can buy from China or Mexico.

The Mexican shirt costs $6.00 FOB. For the purpose of this case study, assume there is no duty or quota.[9]

Current market price for quota Cat. 338/339 in China is $2.25 per piece.

Duty rates for cotton knit shirts to the United States (6109.10.00) is 21%.

COUNTRY	COMPETITIVE FOB	DUTY	QUOTA	TOTAL	PCT FOB DIFFERENCE
China	$3.10	$0.65	$2.25	$6.00	48.4%
Mexico	$6.00	0	0	$6.00	.

To compete, the Chinese T-shirtmaker would have to sell for almost half the FOB price of his Mexican competitor. We haven't even looked at the other advantages of Mexican production: the added freight time and cost of shipping by sea from China, as opposed to shipping by truck from Mexico, and the fact that the Mexican T-shirt will be produced from American cotton yarn, which is far superior to anything available in China.

LEADING GARMENT EXPORTERS TO U.S. 1996–97

Country	Sales 7/95-7/96	Market Share	Change '96	Sales 1/97-12/97	Market Share	Change '97
Mexico	3631	8.31%	40.94%	5050	11.80%	39.08%
China	4126	9.45%	-21.39%	4487	10.50%	8.75%
Hong Kong	4165	9.53%	-9.31%	3934	9.20%	-5.55%
Dominican Rep	1759	4.03%	0.55%	2215	5.20%	25.92%
Taiwan	2681	6.14%	-7.87%	2071	4.80%	-22.75%
Honduras	N/A	N/A	N/A	1659	3.90%	N/A
Philippines	1717	3.93%	5.64%	1596	3.70%	-7.05%
Indonesia	1398	3.20%	9.42%	1596	3.70%	14.16%
S. Korea	2101	4.81%	-13.25%	1517	3.50%	-27.80%
Bangladesh	N/A	N/A	N/A	1447	3.40%	N/A
Canada	1847	4.23%	21.94%	N/A	N/A	N/A
India	1651	3.78%	2.10%	N/A	N/A	N/A
Italy	1571	3.60%	10.40%	N/A	N/A	N/A
Thailand	1376	3.15%	-2.20%	N/A	N/A	N/A

Figures in U.S. $billions. Source U.S. Department of Commerce statistics.

From January to July 1996, textile and garment exports to the U.S. from its NAFTA partners grew at a substantially higher magnitude than exports from outside the NAFTA bloc.

What is remarkable about Mexico's dramatic increase in garment and textile exports is that, unlike Canada, Mexico had no past history of textiles and garments other than ethnic fabrics and embroidered articles. Furthermore, the quality of Mexican production remains relatively poor. Importers have been forced to create an industry from the ground up. Spurring their efforts were the massive macro-cost advantages that Mexico enjoys through NAFTA. By 1997, Mexico had become the world's largest garment exporter to the United States, due entirely to macro-cost advantages.

There is another political aspect to trade blocs which, though very important, is not immediately apparent—the ongoing conflict between local garment and textile interests. Most people look at textiles and garments as parts of a single industry with common goals. For example, we tend to assume that increases in demand for garments will inevitably lead to increased demand for textiles. And so they do—on a global basis. However, in any particular market the relationship is by no means fixed. The average garment may contain over 60% fabric by value; however, there is no reason to assume that any particular garment produced in the United States would be made from American fabric.

In fact, garment factories in the United States, hoping to increase their share of the U.S. market, also want access to foreign fabric to both reduce costs and increase variety of style. Domestic mills, on the other hand, want to reduce fabric imports, even if this leads to reduction in domestic garment production. As U.S. fabric producers possess superior lobbies and traditionally more political influence, American regulations, laws and policy are skewed in their favor against the interests of garmentmakers.

U.S. import duty rates clearly demonstrate this bias. The duty on a wool skirt (6204.52.20) is 17%. The duty on woven wool fabric (5111.20.90, 5111.30.90, 5112.20.30, 5112.30.30) is 32.8% + $0.291/kg.

Case Study XVI—Wool Skirt: Subsidizing Foreign Factories

You are now buying ladies' sportswear for Bloomingdale's. You have to place an order for wool plaid kilts.

The fabric comes from Scotland (Bloomingdale's is a class operation) at a cost of $12.00 per yard and each garment requires 1.25 yards. Total fabric cost is $15.00. You can produce the garments either in Sri Lanka or the United States. If you produce in Sri Lanka, you have to pay a quota premium of $1.00 per kilt. You also have to fly in the fabric at a cost of $1.25 ($1.00 per yard). Finally, you must airfreight the finished garments to the United States at a cost of $1.75 per piece. If you produce the skirts in the United States, freight for the fabric is only $0.38 ($0.25 per yard). You have no duty for the garments. You have no external freight. You have only the duty on the fabric.

COUNTRY	FAB	FAB FRT	FAB DUTY	FAB TOTAL	CMT	GMT FOB	GMT QUOTA	GMT FRT	GMT DUTY	TOTAL
Sri Lanka	$15.00	$1.25	0	$16.25	$4.00	$20.25	$1.00	$1.75	$3.44	$26.44
U.S.	$15.00	$0.38	$6.00	$21.38	$8.00	$29.38	0	0	0	$29.38

The kilt produced in Sri Lanka is almost $3.00 cheaper than the same item produced in the United States, even though:

- The fabric had to be flown 8,000 miles from Scotland to Colombo and the finished garment flown 9,000 miles from Colombo to New York;
- The kilt produced in Sri Lanka required a surcharge for quota;
- The kilt produced in Sri Lanka was subject to duty on the full garment price while the kilt produced in the U.S. was subject to duty only on the fabric.

Much of the cost difference is attributed to the lower manufacturing cost (CMT) in Sri Lanka, only 50% of U.S. costs. But that advantage was only maintained because of the duty difference between imports of fabric and garments to the United States. If the duty rate were identical, the garment produced in the United States would have cost only 2% more than the one from Sri Lanka. In that case, it would have been clearly illogical to ship the fabric all around the world just to save $0.51.

What makes production in Sri Lanka profitable is the U.S. duty difference between fabric and finished garments which ultimately subsidizes overseas factories. The U.S. government would rather subsidize overseas garment exports to the United States than allow domestic makers to produce using imported fabrics.

The textile industry is capital-intensive, giving Western countries a distinct advantage over China and other Third World nations. In recent decades, textile manufacturers in Western Europe and the United States have periodically made the necessary investments to upgrade machinery, skills and technology and have remained competitive with their lower labor-cost counterparts.

For the U.S. textile industry, NAFTA offers a golden opportunity to lock in its position as the main raw materials supplier for all garments sold in the United States. Remember, by NAFTA regulations, country of origin for garments does not refer to the country where the garment is produced. It does not even refer to the country where the fabric is woven and finished. To qualify for duty-free status, a garment has to be produced in a NAFTA country of fabric woven and finished in a NAFTA country, in turn woven of 100% NAFTA yarn.

As a sop to domestic U.S. garmentmakers, NAFTA did not immediately end tariffs and quotas for all garments. There is a schedule allowing for gradual transition. However, by December 31, 2004, all NAFTA trade will be theoretically free.[10]

Further weighing the scales in favor of the textile sector is the widespread sentiment in the United States and the EU that a strong textile industry is a real national asset. Since at least 60% of every garment is fabric cost, every time Mexico exports a garment to the United States produced from American fabric, almost two-thirds of that import is actually domestic production. Every time a factory in Eastern Europe or North Africa exports a garment to the EU, 60% of the value never left home.

Tariffs, quotas, country-of-origin regulations and trade disputes all exist in the real world and each can greatly affect product macro costs. Yet there is one factor with the greatest potential impact on macro costs which does not exist at all—this is perception. We live in a world where perception has more impact than reality. When professionals state that the consumer does not care what country a product is made in or about factory working conditions in that country, they are fooling themselves. If people decide that something is bad or that a particular government is evil, they will simply stop buying. These perceptions have already destroyed Burma's nascent export-garment industry. They now threaten China.

NOBODY LIKES CHINA

The greatest international success story of the past two decades has been China. However you measure progress, China has excelled. Despite the many social and political problems which persist today, when you consider that in 1976 China was just emerging from the Cultural Revolution, a decade of tragedy and destruction unequaled since the era of Genghis Khan, here is a country worthy of respect.

Yet the perceptions we have about China currently threaten to dramatically raise the macro costs of doing business there. It is as if every individual and group from every facet of American thinking, from

53

...Nobody Likes China...

reactionaries still fighting the anticommunist crusade to liberals looking to protect human rights, have converged in agreement on a single point: *We do not like China*. The Christian right accuses the Chinese of committing wholesale infanticide (abortion) and makes common cause with women's rights movements who charge them with female infanticide (murder of girl children). In the U.S. Congress, liberal members join with conservative Sen. Jesse Helms to castigate the Chinese over excesses in Tibet. Corporations looking to jump on the Chinese investment bandwagon temporarily leap off to attack the Chinese over trade restrictions, copyright piracy and illegal transshipments.

If it were not for rising macro costs, in the near future, China would certainly dominate the international textile and garment industries. China—particularly now that it includes Hong Kong—has the most competitive full-value cost structure of any country in the world.

The government of China and the more progressive parts of its industry are doing everything possible to make buying garments in China user-friendly. Thanks to enormous investments of capital and expertise on the part of Hong Kong and Taiwanese companies, working in Shanghai, Dalian and the areas adjacent to Hong Kong is easier than almost anywhere else in the world. If it were left to the producers, China would have the lowest macro costs of any garment and textile producer worldwide.

But macro costs are affected by perceptions in the importing countries. These perceptions are inflating macro costs to a point where doing business in China will become simply too expensive. These perceptions alone raise macro costs. Unfortunately, no one stops to consider how accurate these perceptions are. Here are but a few examples:

- China is a predator in the world trade arena.

China is allowed almost unlimited access to U.S. markets, while severely restricting U.S. imports. China has the second largest trade surplus in the world with the United States, after Japan. In 1996, China exported $51 billion worth of merchandise to the United States and imported only $12 billion worth,[11] leaving a deficit of over $39 billion.

The Chinese argue that these figures are incorrect. They maintain that although the United States has a trade deficit with China, it is only about $12 billion—less than one-third the amount claimed by Washington.

In fact, neither claim has real merit—it is all a question of statistical definitions. The United States computes exports on the basis of the country to where the goods are shipped. If merchandise is then reexported to a third country, the United States statistics do not record these movements. On the other hand, imports are listed by country of origin. As a result, when the United States exports merchandise to Hong Kong, which in turn reexports those same goods to China, the United States still considers the goods to be part of exports to Hong Kong. However, if China exports goods to Hong Kong, which in turn reexports those same goods to the United States, the United States counts this as imports from China.

The Chinese take the same approach—with the opposite results. When they export goods to Hong Kong, which in turn reexports the same goods to the United States, China calls this 'exports to Hong Kong'. However, when they import goods from the United States through a third country, they calculate this as imports from the United States.

The amounts involved are considerable. Because Hong Kong has some of the largest and most efficient port facilities in the world, most imports and exports from southern China come through Hong Kong, creating one of the world's largest trading areas. Hong Kong does the largest volume of reexports in the world. It also has—after the Netherlands, Australia and Belgium—the fourth largest trade deficit with the United States, due almost entirely to imported U.S. goods re-exported to China.

- China uses prison labor—many prisoners are held on political grounds—to produce merchandise which it then exports to the other countries.

It is certainly true that people work in Chinese jails. The late Chiang Ching, wife of Mao Zedong and leader of the 'Gang of Four', worked in a prison doll factory after her conviction in the late 1970s. It is also true that China, to its discredit, imprisons political dissidents.

In fact, the reality differs greatly from the perception. Most people in Chinese jails—probably 99 out of every 100—are criminals in the widely accepted meaning of the word. China puts its prisoners to work. Putting prisoners to work is a perfectly reasonable idea. In the United States, it costs more money to send someone to jail for four years than to Harvard University to receive a B.A. degree. The United States increasingly spends more money on building prisons than building schools. The United States has a higher percentage of its population in jail than any other country in the world, including China.

The United States would do well to copy the Chinese and put its jailed drug pushers, child molesters and other criminals to work. Why should they not defray at least a part of their costs?

- Chinese industry is based on workers who are forced to work unreasonably long hours in terrible conditions for slave wages.

Certainly by U.S. standards, wages in China are low. But, in fact, the factories that produce most export garments are not the giant state factories with their antiquated machinery covered with decades of grime and sewers working seven days a week for subsistence wages. Those factories are going broke because of poor machinery and an equally poor management that has permitted valuable industrial assets, both human and mechanical, to deteriorate badly. Approximately 90% of garment exports are actually produced by township, cooperative and joint-venture factories in the areas around Hong Kong, Shanghai and several northern cities.

In these factories, for the most part equipment is modern, buildings are often air-conditioned and workers are paid about $0.50 per hour. By U.S. standards, this is quite low. But by Third World standards, wages are quite high—particularly when compared with the cost of living. Wages in Chinese export factories are twice those paid to similar workers in Indonesia and Sri Lanka—and three times that paid to workers in Bangladesh, India and Vietnam. In addition, wages in export-garment factories are rising by well over 10% per annum. People have to start somewhere. We should not be outraged to discover that countries that began economic development hundreds of years after us have not caught up immediately.

- China is an economic thief that steals our secrets through copyright piracy.

There is no question that copyright piracy is rampant in China. Individuals in the highest-level of provincial governments are involved as are senior officers in the People's Liberation Army (PLA). Nevertheless, there is general consensus among knowledgeable professionals that the central government is making a real effort to put an end to piracy, although admittedly, many believe more can be done.

The reality is that even at its worst, copyright piracy in China never reached the levels it attained in the former Soviet Union, where perhaps over 90% of all software is pirated. In terms of value, Chinese copyright piracy is lower than that in Germany. Yet we do not castigate the Russians; we do not even mention the Germans at all. Copyright piracy is certainly theft. But it isn't a peculiarly Chinese problem—it is a worldwide one.

- The Chinese do not allow political dissent. Those who disagree with the politics of the ruling elite and who speak out are severely penalized.

Anyone in China who is an activist dissenter runs the risk of being sent to jail. However, this is not unique to China. There are very few places in Asia where I would choose to be an activist dissenter. There is no question that if I raised the cry of 'freedom' in China and were not American, I, too, would quickly find myself in deep trouble—probably in jail. Then again, if I did the same thing in most countries of Eastern Europe or Central or South America as a local, I would also find myself in prison.

Most countries have serious human rights problems. China, while certainly deserving of criticism, should in no way be singled out for opprobrium.

- Tibet

While there is no justification for Chinese policy in Tibet, the debate here concerns not only our perceptions but our reactions. To many well-meaning people, the only solution is total isolation—we should stop all relations and certainly all trade with China. Yet there are those—including the Dalai Lama himself—who believe that the best hope for a satisfactory solution to the problems in Tibet is in continued engagement with the Chinese authorities.

Unacceptable working conditions, predatory trade policies, copyright piracy, human rights and foreign aggression—the morality of these problems is not at issue. For our purposes, these problems are questions of cost. What is at issue is how many people are making business decisions based solely on moral stands. Regardless of the truth or falsity of any of these perceptions, more and more Americans believe that these perceptions are accurate and that doing business in China is immoral.

There is a growing number of consumers who do not buy made-in-China products, who want the U.S. government to take more direct action to penalize China, and eventually to cease all business. This in itself raises the cost of doing business in China and of buying made-in-China garments. Even now there are companies in the United States that refuse to work in China.

The Chinese government believes that anti-China feeling is the result of U.S. government propaganda. Senior officials in the Chinese government believe these to be matters of foreign policy and, as such, solvable on a government-to-government basis. What they fail to understand is that in the United States few people believe anything government tells them. The Chinese don't realize that most American social policy—whether it involves antipollution laws, protection from crime, or foreign policy—is the result of people pushing government. In the United States, government realizes that the first step in leadership is to catch up with those you plan to lead.

CONCLUSIONS

In most cases, macro costs are the most important factors determining total garment cost. In some cases, macro costs might be the only important factor. Let's face it—you are not going to North Korea to buy goods, even if they gave you the garments for nothing.

However, macro costs are not the only factors determining product cost and high macro costs can be offset. Garment duties from Vietnam, until it gains most-favored-nation status as currently under discussion in the U.S. Congress, average 70% compared with 18% for the rest of the world. Nevertheless, that added cost can be overcome, where Vietnamese factories are able to offer other advantages that offset their very high macro costs.

Besides the obvious—cheap labor—a factory can possess other advantages which can compensate for high macro costs:

- The factory might have facilities that allow them to carry out necessary manufacturing tasks, such as patternmaking or samplemaking, that you are now performing in the United States.

- The factory might own or have access to specialized or hard-to-find facilities, such as handembroidery or space-dye techniques, which you require.

- The factory might just be very dependable, which in itself can offer great cost savings.

Those advantages that are specific to suppliers and factories are indirect costs. After macro costs, they are the key factors which determine product cost and are the subject of the next three chapters.

Chapter 4
Indirect Costs: Facilities

If your business is the manufacture, purchase or importing of garments, then all the costs in your business have to come out of those garments. However, if those costs are to come out of the garments, they first need to be included—this means, not only macro costs, but also the FOB price, the company car you drive, and the theater tickets you bought for your buyers. Your accountant may insist that these be listed as cost of goods, administrative expenses and selling expenses. That is his problem. He can call them anything he wants. He does not have to pay the bills. As far as you are concerned, each T-shirt must include a few cents for your car and everything else you charge to your business.

One important part of product cost is manufacturing, which includes all the materials and processes required to produce the product. In fact, anything or anybody that brings physical change to the product is a part of the manufacturing process and must be included in manufacturing costs.

But while the rent you pay for your Broadway showroom, your bookkeeper's salary and the trip you made to Indianapolis to do the show at L.S. Ayers are all product costs, they are not manufacturing costs. Likewise, macro costs such as import duties, quota premiums, the cost of working in countries with poor infrastructure and human rights records, are also product costs. However, since none of these physically change the product, they are not part of your manufacturing costs.

Contrast these expenses with the cost of your patternmaking department, your designers, the woman who makes your specs, your samplemakers, the rent you pay for the space they occupy and the cost of the electricity they consume. Since all of these produce physical change in the garment, they are as much a part of the manufacturing process as the cutting department in the factory making the stock garments and the buttons and other materials that go into those garments.

This concept is exceedingly difficult to grasp because we are all taught to think in terms of definition. We believe that a factory *is* a room full of machines or that the designer is that woman who comes in every day and sits behind that sketching table. In fact, both factory and designer are functions. A factory *does* manufacturing just as a designer *does* design work; any place where manufacturing takes place is a factory just as anyone who does design work is a designer. All are part of the manufacturing process and must be included as manufacturing costs.

We have been taught to believe that manufacturing takes place only in the *factory* where the garments are *made*. Unfortunately, this definition leaves out almost all of the most expensive manufacturing costs. This point is not a mere academic discussion of interest only to economists; it is crucial to all garment importers. Unless you include indirect costs in your costings, you have no way to identify the factory with the lowest costs to produce your goods.

For a simple illustration of this premise, look at the following example.

Case Study XVII—The Patternmaker

You import ladies' dresses. Your average order is 2,000 pieces per style. In the course of a year, you import 250 styles totaling 500,000 garments. Since you have a good designer and a good merchandiser, 50% of all the styles you make original samples for actually become orders. You, therefore, require 500 patterns per year. With corrections and grading, you need three patternmakers and one grader. Even if you pay the lowest wages in the industry, your salaries, including benefits, will probably total a minimum of $265,000 per annum. You have to add another $100,000 for rent (patternmakers need space), utilities, equipment, etc. Your pattern room now costs you $365,000 per year. You have to pay these people in slow times and probably overtime in the busy periods. And this is all overhead.

You work at two factories—one in southern China, the other in Thailand. The southern China factory charges CMT $5.00 per dress; the Thai factory, $4.70. All other costs are the same. The quality is the same and both are equally reliable. However, the southern China factory will make and grade your patterns as part of the FOB price. The Thai factory cannot.

Whom do you prefer?

The difference in CMT price is $0.30. On a half-million units, the costs at the Thai factory are $150,000 less than in southern China. However, the southern China factory will do all your patternmaking, thus allowing you to close your U.S. pattern room, saving you an immediate $365,000 per annum, plus changing what was an overhead expense to a direct expense. As an added bonus, this shift allows you to fire Rosenzweig, your so-called chief patternmaker who has been giving you a cancer for the past ten years.

The decision seems obvious, except for one small point. You have not included patternmaking in your costing. Go ahead, look at your costing. Do you see an item marked *patternmaking and grading cost*? No! To you, only fabric and CMT are included. And that is why you have preferred Thailand over southern China all these years. You never knew that the $0.30 per dress in your pocket was really costing you net $215,000 a year.

Patternmaking is not the only function concerned. The discussion involves the entire manufacturing process, which can be divided into two parts—the actual making of stock garments, the direct costs; and everything else, the indirect costs. Limiting manufacturing costs to only the direct costs of material plus garmentmaking is to exclude the indirect costs, by far the most time-consuming and expensive part of the manufacturing process.

61

Indirect costs are the expenses required for all the operations included in the manufacturing process other than making charges. Someone must perform these operations if the stock order is ever to be completed. That someone is either you or your supplier. For your supplier to do the required work, he must have special facilities such as patternmakers or access to good dyers and printers. If the supplier has the facilities, the cost of that operation can be included in the FOB price of the garment. You save money on your end because you no longer have to pay for those specific items separately. Naturally, a factory with special facilities will charge more for the garments than a factory that lacks those facilities. However, when the amount added by the factory costs is less than the amount you would have had to pay to do the work yourself, you have a net saving and the factory has provided an indirect-cost advantage.

You have a similar problem dealing with indirect costs as you did with macro costs. You can't negotiate macro costs because macro-cost expenses are countrywide expenses. The factory has no control over them. Only the government does. Likewise, you cannot negotiate indirect costs unless the factory has the specific facilities you require. Without those facilities, you have nothing to negotiate about. You cannot negotiate for the factory to make patterns or to print greige goods unless the factory has patternmakers or access to quality printers. Because of this reality, traditionally few buyers in the industry include indirect costs as part of either product or manufacturing costs.

Nevertheless, indirect costs cover a very wide area and after macro costs, are the most important factors in the total cost of the product. Once you have decided which country to make your goods in, your decision on which factory to give your work to should be based on indirect-cost advantages.

At the back of this book is a flow chart which lists all the steps you, your agent or the maker go through to produce a single style. There are 101 steps starting with *Designer attends fabric show* (1) to *Order ready for shipment* (101). The first sample you sewed in New York is the box marked Step 14. The first duplicate the factory sewed for you is the box listed as Step 39. Did you supply fabric for the sample? Look at the diamond marked Step 25. If yes (Y), the factory should have inspected the fabric on receipt as marked in the diamond marked Step 33. On the other hand, if you did not send sample fabric, the factory had to locate the fabric for you. After all, someone had to supply the fabric; in this case, the factory carried out their work in the boxes marked Steps 34-37.

You will also note that there are additional Steps 96-100 which include *Prepare shipping documents* and *Final inspection*, marked with broken lines. These operations are separate because, although they are normally carried out at the factory location, they do not physically change the garment and, therefore, are not part of the manufacturing process. Licenses, invoices and packing lists are necessary to clear the goods; however, they do not change the goods. The same is true of final inspection. On the other hand, *In-process inspection*, Step 93, is carried out to make necessary changes in the garmentmaking process and is therefore an integral part of the manufacturing process. However, by the time you reach final inspection, it is too late to make any changes. The garments are complete. As a result, final inspection is irrelevant to the manufacturing process. Final inspection does not help improve garment quality, but tells you much about the quality of your agent and maker.

The first thing that becomes clear is just how much manufacturing time and work is necessary before *Stock order ready to cut* (87). In the entire flow chart, only 28 days and nine operations involve actually making the garment. The second thing that becomes clear is that all the expensive people and work are involved in Steps 1-86. Surely if you want to save money, the place to do it is the earlier stages of the manufacturing process.

The direct costs of making the garment compose less than 15% of the total number of operations and take up less than 15% of the manufacturing period, yet almost all importers exclude the remaining 85% of manufacturing costs from their calculations.

These next three chapters deal with indirect costs—the forgotten 85% of the cost of the manufacturing process.

The ability to provide garments with low indirect costs is in the hands of the factory: the buyer can not control these costs. I am sure you would like the factory to make, correct and grade your patterns. You would also like the factory to make your samples. If your maker produces the patterns and the samples, then you no longer need a sample, patternmaking or grading department. However, this is not something you can negotiate with the factory. There is no sense arguing about samples and patterns if the factory has no sample department or patternmakers. What you can do as an intelligent importer is select your suppliers on the basis of what facilities they can offer to reduce your indirect costs.

This is how you save money—you find the factory that has the necessary facilities. It is these facilities that reduce your indirect costs and allow you to buy your garments at the lowest cost. Indirect costs affect price far more than direct costs. If you disregard indirect-cost factors, you will inevitably wind up first with Louie the Lip and The World's Greatest T-shirt Factory and shortly thereafter at a Chapter 11 hearing.

HORIZONTAL INTEGRATION

One way to look at indirect costs is as horizontal integration. Everyone knows about vertical integration. This is where you start with a sheep and you wind up with an overcoat. If you own the sheep, the spinning mill, the weaving mill, the dyer and the garment factory, you are vertically integrated.

Horizontal integration is a little more complicated. Here the factory does only the garments, but it does everything there is to do in this single area. For example, for a single blouse order there are 86 steps required before you can begin to produce your stock blouses. This includes samples, patterns, lab dips or strikeoffs, trims purchase, etc. Someone must do this work, either you the buyer or your supplier. If the buyer is willing to make the investment to have his own preproduction facilities, he can work with less developed makers who will charge on a direct-cost basis only. However, to the degree the buyer does not have these facilities and does not want to make the investment necessary to create them, he must work with more developed factories able to provide these required services. The ultimate full-service factory is one that is totally horizontally integrated—you give them the sketch, they deliver the stock order. In reality, no factory is capable of carrying out all manufacturing functions. However, a full-service factory comes close. Naturally, a full-service factory charges more than Louie the Lip.

The question is: Which is cheaper for the buyer (and more profitable for the factory?)

PREPRODUCTION EXPENSES

Most importers have been told by their accountants to divide expenses between direct product costs and the indirect expenses of doing business. All home expenses, including showroom, staff, selling, etc., are part of the expense of doing business. Only landed-duty-paid (LDP) costs are product costs.

Full Value Cost Analysis (FVCA) looks at costs from the other direction. If your business is importing garments, all of your costs must be included in those garments since the garments are your only source of income. Likewise, all cost reductions incur garment cost reductions. Nowhere is this premise more evident than in preproduction expenses. Every expense that you can take out of your domestic cost of doing business and push on to the supplier as garment cost saves money in two ways:

1. The maker can probably do the work cheaper than you can—not just because he may pay his workers less than you do, but more importantly because he works in scale. You cannot. If, for example, you make samples, you do so only for yourself. Your sample department may have five in-house staff but sufficient work for only eight months a year. Your supplier, meanwhile, may make samples for twenty customers like you. If he has a reasonably large operation, his sample department probably resembles a full-size factory. When you have insufficient work to keep your five sample workers busy, you simply grit your teeth and pay their wages. When he has insufficient work for his sample department, he covers his expenses by putting small stock orders in his sample department.

2. By giving the samples to the factory to produce, you take samplemaking out of your overhead. Your sample department in New York has virtually the same monthly expenses—rent, salaries, etc.— regardless of how many samples are produced. The maker, on the

...your New York samplemaking department refuses to travel to Laos...

other hand, will charge only on a per-sample basis. If you have a lot of samples to produce, you pay more; fewer samples, you pay less. Furthermore, the maker's sample charges are based on a factor of FOB price—typically the charges are *FOB x 2* for the first sample and *fabric + CMT x 2* for each subsequent sample. These charges do not even begin to cover the factory's real costs. By giving the maker the sample work, you are transferring your overhead to his.

Any part of preproduction can be transferred from your place in New York or Los Angeles to the maker in Asia or Latin America. It takes only a change in perspective: you must simply learn to look at manufacturing not as a series of definitions but rather as functions.

• Definition: A samplemaker is a person who makes samples—in your case, one of the four horrible sisters who deign to come to your sample room each day albeit a half-hour late and who, if she works fast, will sew one pair of pants in three days.

• Function: Samplemaking is a process involving certain specific steps. These steps need not all be performed at the same place or even by the same people. All that matters is that the samplemaking process take place efficiently.

You can transport your entire samplemaking process to a factory in Laos, provided the factory in Laos has the proper samplemaking facilities. However, you cannot teleport the four horrible sisters to Laos, as much as you would like to do so. They will not go.

Now comes the interesting part. We are going to take several preproduction processes, as shown in the flowchart, and break them down to compare indirect costs.

Design—Flow Chart Steps: 1-8

For your design room, you require one designer. Since you are an importer, you require an import designer. Import designers have experience working outside the United States. They can communicate effectively through translators and are accustomed to extensive travel. The going price is $125,000.

Your designer requires an assistant. She does specs and follow-up, and runs the room when the designer is away. Price $25,000.

Overseas travel and other design-related expenses, not including fabric sampling, usually equal the full salary of the designer. Add $125,000.

The greatest—and widest range—of expense here is fabric sampling. A couture designer will require over a $1 million per collection for sample fabric he may not even use. On the other hand, a T-shirt designer can get along on about $1.65. After all, how expensive is cotton jersey? For our purposes, let's say you need $250,000 per annum.

Your designer has to sit somewhere, use a telephone, and has other overheads. Add $25,000 per year.

Your design room up to now costs $550,000. For this, you can have detailed sketches, with sample fabric swatches, for about 500 styles a year. But you cannot have any samples, since we haven't yet included costs for patternmakers or samplemakers.

What I have described here is not a large design room. Based on projected sales of 500,000 garments per year, it already adds $1.10 per unit to the cost of each garment sold—provided you meet your projections.

The accepted wisdom is that fashion design can take place only in the country where merchandise is sold. Designers, it is claimed, need continuous input from the market. From the point of view of many importers, since Asian suppliers do not have qualified designers, they cannot provide design. The mistake the importer makes is to confuse definition with function. There is much more to *design* than the *designer*. Of the annual design costs of $550,000, the designer's salary is under 25%. Even with her travel and other expenses, her total is less than one-half of the total cost of design.

Once you look at design as a function, it becomes clear that many of the processes can indeed be transferred to the supplier.

Fabric sampling is the single greatest cost for most woven garment design. If you are going to produce samples, particularly salesman samples, you must order anywhere between 50 to 100 yards of every fabric and in some cases in more than one color. Furthermore, you know in advance that most of the sample fabric will never be used. It will simply be discarded, either because the style is not right, or if the style is right, it might not go with the fabric selected. Someone has to supply this fabric. As long as you assume that *design* is synonymous with *designer* that somebody will always be you. Therefore, either at the fabric shows or immediately upon your return to New York, sample orders must be placed with the mills that designed and produced the original fabric.

But there is another possibility. Once you realize that sample fabric selection and purchase are both parts of the design process, you can begin planning how to foist the work on the maker. Silk fabrics need not be sampled by you from the original European mill. These fabrics can cost over $20 per yard. Let's face—it you aren't going to buy the stock fabric from the Italian or French mill in any case. Why bother sampling $2,000 worth of fabric for every pattern and colorway your designer thinks she may use when you can have your Asian supplier copy the sample yardage for $9 per yard in Korea or $5 in China? Plain, jacquard, yarn-dyed, solid or print—you can save at least half and perhaps as much as three-quarters of costs by sourcing sample fabric through your supplier. The same can be said for many cotton and linen fabrics.

Even if fabric has to be sampled at source, why should you be the one who is always stuck laying out the money? Provided you are working with a normal or full-service factory, they can pay for the sample fabric. Any fabric used for samplemaking will be billed as part of the sample garments. You can even get rid of the leftover fabric by instructing the maker to cut it up as part of stock orders. Cutting 5-50 yard cuts can be a real pain, but it is not your worry—let the maker do it. As long as you understand that fabric sampling is just one more process—and provided you have a good maker—you can avoid paying up front for all samples and at least recover your costs on any unused fabric.

Obviously each case scenario involves other, sometimes overriding considerations. For example, of the $250,000 allocated for fabric sampling, you could theoretically save one-third of costs, provided your supplier has the facilities available. But if the factory is in central China or Indonesia, there is no sense looking to that supplier to provide any sample fabric at all. All he can offer is cheap labor.

Fabric sampling is just one area where costly parts of the design process can be transferred from your overhead to the maker. For example, why waste your time and money on rehashed styles? Many styles are identical to previous seasons—only the fabric has changed. For these styles, nothing is required by the factory except a two-line fax and a swatch of the new fabric. The factory can adjust patterns and make first samples. Your designer can then decide to reject the style altogether or instruct the factory to make necessary changes.

In some cases, if you are working with a top quality maker, you can send sketches and they will make a first sample altogether. At that point, your design overhead is reduced to the designer and her assistant. However, it is possible to go even further and transfer the entire design process to the agent. It has been done.

The Agent as Designer

Despite the accepted wisdom that the designer must live in the country where the merchandise is sold, there are some companies which design in the country where the garments are supplied. The facilities and savings are considerable.

Case Study XVIII—Ann Tjian & Kenar

The best example of agent as designer is Geiss & Tjian, agents for Kenar. In this case, the Hong Kong office acts not only as the agent and designer, but also provides patternmaking, samplemaking as well as fabric and trim purchasing. In fact, Geiss & Tjian provide almost all the facilities of a full-service factory.

Kenar was, until they overexpanded, a large importer of ladies' sportswear covering nearly the entire range of ladies' items. For a considerable number of styles designed and produced in Asia, Kenar had no design overhead whatsoever. Kenar did not require a sample department. All samples were made by the agent. All trim was selected by the agent. In terms of efficiency, this method of working was unbeatable. There were few surprises at Kenar when stock shipments arrived. The garments looked the way they were supposed to look because the designer's staff was at the factory inspecting Kenar's production and if design changes were necessary, the designer was always near the maker to make the required changes.

The agent was paid two commissions, one for design and one for overseeing production. The result was that Kenar had one of the lowest overheads per unit in the industry, and Geiss & Tjian did very well indeed.

Several companies have tried to duplicate this formula. They have been successful, provided they set limited goals. Only Kenar was able to carry out full design work; unfortunately, it is extremely rare to find a designer with both sufficient skills and the single-minded dedication necessary to perform both tasks.

Merchandising—Flow Chart Steps: 9-10, 48, 66, 79

Despite its crucial role in the process, merchandising is another design area often overlooked as a manufacturing function. To produce saleable garments, it is not enough to have good designers—you need good merchandisers. Some of the best labels in the United States are successful not because of exceptional design, but because of great merchandising.

Case Study XIX—The Gap as Merchants

For this case study, you do not even work in the industry. In fact, you know nothing about garment production at all. You are a CPA. You are divorced with two children.

You are at Kids Gap checking out the latest spring collection. You might think you go there because the salespeople are nice. They realize you have no idea of what you are doing and they try to help. You might think you go there because Gap clothes last longer or that they are good value—all this is also true. Yet, in actual fact, these are only secondary reasons.

The real reason you go there is because The Gap has some of the best merchandisers in the world. Individually, the garments are not all that great. The jeans and shorts are nice, but nothing exceptional. A T-shirt with a screenprint of a giant fly is not the sort of thing you would choose for your 8-year-old son, but when you put it all together—the socks, pants, T-shirts—somehow everything works. Your son looks pretty good, even with the giant fly on his T-shirt.

The Gap's total merchandising delivers a distinct look—in this case, clean-cut American kid, but not dumb (the giant fly takes care of that).

Good merchandising looks at the collection as a complete unit in order to maximize sales and profit. Is the style aimed at your target market? Does each style look as if it has greater value than its listed price? Most importantly, does each group have integrity? Does each style in a group fit into that group? Does the group possess sufficient strength to ensure that all materials committed will be used up?

Merchandising work continues well after the collection has been completed. For example, as periodic sales information comes in, production orders should be modified to increase orders for the better-selling styles while reducing those where sales aren't meeting targets. If sales are far above projections, attempts can be made to purchase additional materials for last minute reorders; where sales are far below projections, it might be possible to cancel existing material orders.

In the traditional company where there is a 'designer' and a 'merchandiser', the two persons collaborated closely and often traveled overseas together to work with the factories. The designer would check the factory duplicates, while the merchandiser considered the integrity of the line and negotiated prices. In knitwear, where generally all samples were made at the factory, both designer and merchandiser did most of their work there.

In a modern organization in which design and merchandising are functions and not titles, both can be broken up so that at least some of the work is carried out by the supplier. Functions that are design-oriented may continue to be performed best by the customer, while those relating to maximizing profit and minimizing loss might be better suited to the supplier—provided the supplier has the facilities.

In a full-service factory, the customer can make changes not only in size assortments, but even from one style to another, up to the moment the fabric has physically been spread on the cutting table. This is not an easy task—but your maker can work much more efficiently than you can. Take this example.

Case Study XX—Merchandising to the Last Drop

You are a merchandiser at a medium-sized sportswear company.

One of your groups is made of Chinese linen. You have four colors: white, black, navy and orange. The line plan consists of two jackets, two skirts and one pants.

This is your initial order.

STYLE	CONSUMPTION IN YARDS	TOTAL UNITS	COLORS			
			White	Black	Navy	Orange
Jacket 1	1.60	1,000	250	250	400	100
Jacket 2	1.50	500	125	125	125	125

Skirt 1	1.25	800	300	100	300	100
Skirt 2	2.00	600	150	150	150	150
Pants	1.40	600	150	150	150	150
TOTAL UNITS		3,500	975	775	1,125	625
TOTAL YARDS REQUIRED		5,390	1,473	1,223	1,713	983
TOTAL YARDS ORDERED		5,450	1,500	1,250	1,700	1,000

It is three weeks into the selling season and you have better information. Jacket 1 is not doing well. Jacket 2 is doing really well. You want to cancel Skirt 1 altogether (you told the designer that nobody would be caught dead in that abomination). Finally, Skirt 2—the one you told her all along would be a winner—is selling well. The pants are also moving, but only in white and navy.

It is time to change your order.

STYLE	CONSUMPTION IN YARDS	TOTAL UNITS	COLORS			
			White	Black	Navy	Orange
Jacket 1	1.60	500	125	125	500	50
Jacket 2	1.50	1,000	250	250	250	250
Skirt 2	2.00	935	250	230	290	165
Pants	1.40	900	300	150	300	150
TOTAL UNITS		3,335	925	755	1,040	615
TOTAL YARDS REQUIRED		5,430	1,495	1,245	1,695	995
TOTAL YARDAGE ORDERED		5,450	1,500	1,250	1,700	1,000

Only a great factory which understands that the change in assortment will ultimately bring more sales and more future business to everyone involved will accept changes like this at the last moment. It would also help if the factory loved you. There is only one problem with this solution so far—it will not work.

You forgot about the buttons—and also the interlining, lining, thread, zippers, shoulder pads, main labels, care labels, polybags, hangers and cartons—to say nothing of the quota. When you changed the assortment, these all changed as well. Would you like to remerchandise all these items as well? Don't even try it. Now you understand why you split merchandising functions between your people and the maker—only he can do something at this point.

This is one reason why you went to the full-service factory in the first place. They might charge more on CMT, but you make it back on indirect-cost savings.

A normal-service factory might be willing to change size assortments, but they cannot cope with changing trim orders. More than likely the factory would make mistakes and the entire order would be delayed while they try to correct their errors and reorder trim.

As far as the 0-service factory is concerned, forget about it. You are stuck. Change one item in your order and your delivery will be lucky to make it to the stores for the next season.

Patternmaking and Samplemaking—Flow Chart Steps: 13-16, 23-26, 50, 54-65, 69-71

Overlapping design and the later steps in the manufacturing process are patternmaking and samplemaking. Most garment importers classify these major cost areas as 'overhead'. Using FVCA, they are some of the best places to achieve indirect-cost savings. A quarter of the steps in the total manufacturing process are made up by patternmaking and samplemaking. This is excluding the preproduction duplicate stage (Steps 21-22, 38-41, 75-78) which every factory, whether full or 0-service, must be able to perform.

To run any sort of sample department in New York, the costs are enormous. You require patternmakers and sample sewers. Note that the only real difference between a sample room and a complete production department is that the latter has the ability to adjust patterns for different sizes (grading) and a production manager.

To transfer any appreciable portion of this work to the maker is not an easy undertaking. The quality of the maker is often found in the strength of his pattern and samplemakers. A 0-service factory will offer neither. A full-service factory will have experienced technicians equal to anything available in the United States.

Furthermore, the ability of the maker to make your patterns and samples satisfactorily is based not only on the quality of his factory but also on the nature of your garments. The least difficult are sweaters— where there are no patterns and where, as a rule, the maker produces all the samples anyway—and T-shirts, where only rudimentary patternmaking and samplemaking skills are required. In almost all other cases, there are special problems unique to the garment design process that require specific skills and factories able to provide the necessary service.

The first problem is fit. For a garment to have any value, it has to fit. Both the measurements and shape have to be correct. The relative importance of measurement to shape is not fixed; it changes with garment type and garment cost. The problem concerns dimension. Knitted garments such as T-shirts and sweaters are two-dimensional in nature. Put a T-shirt on a table and it will lay perfectly flat. For two-dimensional garments the measurements are all-important. If the garment conforms to the series of measurements shown on the specification sheet, it will fit. However, three-dimensional garments such as woven jackets, coats and most skirts, also require shape. For these garments, all the measurements listed on the spec sheet could be correct, yet the fit might still be totally wrong.

There are reasons why three-dimensional garments bring greater problems. Fabric cut with curves or on the bias can be stretched and eased in. Two curved pieces, each measuring six inches, can be sewn together in a seam six inches long. They could also be sewn together in a seam four inches long or seven inches long, and in each case the seam should be flat and unpuckered. Easing and stretching provide shape, resulting in a finer garment with a better look. But handled poorly, these same techniques can create potentially gross errors in which the same measurements and pattern pieces will produce very different results.

Three-dimensional garments require not only great skill on the part of the design team, they also demand a very well-run factory. Obviously, only designers of more expensive garments—ladies' high fashion apparel and eveningwear as well as fine men's suits—can afford better factories which offer these more sophisticated techniques, just as the success of the actual production depends very much on the extent of those skills at the chosen factory.

The first person called upon to perform is the patternmaker. Once a designer has selected fabric and made her sketch, someone must make a pattern and then use that pattern to cut and later sew a sample garment. However, a pattern is not like a blueprint, a detailed drawing of a building. A pattern is a two-dimensional template from which fabric has to be cut and a three-dimensional garment sewn. This change from two to three dimensions causes distortion—the finished garment never looks precisely like the sketch.

The procedure involves making a pattern, cutting the fabric against that pattern, correcting the sample sewn from the cut fabric, and then altering the pattern in accordance with those corrections. The alteration and correction process can be repeated several times; in each instance, the sample will correspond more closely to the designer's ideas and sketch. There are, however, two problems. First, the process requires both a skilled designer and an equally skilled patternmaker. Secondly, the time required to make the amended sample is the same as making a new sample. Thus if every style has to be corrected one time, the samplemakers can produce only half the number of styles. Even in optimal conditions, most styles must be corrected at least once. You can reduce the load by rejecting the obvious dogs early on, but this savings is soon lost once you consider that some styles may need correction three, four, or even more times.

Even so, the indirect-cost savings derived from successfully making your patterns and samples at the maker's facilities are just too good to pass up.

Consider these calculations. A patternmaker can make one dress pattern per day. A further half-day is required for corrections. Therefore, if you require 500 dress patterns per year, you will need three full-time patternmakers. Even a mediocre patternmaker in New York costs $75,000 per year, right up there with lawyers, accountants and plumbers. Cost: $225,000

Next, we need samplemakers. A samplemaker will make one sample dress per day. (Already I can hear the professionals laughing. All right, I have never seen a sample sewer make one sample per day, but I don't want to be too depressing.) Assuming an average of two samples per style, you therefore require 1,000 samples and four sample sewers. They cost $30,000 per annum each, with benefits. You can find people for less, but they will not be of the same quality or speed. Cost: $120,000

They also need a room to work in as well as materials. Cost: $50,000

Add the grader. Cost: $50,000

The total cost of your New York sample department plus grader equals $435,000 per year or $870 per style. Based on sales of 500,000 units per year, the cost of first (and corrected) samples adds $0.87 per stock garment. Added to the $1.10 per unit for design expenses, total design expenses are now $1.97 per unit. And yet you've never listed these costs in your costings. To you, they are just 'the cost of doing business'.

In FVCA, they are part of your manufacturing costs and are about to be slashed..

The obvious solution is to pay the overseas factory to make the patterns and the sample. Most overseas factories do not charge for patternmaking and the charge for samples is usually twice CMT per unit when you supply the fabric. If the CMT is $10, you pay only $20 for the factory to make your patterns and samples—a mere 2.2% of your $870 per sample average cost. The savings are tremendous, provided the factory has good patternmakers and a large sample department. Not only can you save $395,000 per annum in salaries, you can also save on the overhead of the pattern and samplemaking rooms and automatically have facilities for expansion with no additional overhead. If the factory has the facilities, it is cheaper to work at the factory, even if they charge more to assemble the garment.

In addition to designer samples, you will require other samples—the most important being salesman samples. Without them, you cannot sell. The ability to provide acceptable samples efficiently and at reasonable prices is a good yardstick for determining whether or not a factory can help you reduce indirect costs.

The preproduction process begins with the factory's first sample. The buyer provides the details, the factory produces a garment. Every factory must be able to make a countersample. Without a sample, there will be no order. Even Louie the Lip will make a sample, provided you give him written guarantee of an order for not less than 500 dozen, signed in blood.

The depth of details provided by the buyer and how the actual samplemaking process takes place is based on the relative abilities of buyer and factory. Read on.

Case Study XXI—The 0-Service Factory or Working Down

You are production director for Liz Claiborne (an extremely knowledgeable importer) and for some reason you are committed to working with a factory in Tierra del Fuego (the closest land mass to Antarctica). Without ever having gone to Lower Patagonia, you know that whatever this garment requires, the factory will not have it. You start what you know will be a lengthy process.

As an experienced and professional importer, your samplemaking package will contain the following for each style:

- One completed sample;

- One complete pattern, with markers for any piece you think may cause difficulty;

- Fabric sufficient for three samples: the one they send you, their keep sample, and their first effort which they did not send you for obvious reasons;

- A complete set of trim sufficient for three samples, with instructions to send you examples of the closest items available locally;

- Sewn muslin pieces showing any special stitch or treatment such as shirring, pleating, or unusual darts;

- Detailed notes.

One month later you receive the factory's duplicate which looks nothing like your sample. There are three possible reasons:

- They did not understand your instructions;

- They understood what you wanted but lacked the required machinery;

- They understood what you wanted but lacked the required ability.

Since we know just how competent you are, we can immediately discard Possibility 1. This leaves you with the choice of either dropping the factory or working the garment down to conform to the ability and machinery of the factory, hopefully with little change to the look.

Eventually, three or four cycles later, the factory produces a sample that looks acceptable and you are confident they are capable of producing for stock.

But given the amount of effort required to produce the first sample, direct costs at the Patagonian factory had better be very low indeed.

Most normal-service factories are capable of producing a decent sample after the first or second attempt. Depending on the relative abilities of buyer and factory and the style's degree of difficulty, the buyer provides either a sample with pattern or a detailed sketch with a spec sheet (giving size measurements) and tech sheet (giving seam types and allowances, etc.). As a rule, better organized importers will provide patterns to less sophisticated factories, unless they involve T-shirts or sweaters, for reasons already explained above.

The normal-service factory will strive to duplicate the buyer's sample as closely as possible, both in appearance and quality standard. Success is relative and measured by the degree to which the factory is able to meet those goals.

Case Study XXII—The Full-Service Super-Factory

At the top level, factories have sample and patternmaking facilities far more sophisticated than those operated by any importer. Here each patternmaker is assigned to work exclusively for a single customer. Even if the European or American designer and a patternmaker work 10,000 miles away from each other and speak a totally different language, their relationship is intimate. Patternmaker and designer rarely meet; yet over a period of time, by looking at the designer's sample and pattern, the patternmaker will understand what the designer wants, even when the designer's own sample and pattern do not.

For a full-service factory, it would be far cheaper to produce a sample in a fine tailor shop than in their own factory. Typically, a first duplicate takes twelve times longer to sew than the same style in production.

Of course, first the factory must make their duplicate to show the customer what the production will look like. But at the best factories, already other production considerations will be entering the formula, and the countersample may not be a precise replica of the customer's first sample.

The full-service factory not only has greater assets than other garment suppliers, but often has more than the customer himself. Rather than talking down to a full-service factory, you should treat it like a true partner and defer to their greater knowledge, production experience or ability to access special trim or machinery. The result will be a better quality garment, where costs have been reduced because time-consuming production operations are now more efficient, or where incorrect materials used in your first sample have been replaced with more suitable ones.

Samples are so important to the manufacturing process that, in many cases, the ability to make good samples alone may be a determining factor in factory selection. After all, unless the sample is correct, the designer's work is useless, and unless you can have salesman samples in the correct quality and shipped on time, you will never sell the style.

Although everyone wants good samples, importers don't all go about it the same way. While most buyers try to lower indirect costs by developing long-term relationships with their major suppliers, others prefer the something-for-nothing method. The Wendell Wasp method of sample acquisition is well known in the industry.

Case Study XXIII—Wendell's Ploy

Wendell Wasp had a simple solution to the entire sample problem, which simultaneously minimized both his indirect and direct costs.

Wendell would search out the best factory he could find, preferably one that had never heard of him nor his company Schmidlap Enterprises. He would introduce himself and begin his spiel. Wendell Wasp talked only in telephone numbers—all order quantities would be seven-digit figures.

Naturally, if the factory wanted these wonderful orders, they would have to do their part—usually consisting of immediately stopping all other sample production to make room for Wendell's collection. Although Wendell seldom met with complete success, he usually managed to take over more than half the sample department.

Wendell would then give the factory his sketches and spec sheets and the work would begin. Wendell's designer would fly in from the United States to start working with the factory. Unfortunately, it was difficult for her to work. She knew from past experience what was about to occur and working for two weeks in a permanently cringing position was bad for her back.

The sample work would proceed. Meanwhile, Wendell would alternate between constantly carping about the slow speed of samplemaking and expressing unbounded optimism as each style was completed. "This is the greatest group I have seen in all my seventeen years in business. We will sell millions. We must go faster. Don't you know what an opportunity this collection will be for your factory?" was a normal Wendell comment. Working the factory to a fever pitch of excitement was Wendell's stock-in-trade. Even the most skeptical factory managers would become enthusiastic as Wendell raved over each successive sample.

Eventually the samples and salesman samples were finished. They usually looked beautiful, as you would expect when a top-quality factory commits their entire resources to a single collection. Everything would be packed up. Wendell, taking the samples himself, would congratulate the factory as he left the building, calling over his shoulder, "Greatest collection I have ever seen...millions in orders...you are going to make a fortune...you will be hearing from me short..."

That was the last the factory ever saw of Wendell or their samples.

The salesman samples were sent to New York where the buyers could marvel over the style and the quality. The first samples were sent to Honduras where, in a reconverted pajama factory, the manager scratched his head while trying to figure how it was possible for any factory to make such garments. Wendell had what he wanted. Another season.

There is some debate as to whether Wendell will ever run out of factories willing to make his samples. After all, he is fairly well known. There is equally debate over whether buyers will ever get tired of receiving stock that looks nothing like the samples, but that is what Chapter 11 is for.

Material Selection and Purchase—Flow Chart Steps: 1-2, 5-6, 28-32, 33-37, 45-46, 51-53, 54-61, 81-83, 84-86

Material selection and purchasing is every bit as costly as pattern and samplemaking. In the past, buyers used to draw distinctions between (1) FOB factories that supply all fabric and trim; (2) CMT factories for which the customer provides fabric and the factory supplies trim; and (3) CM factories which supply nothing at all. While these distinctions are still important, there is an additional consideration to be made—not only who pays for the material but also who is actually ordering and responsible for it.

With a 0-service factory, who actually pays for the fabric is critical. If you the buyer are paying, either you or your agent must closely follow up every step in the production process for every shipment. You cannot expect the 0-service factory to be responsible for anything. If, however, you insist that the factory pay for the material, you are protecting your company from the very real possibility that the factory production will be so poor that you will have to reject the order and still be stuck with the cost of the material.

When working with a normal-service factory, at least you don't begin each order with the expectation that the factory will destroy your material. But the material might still have quality or delivery problems. In this situation, who actually pays for the fabric is irrelevant. If you order the fabric and then ask the maker to pay the mill directly, the maker may be classified as an FOB factory, but if the fabric is late or the quality unacceptable, responsibility still rests with you the customer. As a result, unless you are working with Louie the Lip, you want the factory to both order the material and be responsible for it. The risks otherwise become much too great.

Nowhere is this premise more apparent than in trim sourcing.

When the factory stands responsible for all trim, the buyer's costs are markedly reduced. Direct costs go down to some degree simply because the factory is better equipped to negotiate local trim prices than either the buyer or his agent. However, the real savings are in the indirect costs. Anywhere between 15 to 25 trim items may be required for one particular style. With so many items, it is quite normal for at least one item to be shipped late or in insufficient quantity, incorrectly or not at all. Obviously, if the buyer or his agent is responsible for trims sourcing, the buyer must accept delayed shipment. But when the factory is responsible for trim, late arrival of an item is clearly the factory's problem. They must make up the lost time.

Case Study XXIV—The Label Disaster

Some European design houses still insist on supplying their own labels, in most cases to protect against counterfeit garments. Each label is marked with a serial number on the side selvage. The system usually works well—except when it leads to catastrophe.

After producing all their garments in Scotland for 130 years, one of the U.K.'s best-known labels and most conservative companies finally decided to try importing. Through one of Hong Kong's most reliable agents, they approached one of the best factories in Asia to produce 3,000 silk blouses.

Their requirements were very strict. Few factories could have produced to their standard and fewer still would have made the effort for only 3,000 blouses. But having dealt previously with many of Europe's most expensive labels and difficult designers, the factory simply factored the buyer's requirements into their costing formula and quoted a price. The buyer agreed and the factory started its work.

At first all went well. Fabric and trim were accepted and production began. No one noticed the absence of labels. Normally, since label sewing is the first operation in the sewing process, the factory would have been immediately alert to the problem. In this case, however, the labels were to be sewn on by hand and were, therefore, the final sewing operation.

Eventually, the factory contacted the agent, who contacted their client, who exclaimed: "What labels?" And then followed with: "Oh, those labels."

Unfortunately, the blouses were meant to be sold with sweaters, the buyer's main business. Without the blouses, the sweaters were also delayed—all because of a label.

For the purposes of production planning, trim is divided into two categories: early and late order. Late-order trim is available either in the spot market, or within a fairly short period of time. Early-order trim must be ordered well in advance, in some cases by as much as 60-90 days. Long lead times are not only a scheduling nuisance but, more importantly, severely restrict the buyer's flexibility. These restrictions can have serious and costly consequences.

A buyer will normally order a range of styles in a particular fabric, each style having its own trim requirements. To ensure the best assortment of colors and sizes, the buyer will try to finalize his order as late as possible. Under normal circumstances, the factory is usually quite willing to allow the buyer the additional flexibility, providing all fabric ordered is used.

However, where trim must be on early order, particularly when a trim item must be dyed to match, the buyer is forced to decide on not only style assortments but color assortments for each style far in advance of actual production. At the retail end, this rigidity results in some styles selling out early while others must be marked down. Actual losses to the importer far outweigh any savings he could make by lowering direct costs.

We look at a label or a piece of lining as something of secondary importance until we discover the label is missing or the color of the lining is wrong. It is only then that we look at the exceedingly high indirect costs related to trims purchasing.

Organizing trim for a 0-service factory with no facilities can be a nightmare. Not only is the factory unable to offer any real assistance but, as most such factories are located in underdeveloped countries, many trim items are unavailable locally and must be imported.

The normal service factory can supply normal trim items, including plain buttons, simple interlining, thread and polybags. The difficulty arises when it is not possible to locate special trim items in the supplier's country. Indeed, some special items will almost always have to be imported unless the factory is full-service and located in Italy. The question here is one of degree. Can you count on the supplier to find most relatively difficult trim items, or must you plan on importing anything out of the ordinary?

Once you have to import items on behalf of the supplier, you are trapped. Your direct costs go up and so do your indirect costs, since any delay in arrival will be your responsibility. Also, don't forget that in almost all cases, you or your agent have to check all trim to ensure that the quality and color are correct.

The full-service factory overcomes this difficulty. If it is located in a well-developed country, almost anything is available in stock, either from local producers or existing specialist importers. If an item must be imported, the full-service factory will get it from your designated supplier, whether it be special lace from Belgium or a button from a supplier located three blocks from your showroom on 39th Street in New York City. In both cases the full-service factory takes responsibility.

The full-service factory can also be trusted to check trim. As an extra precaution, however, reliable factories will prepare a special trim sheet for each style, showing samples of all trim in all colors which is then sent either to the buyer or his agent. This way everyone has a record of what is being used.

Equally important, as already discussed in Case Study XX, the full-service factory has the ability to merchandise trim in order to provide the customer with the greatest flexibility to change assortments up to the last possible moment.

Other Facilities

What is most remarkable about indirect costs is how few people realize their importance—or just how many important elements in your business are a part of indirect costs. For example, financing charges and letters of credit are an integral part of indirect costs, yet most importers don't consider their letters of credit to be part of the manufacturing process.

On the one hand, everyone acknowledges that the time of trim arrival is part of indirect costs. If the button or label does not arrive at the factory on time, manufacturing work will cease and the order will be shipped late. Late delivery costs money. However, these same importers do not realize that if their letter of credit arrives late, this too will cause the manufacturing process to cease, resulting in delayed shipment of their order.

In a sense, a letter of credit is even more of an indirect cost than a button or label. If the button arrives late, the order will be late: this is beyond anyone's control. But a factory can overcome late arrival of a letter of credit, provided the customer is trusted and the factory has its own credit facilities. Furthermore, if your relations with the factory are so good that they do not even require you to open a letter of credit months in advance of shipment, they are giving you an indirect cost advantage far greater than any savings you could get by reducing direct costs.

Case Study XXV—Letters of Credit

You own a moderate-sized company. Your total sales volume is $10 million a year. Like most people at this level, you are constrained by a limited credit line. You currently have a choice between two factories:

Factory A: A Chinese state-owned factory that requires letters of credit 90 days before shipment.

Factory B: A Hong Kong-controlled China factory that allows a favored customer to open the letter of credit immediately before stock shipment.

Since you have limited credit, the choice is obvious.

If you go with Factory A, your bank will automatically block a part of your loan facility equivalent to the size of the open letter of credit. You can only turn your money three times a year, after allowing an additional 30 days for shipping and customs clearance. If you go to Factory B, you can turn your money 10 times a year.

In fact, once you consider the importance of later payment, you have no choice. You cannot afford to deal with Factory A unless it gives you a price which would allow you to make three-and-a-half times the net profit as with Factory B. To put it another way, by allowing a more liberal payment policy, Factory B has a lower cost than Factory A, even if their direct costs are appreciably higher.

Even factoring in other calculations, including duty, freight, selling expenses, etc., Factory A would still have to come in at less than 50% of the FOB price of Factory B to be competitive.

Furthermore, Factory B has not even extended you any actual credit. Imagine the savings you could enjoy if they shipped you on an LDP basis and then allowed you to pay 60 days after shipment. For reliable customers working with full-service factories this scenario is not that uncommon.

Once again, while the indirect-cost advantage discussed in this case study is greater than the entire labor-cost savings between working in say, Hong Kong and Indonesia, if you check your costing sheet, letter-of-credit timing and credit facilities are probably nowhere to be seen.

QUANTIFYING INDIRECT COSTS—BIRNBAUM RATIOS

Understanding the importance of the facilities that go into indirect costs is only the first step. To be of any real value, indirect-cost savings must be included in your costings and therefore, must be quantifiable. For example, a factory that will make patterns and samples will have a higher CMT than a 0-service factory, if only because full-service factories tend to operate in more developed countries where labor is more expensive. The question that you, the importer, must ask is: Do the indirect-cost savings of factory patternmaking and samplemaking compensate for the higher CMT? Likewise you, the factory owner, must ask: Will my investment in good patternmaking and samplemaking result in lower overall costs? These are not easy questions, but they are central to indirect-cost calculations.

Case Study XXVI—Cheap Labor vs. Cheap Patterns and Samples

A cheap sewer costs less than a more expensive sewer, provided she sews fast enough.

A cheap patternmaker or samplemaker, however, saves you a lot more money than a cheap sewer, simply because the former are paid a lot more to begin with than the latter—particularly when the patternmaker and the samplemaker are located in the United States and the sewers are in southern China. As already discussed, the savings are even larger if the Asian factory offers patterns and samples as a combined facility. This way you pay only for the work you need and have no overhead at all.

The purpose of this case study is to enable you to calculate potential indirect-cost savings and compare them to final costs at factories working with lower direct costs (labor, fabric and perhaps trim). At what specific point do indirect-cost savings—in this case, pattern and samplemaking facilities—gained by working in one country overcome the lower direct costs offered by working with another. First, you must consider several factors:

- How long does it take to make a pattern or a sample? Obviously, the faster the pattern and samplemaking, the cheaper the operation.

- How fast does it take to sew the stock garment? The faster the production, the greater the number of garments can be produced in the same period of time, which in turn helps offset the cost of patterns and samples.

Take a dress which, compared to a T-shirt or a simple skirt, is a relatively complicated garment. Assume the patternmaker requires one day to make the pattern and an additional half-day to correct the pattern. The samplemaker requires two days to sew the first sample and another two days to sew the corrected sample.

A sewer in Bangladesh is paid $1.20 for a 10-hour day. The same sewer in Italy is paid 139 times more—$133.20 for an 8-hour day. Even allowing for the greater productivity of the Italian worker, the sewing cost a of dress is 98 times higher in Italy than in Bangladesh—$20.48 compared to $0.21. As a result, the direct-sewing cost of 100-dozen Italian garments is $24,575 compared to $256 in Bangladesh. Let's say that if Italian sewing costs equal 100, the Bangladeshi costs would be 1.

However, the factory in Italy provides certain indirect-cost savings not available in Bangladesh. Among these are qualified patternmakers and a full samplemaking department. As a result, if you buy the dresses in Bangladesh you have to add the cost of making the patterns and samples in New York. The cost of the New York-made pattern works out to $468.75—not including overhead. The cost of two samples is $500—again, not including overhead. The cost of 100-dozen dresses sewn in Bangladesh therefore rises from $256 to $1225.75 while the Italian costs remain the same.

If Italian costs remain 100, Bangladesh now increases to approximately 5. The addition of just two indirect-cost factors pattern and samplemaking—raises the cost of the garments made in the Bangladeshi factory 5 times relative to the Italian factory

Factoring in indirect costs creates the *Birnbaum Ratio*—5:1. It redefines the cost indices once indirect-cost facilities have been added in. Obviously, pattern and samplemaking facilities alone will not make the Italian factory competitive with the factory in Bangladesh. The direct-cost advantage for sewing in Bangladesh is still over $24,000. A difference of only $968.75 will not override that advantage (which is why Kmart still buys from Bangladesh and not Italy).

But patternmaking and samplemaking are only two of many possible indirect-cost facilities available in the Italian factory which are generally not found in Bangladesh. That is why Italy remains the world's third largest garment exporter, while Bangladesh's garment exports, while substantial, are much lower in value.

Furthermore, Italy is not unique in its ability to gain indirect-cost advantages by providing pattern and samplemaking facilities. Consider the advantages if a factory in Sri Lanka were to invest in a qualified patternmaker and a full sample department. Sri Lanka may be a cheap-labor area by Italian standards—$2.40 for a 10-hour day—but sewers earn twice as much as their Bangladeshi counterparts. One hundred dozen dresses in Sri Lanka have a direct-sewing cost of $513 compared with $256 in Bangladesh. Sri Lankan factories simply cannot compete with Bangladeshi factories on direct cost. If Sri Lanka equals 100, Bangladesh is at 50.

But when the factory in Sri Lanka is able to provide patternmaking and samplemaking, the costs in Bangladesh rise to $1225 while the Sri Lankan costs remain fixed at $513. In this case, if Sri Lanka equals 100, Bangladesh adjusted costs now equal 478 (see Birnbaum Ratios in following tables). Now it is the factory in Bangladesh that is unable to compete.

Country	Daily Wage	Working Hours	Hours to Sew 1 Unit	Cost per Unit	Direct Cost 1200 Units	Add Pattern & Sample Cost	Total
Italy	$133.20	8	1.23	$20.48	$24,575	$968.75	$25544
Hong Kong	$ 39.20	8	1.23	$ 6.03	$ 7,232	$968.75	$ 8201
Thailand	$ 7.20	10	1.60	$ 1.15	$ 1,382	$968.75	$ 2351
China SEZ	$ 4.00	10	1.33	$ 0.53	$ 638	$968.75	$ 1607
India	$ 2.00	10	2.29	$ 0.43	$ 550	$968.75	$ 1519
Sri Lanka	$ 2.40	10	2.29	$ 0.43	$ 513	$968.75	$ 1482
Indonesia	$ 1.80	10	2.00	$ 0.36	$ 442	$968.75	$ 1411
Pakistan	$ 1.60	10	2.29	$ 0.37	$ 440	$968.75	$ 1408
Vietnam	$ 2.00	10	1.45	$ 0.29	$ 348	$968.75	$ 1316
Bangladesh	$ 1.20	10	1.78	$ 0.21	$ 256	$968.75	$ 1225

Job Function	Annual Salary	Days Worked per year	Days to make 1 Unit	Cost per Unit
Patternmaker	$75,000	240	1.5	$468.75
Samplemaker	$30,000	240	2	$500.00

COST COMPARISONS							
	Index Direct Costs Only (A)	Adjusted Index with Add. Indirect Costs (B)	Birnbaum Ratio (A:B)	(A/B)			
CASE I: Italy is the only country with patternmakers & samplemakers							
Italy	100	100	100:100	1.00			
Hong Kong	29	33	33:29	1.13			
Thailand	6	10	10:6	1.70			
China SEZ	3	7	7:3	2.52			
Sri Lanka	2	6	6:2	2.89			
India	2	6	6:2	2.76			
Indonesia	2	6	6:2	3.24			
Pakistan	2	6	6:2	3.20			
Vietnam	1	5	5:1	3.78			
Bangladesh	1	5	5:1	4.78			
CASE II:	All countries in bold have patternmakers and samplemakers (Sri Lanka = 100)						
Italy	4794	4794	4794:4794	1.00			
Hong Kong	1411	1411	1411:1411	1.00			
Thailand	270	270	270:270	1.00			
China SEZ	125	125	125:125	1.00			
Sri Lanka	100	100	100:100	1.00			
India	107	296	296:107	2.76			
Indonesia	84	273	273:84	3.24			
Pakistan	86	275	275:86	3.20			
Vietnam	68	257	257:68	3.78			
Bangladesh	50	239	239:50	4.78			

Birnbaum Ratios are useful tools for measuring any advantages offered by factoring in indirect-cost savings. They can quantify not only tangible facilities such as skilled workers and specialized machinery but also intangible ones such as better quality, better delivery and lower minimums. The following case study gives an example.

Case Study XXVII—Birnbaum Ratios: Factory Minimums

Once again you are importing dresses. Clearly you want to achieve the highest net profit for each style—which means buying at the lowest cost.

You are very lucky. Your designer has created a group of sleeveless, collarless, hemless dresses, with no shoulderpads, zippers, facings, plackets snaps or buttons. They are unbelievably easy to make. In fact, there is no maker in the world so incompetent that he is unable to produce your dresses. You can choose any factory, in any country, and be assured of a perfect garment every time. You list factories in ten countries, from Italy to Bangladesh. (Italy is on the list only to satisfy your wife.) You have only one problem and it's a big one. You can sell only 1200 pieces of a style. Anything more will have to sold off-price at 50% of wholesale.

Only two factors concern you: cost and minimums.

Your wholesale price is $50 per dress; there are factories where you can produce and land with a gross markup of over 80%. The problem is that the cheaper the CMT, the greater the minimums, but at 80% markup, how can you go wrong?

In any case, since you know about *Birnbaum Ratios*, you can work out the lowest-cost solution. You first calculate the direct costs (materials, labor, factory overhead and profit) to reach your FOB price for the selected factory in each country.

You then add duty, freight, insurance and customs clearance to reach your LDP price. Things look very good indeed. With the exception of Hong Kong, which works out at 52%, everywhere else still gives you over 75% potential markup (see table below).

However, now you have to factor in the minimums problem. With the exception of Italy and Hong Kong, every factory requires minimums ranging from 200 to 1000 dozen per style. Now things are not looking so good. The *Birnbaum Ratios* are all showing large cost increases due to excessive minimums. Where Bangladesh previously worked out at 83% gross markup, it has now been reduced to 38% with a ratio of 137:63. In fact, every cheap labor country with the exception of Thailand has now become uncompetitive.

Here is your group of sleeveless, collarless, hemless dresses, with no shoulderpads, zippers, facings, plackets snaps or buttons which are so unbelievably easy to make that you can go anywhere in the world and you wind up back in Hong Kong. All because of minimums.

Country	Daily Wage	Working Hours	Hours to Sew Unit	Sewing Cost per Unit	Other Labor	Material Cost per Unit	Factory O/Head	FOB
Italy	$133.20	8	1.23	$20.48	$5.12	$5.00	$6.40	$37.00
Hong Kong	$ 39.20	8	1.23	$ 6.03	$1.51	$5.00	$5.65	$18.18
Thailand	$ 7.20	10	1.60	$ 1.15	$0.29	$5.00	$1.44	$ 7.85
China SEZ	$ 4.00	10	1.33	$ 0.53	$0.13	$5.00	$1.66	$ 7.33
Sri Lanka	$ 2.40	10	1.78	$ 0.43	$0.11	$5.00	$1.34	$ 6.87
India	$ 2.00	10	2.29	$ 0.46	$0.11	$5.00	$1.57	$ 7.15
Indonesia	$ 1.80	10	2.00	$ 0.36	$0.09	$5.00	$1.35	$ 6.80
Pakistan	$ 1.60	10	2.29	$ 0.37	$0.09	$5.00	$1.37	$ 6.83
Vietnam	$ 2.00	10	1.45	$ 0.29	$0.07	$5.00	$1.09	$ 6.45
Bangladesh	$ 1.20	10	1.78	$ 0.21	$0.05	$5.00	$0.80	$ 6.07

Country	FOB	LDP	Minimum Pieces	Total Cost	W/Sale Price	Total W/S Value	Gross Profit	Pct Markup
Italy	$37.00	$48.02	1200	$ 57,619	$50.00	$ 60,000	$ 2,380	4%
Hong Kong	$18.18	$23.98	1200	$ 28,776	$50.00	$ 60,000	$ 31,224	52%
Thailand	$ 7.88	$10.82	2400	$ 25,960	$50.00	$120,000	$ 94,040	78%
China SEZ	$ 7.33	$10.11	3600	$ 36,399	$50.00	$180,000	$143,601	80%
Sri Lanka	$ 6.87	$ 9.53	4800	$ 45,721	$50.00	$240,000	$194,279	81%
India	$ 7.15	$ 9.88	6000	$ 59,281	$50.00	$300,000	$240,719	80%
Indonesia	$ 6.80	$ 9.44	6000	$ 56,622	$50.00	$300,000	$243,378	81%
Pakistan	$ 6.83	$ 9.48	12000	$113,735	$50.00	$600,000	$486,265	81%
Vietnam	$ 6.45	$ 8.99	12000	$107,879	$50.00	$600,000	$492,122	82%
Bangladesh	$ 6.07	$ 8.50	12000	$102,022	$50.00	$600,000	$497,978	83%

Country	Gross Profit	Mark-down	Net Profit	Adj. Pct Markup
Italy	$ 2,380	$ 0	$ 2,380	4%
Hong Kong	$ 31,224	$ 0	$ 31,224	52%
Thailand	$ 94,040	$ 30,000	$ 64,040	53%
China SEZ	$143,601	$ 60,000	$ 83,601	46%
Sri Lanka	$194,279	$ 90,000	$104,279	43%
India	$240,719	$120,000	$120,719	40%
Indonesia	$243,378	$120,000	$123,378	41%
Pakistan	$486,265	$270,000	$216,265	36%
Vietnam	$492,122	$270,000	$222.122	37%
Bangladesh	$497,978	$270,000	$227,978	38%

Country	Index Direct Cost Only (A)	Index Adj. with Indirect Cost (B)	Birnbaum Ratios (A:B)	(A/B)
Italy	1312	1312	1312:1312	1.00
Hong Kong	100	100	100:100	1.00
Thailand	66	98	98:66	1.47
China SEZ	65	112	112:65	1.72
Sri Lanka	64	120	120:64	1.86
India	65	129	129:65	1.99
Indonesia	64	127	127:64	1.97
Pakistan	64	144	144:64	2.25
Vietnam	63	141	141:63	2.22
Bangladesh	63	137	137:63	2.18

UNUSUAL FACILITIES

No exporting country has a monopoly on specialized knowledge and facilities. A full-service factory in Hong Kong can provide excellent patternmaking and samplemaking. It may have the facilities to locate trim from all over the world and has developed special relationships with every major mill in Europe and Asia. Its personnel may be skilled to work effectively with all types of designers.

Yet if your interest is importing truly special items, the full-service factory may suddenly be transmogrified into a 0-service factory. Every country has its own special skills that have true commercial value if developed properly.

Indonesian batik and ikat, Chinese handpainted silk and Indian tie-dye all require specialized facilities and skills. Furthermore, these are not just ethnic patterns and designs suitable only for esoteric gifts—they are industrial processes which can be important design assists regardless of the pattern involved.

Do you need prints with 30 colors and no repeat? Do you think it is possible? How about a 30-color print, with no repeat and a minimum of 100 yards? Would you like to buy this in silk for the same price you pay an importer for machine-screened Korean silk print? This technique exists and reputable mills do this work. It is called handpaint—a process that has been going on in China for over 2,000 years.

You might not think about handpaint as a possible tool for your next spring collection because you think of silk hand paint as 'ethnic'—OK for stores like Bergdorf Goodman or for people who want pictures of dragons chasing their tails, but not relevant to commercial design. The problem is not handpaint. The problem is you. Handpaint is simply one more print technique. Correctly executed, it is as commercial as the designer who makes the pattern.

Every country has indigenous techniques relevant to commercial design. Every country has specialized mills and factories with the facilities required to produce finished garments to the necessary level of quality and commercial quantities.

The same silk-printing mill in Hangzhou, with modern European machinery that produces hundreds of thousands of yards per month, also has a fully staffed handpaint department capable of producing thousands of yards of finished fabric or panels in your design. They will also produce as little as 20 yards in your design.

It is for you the buyer to discover the item, locate the country where that item is produced, and find a reputable supplier with the proper facilities.

Bali—The Hidden Design Center

Every country has something to offer the designer. However, there are a few areas that are natural design centers, where people have a taste level and the design background that would be of immediate interest to knowledgeable importers in the West.

Indonesia is a textile and garment production center that has made tremendous investments in the latest textile machinery. But it is Bali that has made a great difference for textile and garment importers. For generations, Bali has been a center for artists and designers. There are fabrics and fabric treatments special to Bali. There are also excellent small garment factories that have a flair for style. Provided you work within the limitations of the island, you will find that while many Asian factories take the style out of production, Balinese factories tend to put more back in.

Bali will never be a major garment producer, but there are some well-known importers who use Bali as a little mine from which each season a little gold is extracted.

India—The Hidden Fashion Center

Working in India has been described as being in hell without the benefit of the good climate. Millennia of poverty and dirt have left an indelible mark on the country. It is impossible to exaggerate the difficulties of working in a country where nothing works. Let me assure you the horror stories you have heard are but faint and mild descriptions of reality.

On the other hand, India is the only country in Asia with its own individual fashion culture. The same culture that has trapped the vast majority of its people in the Dark Ages produces fabrics, textures and colors which are unique, powerful and commercial. These same people, who seem incapable of solving the most basic practical problems, have an understanding of fashion unknown elsewhere in Asia. For professionals, the results do not look ethnic—they simply look special.

Eighty percent of Indian weaving equipment is composed of power looms—old-fashioned shuttle looms that look like handlooms with electric motors attached. The fabric produced is uneven, filled with damages and slubs—totally useless to mass-market importers. But to importers and retailers of fashion at any price point, what India offers is unique. Cottons, woolens, silks and synthetics are all available.

Italian designers such as Romeo Gigli and Giorgio Armani have been using India for a large proportion of their work for years. The results are staggering, but so too are the problems.

India is a continent-sized country with no single textile or garment center. Bangalore, Bombay, Calcutta, Delhi and Madras—each produces textiles and garments special to their area. To take full advantage of what India has to offer, the importer needs to work everywhere. In order to operate successfully, you must either work within disciplined limitations and accept the fact that you will concentrate your efforts in one or at most two places, or be prepared to set up an extremely large organization.

The second problem with working in India relates to the flow of work and material. While there are Indian factories that will work on an FOB basis, and mills and fabric converters who will sell finished fabric, you learn very quickly that you must retain control of every step in the production process. Otherwise your order will either never be completed or it will be completed far differently than ordered.

This means ordering greige fabric, giving it out to be dyed and then finished, taking the finished fabric yourself to the garment factory, and ensuring that garment production proceeds as planned or at least within an acceptable time frame. Needless to say, only a total lunatic would attempt to carry out this work out by himself. The normal procedure is to find a good agent. Every Indian textile-producing area has its own supply of agents, some fairly large, who work with major importers and can provide realistic commercial service. They might not be as good as agents in South Korea or Hong Kong, but using them is a lot better than working on your own.

India also has its own supply of dilettantes, both European and indigenous bored housewives who, having a 'flair for garments', decide that becoming an agent would be interesting, lucrative and worth doing, provided it did not detract from the more important aspects of their lives. Needless to say, the professional importer should avoid these people; the combination of your ignorance of India and their ignorance of production would not result in a successful season.

The two things you do not want in an Indian agent are:

• Someone to introduce you to the factory making for The Gap. If you want a Gap factory, go to China, not India.

• Someone to provide you with a large number of unworkable ideas. For unworkable ideas you can stay home.

Case Study XXVIII—Darshan

Darshan deals in fabrics and garments out of Calcutta. Part agent, part trading company, part supplier, Darshan has knowledge of production at all levels, from greige weaving to finished garments. She has relationships with mills and factories at all levels in the production process required to produce a completed garment.

Most importantly, Darshan understands both European taste levels and the culture of her country. This combination is critical if you are to get anything useful out of India.

Working with Darshan is not like working with your Hong Kong agent. You do not, for example, dump a pile of samples and spec sheets on Darshan's desk and say: "See you in two weeks when the duplicates are finished."

You travel with Darshan. You see what the factories are doing. You see what Darshan is doing. More than your agent, Darshan is your partner in design.

More than any place in the world, India is filled with people like Darshan—skilled, experienced and reasonably practical professionals who would allow professional importers to produce what India has to offer.

The garment industry is going through bad times everywhere and the bad times are here to stay. More people are entering the industry at the very moment consumers are spending less money on clothes. Everything looks the same because everyone is selling the same things.

You either have to design at the extreme edge of fashion, which is an excellent formula guaranteed to achieve bankruptcy, or you have to find something new and interesting. You can also learn to see with new eyes. What is new to New York is a thousand years old some place else. The trick is to see what is different, not as ethnic design, but as new techniques and facilities.

This is a costing problem. 'New, different, and commercial' add both value and costs to your garments. They are as much a part of the manufacturing process as ordering a button. So let's get back now to how else companies can reduce indirect costs.

Chapter 5
Indirect Costs: The Intangibles

The greatest indirect-cost savings occur when the supplier has facilities to ensure the right product is shipped as ordered, on time, and without problems. Reliability is the greatest asset a supplier can have.

QUALITY

Good quality costs money. It is an added direct cost. The supplier requires more skilled people and better techniques, and must make a greater effort. These all cost money which must come out of the FOB price.

Bad quality costs money. It is an added indirect cost—fewer sales, greater numbers of garments returned because of unacceptable defects, and eventually loss of customers. These all cost money and must come out of the wholesale price.

A 10% loss on wholesale cost equals about three times more than a 10% addition to FOB price, if your FOB is about one-third of the wholesale price. The place to save money, or at least not to lose money, is in the wholesale rather than the FOB price. To put it another way, losses due to higher *indirect* costs are much bigger than losses due to higher *direct* costs. It is cheaper to correct a mistake at the factory in the Philippines than to be stuck with the damaged garments in New York. What is cheaper still is to discover the potential mistake before it occurs and avoid it altogether.

Have you ever noticed that certain suppliers are accident prone, while others appear to be unbelievably lucky? The accident-prone supplier always seems to hit problems that are totally beyond his control. Necessary materials arrive late, get lost in transit, or wind up damaged. The factory is already running late. They are trying their very best to catch up, and there's a typhoon. The workers and staff at the so-called lucky factory return the next morning and, with the exception of three pieces of paper which unfortunately fell off a desk, there is no evidence whatsoever of the previous night's storm. The workers at the unlucky factory, located only 30 feet away, have to arrive by dugout canoe just in time to see the last of the semi-completed pieces of your order floating off in the distance.

Don't believe it. There are no *lucky* factories—there are those which are reliable and those which are not. Both have last-minute crises. In the reliable factory, these are limited only to those few events that could not have been foreseen and were by their very nature unavoidable. To the unreliable factory, all events are source potential for last-minute crises. Nothing is foreseen because nothing is planned or even considered in advance. The unlucky factory has no work flow—rather it lurches from one crisis to the next. If you produce your work at such a factory, you will be lucky to receive anything on time and as ordered.

A reliable factory is reliable because it is *committed* to be reliable. Without this commitment, no quality standard is possible regardless of your effort or any skills the factory staff may have. You cannot teach a factory to be committed to reliability. You can only run away as fast as you can when you realize just whom you are dealing with.

Case Study XXIX—Shirts with Holes

Here is a puzzle. You have set up a buying office in Shanghai. The client is a large European retail group with a real commitment to quality. The order is for yarn-dyed cotton shirts, stand-up packed. The client is willing to inspect every garment when it arrives in Italy. This is no small feat. A stand-up packed shirt is folded with tissue paper inside, and pinned in the folded position. The collar sits erect with a special stand. The shirt is placed in a polybag with six shirts to a box, twelve boxes to a carton. The cost of inspection in the European warehouse is $1.00 per shirt, compared to a total FOB price of $6.50.

Clearly, it is your job to set up procedures that would avoid the need for costly inspection on the European side. You set up a complete and detailed inspection process with a manual specifying each QC procedure. With your great system, any problem must come to light.

The first order of 15,000 shirts is completed and shipped. Six weeks later you are asked to come to Europe. Understand, this is not good news. The customer did not ask you to fly in from Shanghai to invite you to the Salzburg Mozart Festival. There has to be a problem and the problem has to be the shirts. What could have gone wrong? In the eighteen hours flying from Shanghai to Rome, you have plenty of time to think. On Style 436B, the pocket placement was a quarter-inch off on 30 pieces. The garments had been sewn before your team caught the error. It is true you passed the pieces. However, the client could not be aggravated about that. The 30 shirts were packed separately, with a note attached. Style 441B had a problem with the hangtags. However, you did notify the client and they approved the replacements. Maybe it was the chest measurements on Style 440. No, the measurement was off only half an inch. That is within tolerance.

Eventually you arrive. The client says "hello" (this is Europe, clients say "hello" before attacking) and you are taken to the warehouse to see the garments. The good news is that only 45 damages have been found—a 0.03% damage rate is very good. The bad news is that the damaged garments have holes actually more like craters. The shirts look like the props used in the closing scenes of an Arnold Schwarzenegger movie. In one case, the hole extends over 80% of the entire back of the shirt.

On the one hand, the garments look very good. Sewing quality is excellent. Measurements are near perfect. Pressing is lovely. In fact, on 14,955 pieces the work is some of the best the client has ever

...shirts with holes...

seen. The problem is that despite the fine goods, your customer cannot risk shipping any garments with 12-inch holes. Their customers will think they are crazy. Is it not possible for you to tighten up your procedures to avoid this problem? After all, there are only 45 pieces and the damage is so obvious that it should be easy to see.

This puzzle has only one solution, and once you understand the situation, that solution is terribly clear. Think about it. How can a garment go through production with a 12-inch hole? Someone would have had to cut the fabric into garment parts. Surely the cutter noticed the hole. Why didn't he cut it out? Why didn't he at least show someone the problem?

After cutting, the garment parts—including the back with the 12-inch hole—went to fusing, where interlining was placed in the collar, cuffs and placket. Those workers had to notice the 12-inch hole. Likewise, the person who sewed the garment had to see something as did the person who overlocked the hem, and the person who made the buttonholes, and the other person who sewed the buttons.

What about the person who pressed the garment? Didn't he think it strange that 80% of the back was missing, or did he simply conclude: "Goody, less fabric means fewer creases"?

Imagine the packer. Didn't he have a problem? The tissue paper would have kept slipping through the hole.

Let's face it. Ten people saw the garment and no one saw anything unusual. As a result, you have two choices—the first, immediately on your return to the factory call a meeting of all staff and controllers. I want you to imagine this meeting. You are standing there and you announce: "In future, we will not ship shirts with 12-inch holes."

The factory manager is standing there, taking notes, and he says: "Thank you, I assure you that we will carry out your instructions. I never knew that our inspectors should reject a garment just because it has a 12-inch hole."

Do you get the message? These people do not care. They have zero commitment to quality. All they want to do is ship the order. There is no way that you are going to stop them from shipping damaged garments. Your inspectors are not policemen. If you need policemen, work someplace else.

It does not matter that only 0.3% of the order was damaged. The low damage rate was due to the high fabric quality. If the fabric had been no good, the factory would still have cut and sewn the garments, and your client would have been faced with a 30% damage rate.

Despite the excellent work the factory is capable of doing, you cannot afford to work there. Without a commitment to quality, the factory will eventually produce and ship damaged garments. The second choice, your only real choice, is to drop the factory—fast, before they cause real problems.

QUALITY ASSURANCE AND QUALITY CONTROL

The 0-service factory is the factory with no commitment to quality at all. Once again, the 0-service factory has the highest indirect costs. This is the factory where, when the buyer specifies interlining, Freudenburg quality 7315, their trim department will look to find a locally produced substitute which they claim is almost the same. The difference can be a reduction in their direct costs and therefore an increase in their profit of as much as eight cents per item. For you, the increase in indirect cost does not manifest itself until your customers ask you why your shirt cuffs feel like plywood. Regretfully, this type of 0-service factory is more common than you would think.

Even with a commitment for quality and the complete assistance of the buyer and his agent, the 0-service factory still cannot improve quality. Many professionals have lived through the same problem. Quality does not change by closer or more complete inspection. Beyond a certain point, increased supervision by the buyer or his agent brings reduction in quality. This is the inspection trap, and at some point every professional has been caught in it.

Case Study XXX—The Inspection Trap

You are director of manufacturing at Schmidlap Enterprises.

You have a large office in Shanghai which is responsible for over $100 million in annual volume at FOB. Working in China is not bad for you. Certainly, you do not have to worry about high macro costs as in Indonesia and Pakistan. Shanghai offers good logistics, satisfactory transportation, and four major textile and garment universities giving you access to English-speaking staff with at least some specialist background. There is not that much corruption and the government generally leaves you alone. That is why your bosses at Schmidlap buy $100 million a year in Shanghai.

The problem is quality control. The factories want to make decent goods. They just do not understand what you want.

The first solution was to bring in more inspectors, particularly for in-process inspection. This did help a little. So you decided to increase the number of inspectors. Surprisingly, this brought no further improvement. Eventually you reached the point where quality was falling and your people were inspecting over 40% of all production.

You were in an inspection trap.

When you inspected 5%-10% of production, you were checking the inspection work previously carried out by the factory inspectors. However, as you increased your level of inspection, you were in fact taking over the factory's own inspection function. As a result, the more you inspected, the less they did.

Furthermore, you took over responsibility. Every garment your inspectors passed was a passed garment. Therefore, even though quality was falling, you had no future grounds for complaint since you had already accepted the production.

The more work you did, the less work the factory did. The more responsibility you took, the less responsibility the factory took. In a sense, you were rewarding their poor work.

The only way to escape from the trap is to stop inspecting the garments. The real solution is to take delivery of the garments in your own Shanghai warehouse. There you can inspect 10%. If the goods fail, send them back to the factory for repair and reinspection. Now instead of inspecting garment quality, you are inspecting factory quality. Factories that fail continually are factories you cannot work with. You may wind up paying more for assembling the garment in another factory, but you will more than make up for it if the move allows you to reduce the size of your Shanghai office, cut overhead, and improve your quality levels.

Very little can be done to ensure any level of quality until either the factory begins to raise itself from 0-service status, or you finally give up and go elsewhere to a normal-service factory. The normal-service factory, through a system of continuous inspection, tries to ensure that quality standards are maintained throughout production. Garments are inspected throughout assembly. This in-process inspection is then combined with a complete final inspection.

As a factory begins to improve its quality level, more time and effort is devoted to inspection. By definition, the purpose of inspection is to ensure that the finished garment meets the customer's requirements. The factory, together with the buyer or his agent, might unpack, measure and scrutinize as much as 10% of a finished order.

However, the factory realizes very quickly that, although the easiest time to find flaws is when the production is complete, it is also no longer possible to do anything about the problems. It does very little good to find out that the sleeve is a half-inch too short when all the garments are finished and packed. Furthermore, it is also too late to ask if a half-inch difference in the sleeve measurement is of importance to the customer. The more developed the factory becomes, the greater emphasis it places on in-process inspection. Particularly in the early stages, production flaws can be remedied. At the same time, when problems arise, the customer can be given options. Perhaps the half-inch difference is not important; or by taking smaller seam allowances at the sleeve head and cuff, the half-inch difference can be reduced to one-quarter inch.

It is at this point that the factory begins to realize that the relationship between a reliable factory and a reliable customer is not competitive, certainly not confrontational, but rather cooperative. When problems occur, the factory realizes that the most profitable course is to notify the customer at once so that a joint solution can be worked out. Both the factory and the customer must realize that the order itself is secondary to the relationship, and that solutions arrived at mutually are in fact most profitable for both in the long term. Naturally, this evolution can take place only between a reliable factory and a reliable customer. If the customer is the legendary Herbie the Mouth, the system immediately breaks down.

Case Study XXXI—Herbie's Choice

Herbie the Mouth has a problem with a style going through production. The shirt called for pocket flaps, and the shirt in production does have the pocket flaps. Unfortunately, the production also has a buttonhole and button closing on the pocket flap. The style does not call for the button closing.

The factory immediately notifies Herbie's agent of the problem and the agent e-mails Herbie the Mouth.

Herbie, being a positive sort of guy, looks at the problem from a positive point of view: "What can I get out of this?" After all, it is not his fault the factory screwed up. Why shouldn't he take advantage of the situation?

Herbie is experienced. He understands these problems and he understands how important they are. Herbie has his own system of analysis. The first thing Herbie does is to discount the possibility that there will be any loss to Herbie arising from the added buttonholes and buttons. "After all, those bastards are getting more than they asked for. Why should they complain? In any case, who can remember six months later whether the style has pockets, let alone flaps with buttonholes?"

Having disposed of any potential downside, Herbie can direct his attention to the upside. Regretfully, he first puts aside the possibility of charging the customers more for the shirts. They wouldn't stand for it.

The next step is to find out how the style is doing. After all, if the style has not sold well, in Herbie's book added buttonholes are definitely grounds for cancellation. Herbie's book of grounds for cancellation has many pages. For example, late delivery is definitely grounds for cancellation, as are early delivery and in some cases even on-time delivery. However, in this instance, the style is selling too well to cancel. Briefly, Herbie toys with the idea of canceling an altogether different style on the grounds that this style has extra buttonholes, but that is just wishful thinking.

In the end, Herbie opts for a claim—25% of the FOB may not be much, but it is better than nothing.

Herbie leaves it to his agent to notify the factory. After all, that is what those good-for-nothing thieves are paid for.

With someone more reliable than Herbie the Mouth, cooperating to achieve quality makes better sense. One of the defining characteristics of the full-service factory is that it relies on complete cooperation to maintain high quality.

The full-service factory also stresses in-process inspection. However, in a full-service factory problems of quality begin long before they start making the stock garments. Quality control becomes less important than quality assurance (QA) and QA begins with the first factory sample where the factory looked at the designer's request. They looked not only from a design point of view, but from that of production as well. Every attempt was made to foresee later problems in bulk production and to correct the first sample to avoid or at least minimize problems down the line. To the full-service factory, since the manufacturing process begins with design, so too must QA.

The full-service factory realizes that for each order it has three customers to satisfy: the designer, whose ideas must be followed; the production manager, whose quality standards must be met; and the merchandiser, who must buy at the right price. The factory uses the samplemaking process as an opportunity to reach consensus. Since difficult or potentially troublesome operations are by their nature costly, changes which make the production flow smoother for the factory will result in cost reductions.

This cooperation between the factory and the customer's various departments is necessary if the customer is to buy at the lowest cost. Regretfully, the problem is often complicated by interdepartmental conflicts, seemingly an inevitable part of both European and American garment import companies. Designers lament that production people destroy their styles because they simply do not understand what the designer was hoping to achieve. Production people resent designers because they ask for the impossible. Sales people dislike them both, claiming that designers insist on creating unsaleable styles which production people cost out at prices that no one can afford to buy. Fortunately, everyone wants to talk to the factory, provided it is a full-service factory, if only to enlist the maker as an ally. The smart factory recognizes these divisions and is able to build consensus.

QA and QC to Achieve 0-Defects

Many manufacturing consultants believe that achieving the highest quality is the same as achieving 0-defects. This may be true for the manufacture of commercial aircraft or coal mining, but the garment industry is different. The world would probably be a much neater place for consultants if the garment industry did not exist. No one really cares what a plane looks like, only that it flies; and certainly no one cares what a piece of coal looks like, only that it produce heat. However, customers do care what a garment looks like. In the fashion industry aesthetics and function must coexist which gives rise to special problems.

No plane manufacturer would use materials and processes that were by their very nature damaged in fact, they insist that everything be uniform to 1/10,000 of an inch. However, garment designers frequently ask for silk fabric, handknit, screen print and draped patterns, all of which differ from piece to piece and are therefore, by definition, defective.

Furthermore, while most industries seek to increase quality by simplifying the manufacturing process, garment designers and their makers improve quality by using more complex techniques requiring greater amounts of skilled labor. The result is that while garment professionals and final consumers alike know that Giorgio Armani produces a higher quality garment than Kmart, the industrial consultant would reject the $1200 Armani jacket as having a greater number of damages than the $50 Kmart version.

This paradox arises because the industrial consultant fails to differentiate between standards of quality and levels of quality. The Armani garment is made to a high standard, requiring many skilled operators and a great deal of handwork. To achieve the look and feel of the garment, Armani must sacrifice uniformity. Levels of quality, which conventionally translate as fewer defects, are much harder to achieve as quality standards rise.

The airplane manufacturer lives in a simple one-dimensional world where only strict quality levels exist. The garment maker operates in a far more complex environment where for each style, he must balance the demands of standards of quality required—if he is to achieve the look the customer desires—with demands of levels of quality to ensure the garment will not be rejected as damaged.

RELIABLE DELIVERY

Factories that ship on time do not rush production. They seldom go into overtime. Reliable delivery is the result of sound production planning, not crisis management. Production planning begins on Day 1, the first time the factory is notified that a style exists and that there may be a future order.

At the same time the first duplicate is being made, the customer notifies the factory of the approximate size of the order and the final stock-shipping date. This date may be six or seven months down the line. To the 0-service factory, most likely working on a CM basis, the delivery date is so far away as to be totally irrelevant. All they care about is that at some point in the far-off distant future, perhaps 30 days before shipment, a truck pulls up at their factory door and disgorges the graded set of patterns (or preferably the marker), the fabric, and more than likely the trim which is unavailable in the 0-service factory's home country.

For the more developed factories, production planning is more complicated. At the top end, the full-service factory will more than likely control the schedule itself since they will be running the entire preproduction process. For them, seven months is a very short time. Each day specific tasks will have to be carried out and 50 separate deadlines will have to be met in accordance with the master schedule if the stock shipment is to be on time.

The complete schedule printout with all details showing what the

100

factory must do and when each task is to be completed, together with what the buyer must do and when each of their tasks must be completed, is sent to the buyer for approval. The buyer will almost always approve the schedule, for both the buyer and the factory are aware of two certainties: the schedule will have to be constantly changed to accommodate unforeseen problems, probably starting as soon as the following day, and whatever happens, the stock will be shipped on time.

The greatest scheduling advantage offered by the full-service factory is flexibility. Things may go wrong, but things never fall apart.

Case Study XXXII—Merrison Garments: Programming for Error

Merrison is a large Hong Kong-based factory group specializing in better ladieswear. With 3,000 sewers in four countries, Merrison is living proof that designer goods need not be produced in small workshop operations. The company ships more than 400 styles per month. At this level, schedules are run by computer. For preproduction work, the entire process is governed by a specially designed program. The program is based on the firm belief that things go wrong. The concept is quite simple.

The customer comes with his sketches, patterns and other paraphernalia. Merrison immediately produces a complete schedule based on 60 days for stock production. This is Schedule A, and very few customers will accept it. However, most customers accept 45 days for stock production, Schedule B.

The schedule is printed out showing specific dates for each step in the process. Naturally, the process soon breaks down. The customer was to have approved strikeoffs on Day 30. They finally approve strikeoffs on Day 36. Automatically, the program shifts from Schedule B to Schedule C with its own specific adjusted dates for each step.

The size/color breakdown was supposed to arrive on Day 84. This is delayed and the program shifts from C to D. Some of the time can be made up by rushing the preproduction steps, but inevitably it is the production time itself that must be telescoped.

Somewhere around Schedule E the company has less than 30 days to produce stock. Past that point, a director must approve further change. But I am sure that somewhere in the computer there even exists Schedule Z, which allows Merrison to produce the stock order in two days.

In a full-service factory, stock is never shipped late.

Few factories are sufficiently well developed to run multiple production schedules. For the normal-service factory, production schedules are relatively fixed. Delays in arrival of material, approval delays, and last-minute corrections and changes in orders inevitably result in delays. The customer and his agent must know at all times at what stage their production is in.

FAST TURN DELIVERY

In a competitive environment late delivery is unacceptable. The costs are too high. On-time delivery is 'acceptable', but in today's cut-throat retail environment, increasingly insufficient to meet the needs of the customer. Importers and retailers can no longer afford the luxury of placing stock orders six months in advance, tying up their capital, holding excessive amounts of inventory and missing the latest fashion changes.

Furthermore, end consumers are becoming more knowledgeable and better shoppers. Until quite recently, women would actually consider it reasonable to buy a winter coat in July when new fall merchandise traditionally arrives in stores. Today, more shoppers are forgoing the dubious advantage of being fashionable and waiting until after Christmas, when goods are marked down, to buy their winter coats. They might not be fashionable in October, November and December, but they will have saved 50%. To the modern consumer, it is better to take the cash and be less fashionable. As a result, the whole concept of season is breaking down. Some retailers are now trying to continually stock new inventory, where clothing inside the shop actually relates to the weather outside. The very successful Spanish-based retail group Zara no longer runs seasons at all.

Today more and more importers are looking at 'fast turn' as a means of staying competitive. If you can provide a steady supply of new merchandise, customer interest is maintained and the till keeps ringing. Unfortunately, few American importers have learned the skills required to work with fast turn. Most mass-market retailers instead seem to subscribe to the Heinrich Himmler school of buying: "You vill do vat I say, or ve vill destroy you."

Typically, the mass-market buying office allows the factory 45 days from time of order to stock shipment. For each day late, a claim of 1% is automatically imposed. After ten days the order is automatically canceled, and after one month, the entire factory staff is sent to the Gulags.

The result of this rigid buying system is garments geared to the lowest common denominator—mediocre everything. Overly simplified styles are combined with basic fabrics readily available in the market and quality is indifferent at best.

All this for 45-day shipment which, when you add 28 days shipping, seven days clearance and inland freight, and seven days sorting, still gives you three-month turns. This is fast turn only when compared to the twelfth century, when camel loads of spices and silks were brought from distant Cathay to Europe via the Silk Road.

Some U.S. companies have mastered fast turn in domestic operations. In California, a group of Eastern Europeans have set up shop using modern facilities and produce spandex knit garments with guaranteed delivery in any color, any style, in the store in 21 days. In Atlanta, there is a company that will deliver T-shirts in eight days, starting from raw cotton through spinning, knitting, dyeing and sewing.

To these companies, direct costs are simply unimportant—the indirect-cost advantages gained in their domestic set-ups overcome any difference in wage rates between China and California.

THE BUYER: DOING YOUR JOB

You, as the buyer, have little control over indirect costs in general, just as it is almost impossible for you to reduce indirect costs in a particular factory. Either the factory has the facilities you require or they do not. Unfortunately, buyers often misuse existing facilities, thus raising their own indirect costs. This happens most often in production planning, almost always as a result of either poor coordination or poor communication or both.

We forget that the manufacturing process occurs simultaneously at the factory and the buyer's place. A good factory may well take over most of the manufacturing responsibilities, but not even a full-service factory can do everything. You must play your part as well. The factory must have the *color/quantity breakdown* (Flow Chart Step 66) if they are to order stock fabric and trim. They must have your *letter of credit* in an acceptable form (Steps 72-74) if they are to proceed with stock production. They need your *style correction* (Steps 49, 68), a *size/quantity breakdown* (Step 67), and *color approvals* (Step 53).

When lab dips arrive for color approval on Friday afternoon and you are anxious to leave for Long Island to play golf over the weekend, you may decide it is not worthwhile to do the work and take a later train since stock delivery is not scheduled for four months, and in any case it is a weekend in Asia as well. However, your decision has just set the clock back three days. Your fax approval sent out on Monday morning will not arrive until Monday night in Asia and cannot be acted on until the following day. Your Friday afternoon is Saturday morning at the factory, but you have forgotten that Asian factories generally work on Saturdays. Now they can do nothing until Tuesday morning. If you had taken that later train, you would have lost four hours but saved three days.

When four months later the stock arrives late and you face cancellations, you may have forgotten that golf weekend on Long Island. You will blame the factory for the losses you now face. But those losses are at least in part due to your own delay. You could have saved time and helped to reach on-time delivery.

MINIMUMS

Minimums are a major indirect-cost factor (see Case Study XXVII).

Most importers are unable to place orders with the majority of Asian suppliers because the minimum quantities per style required by the maker are too high. With the exception of companies in Hong Kong, S. Korea, Taiwan, and the factories in China which they operate or control, minimums range from 500 dozen to 5,000 dozen per style. Unless you are a mass-market retailer or import giant, there is no place for you in these factories. Even someone as big as Calvin Klein can run basic items such as underwear briefs in India, but that is about it.

For most importers, Bangladesh, India, Indonesia, Pakistan, the Philippines and Sri Lanka are simply off-limits. Direct costs may seem attractive, but the minimums are murderous. There are exceptions. Here and there factories are set up to accept more reasonable quantities, but they represent only a small fraction of suppliers.

WORKING CONDITIONS—ETHICAL SOURCING

Child labor, questionable mistreatment of women at the workplace, and excessive overtime are now large and growing factors determining indirect costs. Buyers take great risks when orders are given to factories whose standards of working conditions are unacceptable to the consumer in the buyer's country.

There are many counter-arguments to this view:

- In many parts of the world, putting children to work is part of the culture.

- Families in the poorest countries rely on their children's income for their daily needs.

- Sadly, the alternative to child labor could be child prostitution.

- Child labor exists in even the most developed nations. American children living on family farms traditionally carry out chores. These chores are simply disguised child labor.

- Western cultures have no right to impose their values on other cultures.

These counter-arguments may be correct but they are irrelevant. All that matters is the enormous added cost the buyer will suffer when he is caught.

In the near future you may see an ad that reads:

This Christmas make a child happy—
Don't buy a rug made in Pakistan.

The accompanying photograph shows a 9-year-old girl sitting in total filth hunched over a carpet handloom.

I could be wrong. Instead of child labor and Pakistani rugs, it might be child labor and Indian textiles, prison labor and Chinese tea, or the condition of women in Indonesian garment factories. The list goes on and on.

104

What is interesting is not the almost limitless permutations of terrible conditions in which people are forced to work in many Third World countries, but rather that such ads have become a real possibility. In a time when increased competition coincides with a general and possibly long-term loss of consumer interest, companies are making ever greater efforts to market their products. Anything that turns the consumer off must be avoided at all costs. Public awareness that your child's Christmas toy was produced by undernourished, poorly clothed children maintained in a state of semi-slavery is not going to help sales.

For years, labor unions and human rights groups have lobbied members of the U.S. Congress to tie American trade policy to working conditions in exporting countries. In almost every instance, they were defeated by a coalition of large American companies buying product from and investing capital in the targeted countries. In pursuing these policies, these liberal groups have achieved a record of failure unequaled since the days of the Progressive Party politician William Jennings Bryan in the early part of this century.

The success of the American companies and the failure of these liberal groups were not caused by the nature of the fight but rather its venue. In the United States, decisions of whether or not to buy and from whom are not made by the government. Ultimately, they are made by the consumer. As long as American consumers remained indifferent to the plight of children in India, the problems of women workers in Indonesia, or sanitary conditions in Bangladesh, importers were free to ignore these factors in their purchasing decisions. This is now changing.

Many top line labels have been hurt. Walt Disney, The Gap and Nike have all been accused of producing merchandise in factories with substandard conditions. It is possible that these companies were unaware of the actual conditions of workers at their contracted factories. However, their ignorance of the true situation was an unacceptable argument to some end consumers who stopped buying their products.

Companies such as The Gap, Liz Claiborne and Levi Strauss have regulations that all contractors must follow to ensure a minimum standard of working conditions. All have special departments to ensure these standards are maintained. For example, Gap employees routinely sneak into contracting factories at night to ensure that excessive overtime is not taking place.

While these companies deserve credit for their humanitarian efforts, it is important to understand that what is really involved here is not good ethics, but rather good business. Walt Disney has a reputation as a wholesome group of people dedicated entirely to the entertainment and education of children. To create this image, they have spent millions of dollars. They want to be known as the child's friend, not the exploiter of children.

CONCLUSIONS

More than in any other area of costings, money is lost because buyers fail to adequately consider indirect costs. Macro costs may be larger, but there is a limit to how incompetent one person can be and still survive to see another season. Anybody knows better than to go to North Korea to buy T-shirts, to Burundi to buy lingerie, or to any of the high macro-cost areas where labor is cheapest.

Yet so-called smart people are still lined up waiting for the day when the U.S. government finally grants most-favored-nation (MFN) status to Vietnam. All they can see is the welcoming arms of the Vietnamese government which has promised no interference and abundant cheap labor. They still do not understand that there is more to manufacturing than cutting material and sewing it together. They still haven't learned to add. And because they do not understand about indirect costs, they are going to pay and pay.

Chapter 6
Direct Costs

After having weighed the costs of doing business in one country against another—macro costs—and after selecting the type of factory in that country capable of providing the facilities you need to reduce your expenses—indirect costs—you have finally reached the point where you can begin to discuss the costs of your first style. These are the direct costs. Although importers may place too much emphasis on direct costs, they are still important. Most importantly, unlike other costs, you can negotiate your direct costs.

Direct costs include the following:

1. Material costs

    a. Fabric (top goods)

    b. Trim

2. Making

    a. For wovens and cut-and-sew knits: cutting, sewing, finishing, pressing and packing

    b. For sweaters: knitting, looping and linking, finishing, washing, pressing and packing

3. Agent's commission

ONE-PRICE SHOPPING

In some cases the supplier will give no costs at all, providing only a single price with no breakdowns. Here the supplier looks at 'market price' rather than costs to determine FOB. The factory becomes a trader rather than a maker. Here are some common examples:

India

Many Indian factories work without any costings. I am sure you have seen typical ethnic Indian dresses. The fabric is a yarn-dyed gauze woven on an old shuttle loom where slubs, bars and misweaves give the garment that real Indian flavor. Heaven forbid they should make a mistake and produce a clean piece of fabric. It would be unusable; they would have to call it damaged. The dress itself looks like the polybag it came in—if the polybag had sleeves. The garment has no shape. The bust, waist and hip measurements are all the same—very large. This is definitely a case of one-size-fits-all. For this, the factory wants FOB $14.00. I have no idea how they reach $14.00. We are talking about a country where a trained sewer is paid less than $2.00 a day. It certainly is

*...Triangular Debt Chinese-style—a game where nobody wins.
A owes B, B owes C and C owes A—everybody is waiting to be paid
before paying...*

not the sum of material, which could not exceed $2.50 total; trim, at most $0.25; and making, which could not exceed $2.50 even if overheads were five times the cost of labor. How the factory gets from $5.25 to $14.00 is beyond explanation. By the way, shipment is between 120 and 150 days after order confirmation if all goes well. This is India.

China

Prices without costs also occur in Chinese state factories. Here the situation is somewhat different. You can have a cost breakdown, only the breakdown does not add up. For example, if you buy a raincoat, you have two choices of material. You can buy Chinese nylon, which is inevitably damaged, or you can buy Korean nylon, which is the same cost as the Chinese fabric but of much higher quality. It makes no difference to the state garment factory; they have to buy the fabric from the outside in any case. However, even though there is no difference in fabric cost and the making cost should be identical, the price for the raincoat is 25% higher when made of Korean fabric.

This unexplained difference is not due to a 'buy Chinese' policy, but the result of two factors unique to Chinese state companies. First of all, Chinese state companies truly have no knowledge of costings. They really do not know what the stuff costs, at least partially because up until about three years ago they had no interest in making a profit anyway. Secondly, under the Chinese bookkeeping system, while the state company will owe the same amount of money whether the fabric is purchased locally or from Korea, they actually have to pay for the Korean fabric whereas money owed to another Chinese state company simply becomes triangular debt. (A owes B. B owes C. B can't pay C until A pays him, but A is waiting for C to settle his invoices to A.) The situation may appear confusing, but the results are not. Everybody owes everybody, so nobody gets paid, which is not a good way to run a business.

Trading Companies

In addition to the suppliers in India and China discussed above, there is another even more common type of company that offers no cost information. Trading companies are really agents who, rather than working on a commission, simply add their fees into the FOB price. They quote FOB price only. Trading companies do not provide breakdowns, simply because they do not want you to know just how much they are making—and it can be a lot. Hong Kong trading companies working in China away from the major producing areas can add 100% or more to the FOB price. It is generally not a good idea to work with a trading company.

There are cases, however, when a trading company offers some real advantages. Here are the exceptions:

1. Special products: If your business is handpainted silk, you will need a very special trading company. It is not easy to find suppliers capable of handpaint and it is also very difficult to work with them. Take prices, for example. The handpaint supplier bases

his price on the amount of time required to paint the piece. However, since he does not know how long it will take to paint a particular piece, he will quote price only after having completed the order. Furthermore, if handpainted silk is damaged during processing, these damages would also become rejects and again, the damage rate cannot be estimated in advance. Since the trading company supplies the silk, materials lost through damage—either at greige state or during processing—are for the buyer's account. This is how handpaint has been negotiated for 1,000 years. You cannot fight the system. You certainly cannot change the system. Here it is best to work through a trading company. They will quote a price in advance and the price is negotiable.

2. Special services: There are trading companies which offer such great facilities that your indirect-cost savings more than offset any hidden commission. Asian companies doing private label who provide design, patternmaking, sampling and production facilities would be a case in point, particularly if they are willing to ship on an LDP basis and offer you 90 days credit. This little gem has just cut your overhead by two-thirds. I do not know if one exists, but if you ever come across such a trading company, my advice is to take the deal.

3. Universal buying offices: More easily found are these reliable and giant trading companies that deal in all product lines. The leading Japanese trading houses and South Korean *chaebol* are good examples. All have offices in every major city in the United States, Europe and Asia. A sizable trading house could have over a hundred branch offices worldwide and can, therefore, provide comparative costings from a variety of sources, excellent global communication and local follow-up wherever you decide to work. Many preliminary decisions can be made well before you even leave the United States. Finally, these buying offices perform well when a sourcing chain involves multiple suppliers operating in different countries. For example, if you were interested in nylon raincoats, the global trading company would be better suited to provide alternatives involving Chinese and Korean fabrics than the China state company.

Finally, these trading houses and chaebols are most useful when you are not interested in working long term in any particular country or if your product requires you to work in several countries at the same time. In these cases, by working on your own or through a local agent, you are important to no one. You have spread yourself too thin. However, by selecting one international trading company, you can become an important customer even if your work is divided between many countries.

NEGOTIATING WITHOUT COSTS

Unfortunately, the problem with working without any direct-cost breakdowns is that it is not easy to negotiate blind. Some importers will revert to the Wendell Wasp War method as described in Case Study VII: "Whatever price you quote, I want 25% less." But this is not a particularly good method. In the end, it destroyed Wendell.

There is another negotiating method that is based on total ignorance of direct costs.

Case Study XXXIII—Jerry Shaw: Know What You Can Afford

Someone else may have invented what I call the Shaw Method, but Jerry Shaw himself indisputably brought it to a fine art.

Jerry Shaw is a partner in a leading New York couture house. He is the business side of the business, which means that while his name does not appear on the labels, it does appear on all checks. Some years ago his company decided to introduce a more moderately priced line to be produced in Hong Kong.

Jerry Shaw's approach to price negotiation was modeled on the same approach he had to everything else in business: he knew exactly what he wanted and that was enough for him. He knew his optimum selling price. He knew precisely what he could afford to pay for a garment and still make his normal markup. That was the extent of Jerry Shaw's knowledge and the basis of all negotiations. The vendor was free to argue for as long as he wished. Jerry Shaw would sit there looking very attentive. When the vendor had completed his monologue, Jerry Shaw would repeat the price he was willing to pay. Even $0.25 difference on FOB $60.00 was unacceptable.

The essence of the Shaw method is to go to the vendor and say: "Here is my garment. Please find the fabric, produce the style at such-and-such a price and to my quality standard, and deliver it on or before my required date. In return, I will give you no support or assistance—but I will pay my bills on time, live up to all commitments and guarantee consistent business."

The truth is, while the negotiations may have been one-sided, the work was profitable for both the agent and factory, provided the vendor knew what he was doing. A good vendor could work successfully with Jerry Shaw. His company invariably paid its bills on time and lived up to each and every one of its commitments. Finally, since garment cost did not enter into the negotiation at all, some styles proved to be far more profitable than others. Overall, there definitely was profit for the factory.

An importer could do a whole lot worse than use the Shaw method. For one thing, you need a lot less knowledge to work this way.

Most suppliers who refuse to provide direct-cost breakdowns do so to avoid showing their true commissions. But even if a supplier does offer the lowest price, that advantage will eventually evaporate as customers demand to know more. Costings play a more important role than simply indicating areas of negotiation—they also tell you why a particular style from a particular vendor has a given FOB price. By understanding the details of each costing and comparing costings from different suppliers and for different styles from each supplier, you the buyer can learn how to reduce direct costs effectively.

True direct-cost reduction is not zero-sum negotiation. It is not a situation where each cost savings comes out of your supplier's pocket. It comes from understanding the nature of your suppliers and the nature of your styles.

Some suppliers excel in specific areas. By recognizing this expertise, you are in a position to channel work best suited to each supplier. The factory is given the work they do best (which, by the way, also provides indirect-cost savings), and you receive the benefit of their special skills in the form of reduced prices.

Some styles have particular problems that may involve additional fabric requirements or difficult and, therefore, costly sewing operations. Once you understand the nature of the problem and the exact added cost, you can make necessary changes to reduce the costs yourself.

However, these skills can only be acquired by access to direct-cost breakdowns from each supplier. The more information you have, the easier it is for you to save money on direct costs. Without these breakdowns, you will never know just why things cost what they do.

Direct-cost breakdowns generally include three items: material (fabric and trim), making, and agent's commissions. Of these, the material comprises by far the largest portion.

MATERIAL COSTS

It can be argued that in today's industry, since suppliers source rather than buy, material costs are not direct costs at all. It can also be argued that the industry is no longer the simple place where a customer brought a sample to the factory and said, "Make me that," which in turn took the fabric swatch to the fabric trading company and said, "Make me that," which in its turn swam further upstream to the mill and also said, "Make me that." In those days, few buyers had the ability to source fabric and trim; all material costs were direct costs.

Today, customers—when they have the ability to source product—often assume responsibility for fabric orders. Material becomes in fact both a direct and indirect-cost factor since sourcing requires special facilities and knowledge. For our purposes, however, they have been included as direct costs since most customers and suppliers still consider material as such.

FABRIC

Your largest direct cost is fabric. This is where you can save money, ensure your garments are competitively priced, and where you make profit. Conversely, this is also where you go broke. There is a lot more to buying fabric than sitting in a mill office and signing a contract.

The first question is: Who should pay for the fabric—you or the factory? Should you work FOB or CMT?

FOB vs. CMT Factories:

Many small factories, especially 0-service factories, will not buy fabric. Either they lack the capital or they are simply unwilling to take the risk to finance fabric, representing at least 60% of the total FOB price. But for most buyers, the risk of owning fabric is simply too great.

When a factory owns the fabric, they have a financial investment in your order. If the quality of their production is below standard or if they ship late, they risk cancellation, in which case they lose the money they have invested in your fabric. When the factory owns the fabric, negotiations for claims become much easier.

Furthermore, their investment in your order gives it higher production priority. All factories constantly face problems. Production times can be miscalculated, unforeseen quality problems occur, an operation proves to be more difficult and time-consuming than estimated when the garment was costed. In each case, the factory faces decisions: We are overbooked—whose order should we delay? The quality is at best marginal—should we pass it? Should we replace the correct but more costly sewing operation with an easier one, even though the quality will suffer?

Every factory includes risk as a factor in their calculations. If you own the fabric, you have increased the probability that your order will be the one delayed, that your quality will suffer, and that the factory will often take the easy way out. You cannot cancel because you own the fabric. When the factory owns the fabric, they are the ones who are trapped. It is for this very reason that most customers work with FOB factories.

However, there are notable exceptions:

1. Mass-market customers prefer CMT factories.

These companies cover all indirect costs themselves. They look at the factory only as a room full of machines, necessary to cut and assemble the garments. These customers often block the total production capacity of several CMT factories. Through their agents or wholly-owned overseas buying offices, they are prepared to supervise every step in the production process. In a real sense, they control the factory. If a buyer is willing and able to cover all indirect costs himself, then saving money on direct costs becomes important. An FOB factory makes a profit on fabric.

113

If you control the factory, why allow them to make this added profit?

2. Large agents and trading companies prefer CMT factories.

To the factory, a large agent is a large customer. The same logic that allows the large customer to control the factory and, therefore, ensure reasonable quality and delivery holds true for the large agent. However, the agent also has his own business costs which he must pass on to his customers. This raises the FOB cost of his garments considerably. In a competitive environment where you can work with full-service factories without paying an agent's commission, the agent must work with cheaper factories. A CMT factory, with its lower direct costs, allows the agent to be more competitive.

3. Small high-quality specialist factories do not need to buy fabric.

If you are Donna Karan, you will find many factories that want to produce for DKNY. But no one is standing in line to produce the real Donna Karan designer collection. A Donna Karan jacket requires 40% handwork. The order may not exceed 75 pieces. Every style has its own problem, and every problem requires skilled, experienced tailors. Finally, the price of the fabric may be $50 a yard or more. Only a small, very skilled tailoring factory would take on the work. Whether that factory is located in Hong Kong, France or New York City, you can be certain it is not laying out the money for the fabric.

Ordering vs. Paying:

For an FOB factory, it is not necessary to order the fabric, only to pay for it. On the other hand, if the factory has specialized knowledge of a particular fabric, then once you agree to specific fabric qualities, it may be more advantageous for the factory to contact the mills and place the order. They may have better connections than you. They may be able to negotiate a better price. Most importantly, if the factory places the order, they are responsible for it. If the fabric arrives late, they must make up the lost time during production. If the fabric is damaged, they must take the loss either by cutting out the damages or replacing the fabric altogether.

If you order for the fabric, you are responsible. You have the right to expect the factory to inspect the fabric on arrival. In the event of damages, they should notify you. It is true that if they fail to take these steps and go ahead and begin production, they become responsible if the fabric proves damaged, provided a proper inspection would have revealed the damage. However, once the factory has properly taken these steps, you are left responsible. If the fabric is late, it is your problem. If the fabric is damaged, it is equally your problem.

Yet despite everything I have said until now about the safety of working with FOB factories, in the long run it is still best for you to order the fabric. If you order the fabric, you know the actual price. You know the quality. You also learn about fabric. As long as the factory supplies the fabric, you must go with their existing network of fabric suppliers or start from scratch if you change factories. By standing responsible for fabric purchase, you keep yourself independent. That said, your decisions should also depend on your product. If you import T-shirts, it does not really matter—cotton single jersey or double knit is available on any street corner anywhere in the known world. Places yet undiscovered by Western man have access to 32-count carded cotton yarn and some form of circular knit machinery. On the other hand, if your business is fashion sweaters, I suggest you learn to buy the yarn.

Finally, if you order the material, the factory cannot add their own markup to the fabric cost. You can negotiate directly with the mill, sign a contract, and notify the factory to open its letter of credit. The factory will ask you to pay a finance charge, usually about 5%, to cover the costs of opening the letter of credit and the interest to carry the fabric from the time the mill receives fabric payment until the finished garments have been shipped and the factory receives their payment. As long as you have opened your letter of credit for the FOB price of the garments, the factory will pay for the fabric. In many cases, if you are a known and trusted customer, the factory will open its letter of credit for fabric even before you open yours for the garments.

Analyzing Fabric Cost

There are only two factors determining fabric cost: the yield (the quantity of fabric required to produce one piece or a dozen garments) and the per-yard cost of the fabric.

Calculating fabric yields can be a little complicated. What you want to determine initially is how efficient is the marker.[12] While the marker efficiency depends on the type of garment, the style, as well as fabric width and type, you would expect 85% or better fabric usage. Modern marker technique done by computer will indicate percentage efficiency on the screen.

Granted that markers can be a complicated business, don't let yourself be intimidated. Whatever the complexities involved, you should learn to lay out the patterns either yourself or with the assistance of one of the cutters at your factory. (For sweaters, you need only weigh the finished article to determine the weight of yarn per garment.)

The actual fabric-cost calculation is logical and consistent for all fabrics. Given time and reasonable effort, precise fabric-cost calculation will become second nature. Here is a typical fabric costing sheet.

FABRIC COST SHEET

Fabric Group Name:		
Customer:		
Description:		Date:
PO#	Style #	Yield
PO#	Style #	Yield
PO#	Style #	Yield

Cost of Fabric

FOB/CIF Cost   _____

Freight   _____

Other   _____

Subtotal   _____

Processing Charges

Dyeing/Printing Cost   _____

Finishing Cost   _____

Other   _____

Subtotal   _____

Additional Charges

Finance Charge   _____

Premium I   _____

Premium II   _____

Subtotal   _____

Final Fabric Cost per Yard   _____

Calculated Yield/Garment   _____

Allowance I   _____

Allowance II   _____

Note that fabric cost is not calculated on a style basis, but rather on the basis of the fabric group, which is all the combined styles using that particular fabric. This makes sense since the factory can charge only one cost per fabric type, regardless of what type of garment is purchased. As you are about to see, this seemingly logical axiom definitely puts a crimp in factory costings.

The first category which goes into your final fabric cost is initial *cost of fabric*, followed by *processing* and *additional charges*.

Fabric can be purchased in several states. The easiest calculation occurs when the fabric has already been finished and is purchased on a cost, insurance and freight (CIF) basis; all cost of fabric expenses have already been included in the one price. If finished fabric has been bought on an FOB basis, the overseas freight and insurance must be added separately under the item *freight*.

But when fabric is purchased in loom state (greige), further processing is required before it can be cut into garments. This may include *printing, dyeing* and a variety of *finishing* processes. Each additional processing cost is added here. Obviously, whenever finished fabric has been purchased, the entire processing section is ignored.

Finance charges and *premiums* are the most complicated and controversial items, involving a number of permutations. The most common situation arises when you actually place the order for the fabric, which the factory in turn pays for. Since the price quoted to you does not include letter-of-credit charges or bank interest payments up to the time of garment shipment, the factory must somehow be reimbursed for these expenses. For this, the factory will add a finance charge, normally between 4%-5% of the value of the order, depending on the factory, the payment terms, and the length of time the factory must hold the fabric prior to garment shipment. Five percent is fair. More is exorbitant.

The factory will also add a premium (*premium I*) to cover known losses with regard to the fabric. For example, if, in the course of processing the fabric shrinks 5%, that loss must be made up somewhere. It is customary to include shrinkage in the cost of the fabric. Acceptable charges for added premiums should be worked out in some detail with the vendor in advance.

Besides the listed premiums, the factory will probably include other charges in *premium II*. The items covered here are not unreasonable, but they are hard to explain and justify to the customer. For this reason, they are generally kept hidden. They are closely related to the item *allowance II*, which I will go over in some detail below.

So far, the equation goes something like this: *fabric + processing + additional charges = cost of fabric per yard.*

To calculate the *yield per garment*—simply the marker yardage—you follow similar steps. Once again, if you do not have access to the marker yardage, ask the vendor. If you are not satisfied with the answer, go to the factory and lay the pattern out. The people in the cutting department should help you. You may not get the best or most accurate yield, but you will get a reasonable one. If the factory refuses to cooperate at all, beware—you are probably dealing with crooks.

There are many importers who seldom or ever visit a factory, let alone stand at a cutting table laying out patterns. If you want to be one of these people, then either hire someone to do your work for you or stop now! Go into banking! Bankers do not get their hands dirty. Garment people do.

Direct Costs

There is an old Yiddish expression that says: "The profit of the company is on the floor of the cutting department." If there is a Book of Proverbs for importers, this would certainly be on the first page.

Some basic allowances must be added to marker yardage. *Allowance 1* includes these universally accepted items. First of all, there is basic wastage: after each piece of fabric has been cut, there will be a small uncut balance of perhaps two yards or less. With some fabrics, the leftovers can be used to cut additional garments; with others, piece-to-piece shading makes this impossible. In either case, a balance of small uncut pieces of fabric will always remain. The allowance can be anywhere between from between 2%-5% for all wastage and damage depending on the factory, the nature of the fabric and the type of garment.

The problem with these calculations is that cutting floor realities are more complex than counting the number of remaining fabric pieces. The more you the buyer understand, the more unnecessary it becomes for the factory to hide certain difficulties or even lie to you.

All fabric costings are based on two fundamental axioms, the first already mentioned:

- The factory can charge you only one price per yard for each fabric, regardless of the garment style.

- The same style must always take the same yardage, regardless of the fabric. (Provided the fabric widths are the same, both styles use the same paper patterns and no fabric has yarn-dyed or printed designs requiring special matching.)

The problem with these axioms is that there are a large number of exceptions. These exceptions are the basis for fabric cost *premium II* and garment yield *allowance II*. As soon as two or more styles are produced in two or more fabrics, we immediately see where these axioms fail.

Let's take the example of a blouse and a dress, each cut first in a silk fabric, then in a polyester fabric.

1. Style 1 is the blouse. It takes two yards of fabric including normal wastage but excluding damage.

2. Style 2 is the dress. It takes three yards of fabric including normal wastage but excluding damage.

A. 100% silk charmeuse fabric, 44" width: $10.00 per yard including finance charges and normal shrinkage but excluding damage.

B. 100% polyester fabric, 44" width: $3.00 per yard including finance charges and normal shrinkage but excluding damage.

1A. Charmeuse blouse—$20.00 total fabric
1B. Polyester blouse—$6.00 total fabric

2A. Charmeuse dress—$30.00 total fabric
2B Polyester dress—$9.00 total fabric

So far so good. The factory's difficulty arises when we start calculating the rate of damage, which is very different between silk charmeuse and polyester. Given the quality of silk charmeuse coming from China today, 10% damage is not unreasonable; polyester damage should be under 2%.

Furthermore, this damage rate is not constant. Because dress pattern pieces are longer than blouse pattern pieces, cutting away a fabric damage may require 1.75 times more fabric for a dress than for a blouse.

Take the hypothetical example of a piece of fabric with a barre shading line every yard. In the case of the blouse, the probable yield would be 3 yards.[13] The damage rate for the blouse would therefore be 33%.

However, in the case of the dress, the damage rate would be 100%. Because a barre line exists every yard and the dress pattern pieces are longer than a yard, it would be impossible to cut even a single dress from the roll of fabric. Of course, a 50-yard piece of fabric with 50 damages would not be accepted in the first place. Nevertheless, even if the piece had only eight barres, the damage rate for the dress would still be 1.75 times higher than for the blouse.

Go back to the original estimates (silk = 10% damage, polyester = 2% damage) and now add the fact that the dress damage is 1.75 times the blouse damage or 17.5% damage. The new prices would be as follows:

1A. Charmeuse blouse—2 yards x $11.00 = $22.00
1B. Polyester blouse—2 yards x $3.06 = $6.12
2A. Charmeuse dress—3 yards x $11.75 = $35.25
2B. Polyester dress—3 yards x $3.06 = $9.18

There is no way your supplier can charge you $0.75 per yard more for the same fabric. You would not stand for it. He has only two alternatives— he can fudge the entire costing and hope you do not ask too many questions, or he can keep the price constant and increase wastage in the yardage. However, in that case he hits another problem.

2A. Charmeuse dress—3.205 yards x $11.00 = $35.25
2B. Polyester dress—3.0 yards x $3.06 = $9.18

Now unless you understand his realities, your supplier has to explain why the same dress takes only 3 yards in solid polyester but 7 inches more in solid silk charmeuse.

Your supplier's calculations are further complicated by other factors. Not only is the damage rate greater for a dress than for a blouse, but so too is the wastage rate. A leftover piece of 2.5 yards can still be cut into a blouse; for a dress, however, it is a total loss.

This type of problem is very real and occurs in every garment costing involving fabric groups and/or styles which use the same or different fabrics within the group. Despite the difficulties, learning to calculate real fabric costs is a great investment. Once you understand fabric-cost calculation, you have an accurate measure of the cost of over 60% of your garment. Fabric cost is the area in which most factories try to earn their profit. Overcharging the importer on a zipper is not going to affect the price seriously, but adding 10% to fabric cost is real money.

CMT: CUT, MAKE AND TRIM

Cost savings don't have to cause fights between you and your supplier. Real cost savings occur most often when real costs have been saved. Making an operation easier or finding a quality trim at a lower price saves you money without taking it away from your supplier. Large, successful importers go to great lengths to find ways to allow their suppliers to save money.

Case Study XXXIV—Marks & Spencer: The Lowest CMT

No one pays a lower CMT price than the British retailer Marks & Spencer. At the same time, M & S's level of quality is one of the highest in the industry, as is their markup.

Yet factories stand in line to take M & S work. To work for Marks & Spencer is more than a lifetime commitment—it is a commitment you can pass on to your grandchildren. The rules are very simple. M & S inspectors come into your plant and check it from top to bottom. What sort of quality do you produce? How old are your machines? How are they maintained? Number of workers per lavatory? How clean are the lavatories? How do you treat your workers? In short, are you the type of factory Marks & Spencer wants to associate with?

Provided you pass, they will give you a style. You make a sample and quote a price. They come back with a counteroffer so low it appears ridiculous. Then they show you how you can make that style at their price and still make a profit. Perhaps you need new techniques; they will teach you. Perhaps you need new equipment; they will advise you, and in some instances even lend you the money to buy the required machinery.

Once you are an accepted supplier, provided you keep the faith, you can go on forever. To have Marks & Spencer as a customer is to have guaranteed profit.

To find the lowest CMT is a cooperative effort. Unless you are a Levi Strauss or Marks & Spencer who have enormous staffs of skilled production people, you must rely to a great degree on your supplier's knowledge, skills and experience. As with any other craft, skilled factory people have mastered an economy of motion which is reflected in higher levels of productivity. The small 0-service factory in Bangladesh lacks these skills and experience, and relies on you the customer to bring production know-how to the factory. If you lack professional skills, both you and the factory must struggle together with each new style to reinvent the wheel.

Saving money on CMT involves close examination of the minutia of production time breakdowns and a large number of very small expenses. Anyone who thinks the fashion industry is romantic has never looked past the glitz and glamour to a trim cost sheet.

TRIM COSTS

Talk about saving pennies and inevitably you wind up looking at trim. Trim normally represents from 5%-20% of FOB cost. All raw material that is not top fabric is trim. To calculate trim there are no secret formulas or special tricks, just the trim and the price. Professionals maintain entire libraries of books showing buttons, interlinings, shoulder pads, belt buckles, and countless other items, together with current prices that are updated on a daily basis. Buying trim effectively is simply knowing what you need, what is out there, and what it costs.

For the buyer, the best advice is to stick with the major items with some breakdown of all trim costs and samples of each trim selected for the style. If trim costs appear to be out of line, you should go through a complete trim sheet. Don't be hesitant. The factory will have a trim sheet. If they are unable to produce one, use the trim sheet below and have them fill it in.

TRIM SHEET

Style #_____ | Fabric Group _____ | Date_____

Season _____ | Description _____

Item	Quality	Quantity	Price	Amount
Lining				
Interlining 1				
Interlining 2				
Thread				
Other				
Button				
Other				
Other				
Snap				
Hook & Eye				
Zipper				
Elastic				
Belt				
Shoulder Pad				
Tape				
Other				
Other				
Other				
Main Label				
Care Label				
Content Label				
Hangtag 1				
Hangtag 2				
Hanger				
Foam				
Tissue				
Polybag				
Wastage %				
Ornamentation				
TOTAL				

There is one final group of trim items that requires separate discussion—ornamentation. Embroidery, beading and appliqué are all trim but their complexity can vary substantially. Some categories such as computerized embroidery are widely available and can therefore be treated like any other trim. Others such as handsewn sequins or Schiffly embroidery (broderie anglaise) are so difficult as to form the center point of the entire production process.

Ornamentation is best recognized as a special field of expertise. There are specialist designers, specialist agents, and specialist makers. Areas in India and China are famous for their embroidery and beading; beautiful work of tremendous complexity is routinely and flawlessly mass-produced. Unfortunately, some of the most horrible mistakes can also be made in these places. Inevitably those mistakes are caused by lack of experience, as the following case study will illustrate.

Case Study XXXV —The Great Embroidery Fiasco

Cousin Phil had been around a long time. There was not much that Phil did not know about garments. At least, that's what Phil said. Phil had a customer who did all their designs and samples in the U.S. Phil's job consisted only in having the stock garments produced in Hong Kong and southern China.

The great embroidery fiasco of 1994 began simply enough. The customer sent his designer to Hong Kong to learn what the place had to offer. Phil duly took the designer to visit factories and mills and beading and embroidery and beading and embroidery, because this was the height of the great embroidery boom. Now, in truth, Phil knew very little about embroidery, although he did know embroidery had something to do with little old ladies and big needles. In any case, two weeks later the designer left with pages of notes and swatchbooks of fabrics and beading and embroidery and beading and embroidery, and a fine impression of Cousin Phil's inexhaustible wealth of knowledge.

Three months later, Phil flew to New York to see the completed collection which was opening the following day. That evening the designer brought him to the showroom for a private viewing. The entire collection, every piece, was silk crepe de Chine embroidered with Schiffly. Phil saw at once that he had a problem. Schiffly work is not made by little old ladies and big needles. Schiffly is done with big new machines and many small needles. Phil could not recall ever having seen a Schiffly machine in Hong Kong (in fact, Phil could not recall ever having seen a Schiffly machine at all). The more Phil learned, the less he liked the situation.

Turns out that no Schiffly embroidery is done anywhere in Hong Kong or China. Turns out that Schiffly work is done in such exotic places as New Jersey and North Carolina.

In the end, Phil did make the garments. He simply shipped the fabric half-way round the world to New Jersey, where it was embroidered by these large machines with the many needles. The embroidered fabric was then shipped half-way round the world back to Hong Kong where it was sewn into garments, and then the finished garments were shipped once more half-way round the world back to New York. Phil didn't charge the customer for added freight or work. As a matter of fact, to this day Phil swears that the embroidery was done in China by little old ladies with big needles.

There is a price for ignorance. For embroidery and beading, that price is very high indeed.

LABOR COSTS

No area of costing holds the interest of importers more intensely than labor. To many importers, the only factor worth considering is labor. To find a place where workers are paid less than ten cents per hour seems to be the ambition of 90% of garment importers.

People rush off to Vietnam to wait in line for the U.S. government to grant MFN status to the Hanoi government. Did you know that El Salvador, Guatemala and Honduras are really high-cost-labor areas? The new place is Nicaragua. Go to Somalia, Cambodia and Guinea Bissau. These are the places for cheap labor.

What these importers fail to understand is that grinding poverty is not a rare asset. Most of the world is poor. If all you require is workers willing to work for less than ten cents per hour, board an airplane, choose a direction, and within ten hours you will certainly arrive in a place where your dreams of cheap labor will be fulfilled.

I do not know if Sevenaya Zemyla in the Arctic Ocean, the backwaters of the Amazon River or southern Sudan are places that I would choose to set up my dress factory but, if cheap labor were my only interest, then I would have to admit they all qualify.

Don't forget that low-wage labor does not necessarily translate into low CMT, just as low CMT does not automatically mean low costs. Granted there is a difference between $1 and $10-per-hour labor and granted, labor is an important cost. But like any cost, its importance is relative to how it compares with other costs. In Italy or Germany, where labor costs exceed 60% of total FOB, saving money on labor is very important. However, in Indonesia, where labor costs are under 10% of FOB and about 6% of LDP, there are other areas of far greater importance. How to save money on labor is not just to underpay workers. Rather it is a question of understanding what each operation costs, avoiding unnecessary costly operations, and discovering where increased worker training would effectively reduce labor costs.

Learning the specific labor costs for each style and keeping accurate records for each past season's styles will ensure you ever greater advantages.

LABOR COST SHEET

PO# _____   Date _____

Style# _____   Season _____

Description _____

Sewing Cost			Labor Cost	
Item	Cost		Direct Labor	Amount
			Cutting	
			Fusing	
			Blocking	
			Sewing	
			Overlock	
Hemming				
Buttoning				
Handwork				
Thread Cut				
Underpress				
Final Press				
Checking				
Packing				
Other				
Other				
Other				
TOTAL				
Comment				

FACTORY OVERHEAD

For Third World factories, by far the largest single component of CMT is overhead. In most factories located in developing countries, overhead can run from between 125%-500% of labor. Yet few importers stop to consider factory overhead. After all, what do you know about your Indonesian supplier's electricity bill or his rent? What is more remarkable is that few makers even know how to calculate their own overheads on a per-unit basis (see Chapter 9). Not surprisingly, both customer and factory are often perplexed about the results of any particular costing. For the same order, the customer may feel he has been quoted an excessively high price. Meanwhile, the factory may accept what initially appears to be a very profitable order, only to find that after making extraordinary efforts they have still managed to lose money on the contract.

If a customer understands the factory overhead structure and how he fits into it, he can use this information to obtain a more competitive price. If the maker can accurately compute overhead on a per-unit basis, he might find it profitable to accept some orders with seemingly low CMT prices and reject others with apparently attractive CMT prices.

Everyone knows that garments which are time consuming to produce require higher overheads than garments which are easy to produce, and most people accept that larger orders are charged a lower price as they have a lower per-unit overhead than smaller orders. However, few customers recognize the real cost advantage gained by cooperating effectively with their suppliers. Tough customers are charged more because their inflexible way of working imposes higher costs on the factory. By acting in a reasonable manner, buyers are lowering the overhead costs of their orders and can therefore negotiate better prices. That is why some of the largest buyers in the world pay the highest prices and some not-so-large buyers pay very reasonable prices indeed.

Case Study XXXVI—Talbots: The Best Price

It's not surprising that Marks & Spencer and Levi Strauss buy at very good prices. These are large organizations manned by experienced garment professionals capable of engineering almost any garment into any target price point.

Talbots is a medium-sized American retailer which buys at prices much lower than importers many times their size. You will always find Talbots working in factories that produce to a quality standard a little higher than Talbots actually requires.

But strangely, Talbots doesn't have great garment engineers providing new-state-of-the-art production techniques. Nor does Talbots help its suppliers to invest in the latest equipment.

Talbots' secret is simply to act as a good customer. They do not want to cause trouble. If the factory produces one acceptable countersample, they are ready to go. They do not change their mind every five minutes. They live up to their commitments and pay their bills on time.

In return, they get good prices. Simply because the factory can make a higher profit on the lower price quoted to Talbots than they can from higher prices to some of Talbots' more difficult competitors.

AGENTS' COMMISSIONS

To some degree, commissions to agents are indirect costs. The facilities provided by agents as well as their services will generally create indirect-cost savings. Your agent may have his own pattern and sample room. He may approve lab dips and strikeoffs. He almost certainly follows up to ensure that quality and delivery occur as planned. Most importantly, the agent's primary job is to keep you informed of what is happening at the factory. To the buyer, these facilities all constitute indirect-cost facilities.

However, there are special areas where the agent is better considered as a direct-cost factor. This is when the agent's main role is to actually supervise the garmentmaking process. In effect, he acts as the factory manager's manager.

The agent acts as a connection between you and a variety of factories located in his geographical area. Some agents or trading companies may have offices throughout Asia or even worldwide. The role of the agent can vary depending on the factory. For normal or full-service factories, the agent does less work, while for 0-service factories he does more. The ideal situation for the buyer is where between the agent and the factory, almost all indirect-cost facilities are covered, with the agent picking up the responsibility in any area in which a particular factory is lacking.

In the end, almost everyone needs an agent. You are perhaps 10,000 miles from your suppliers. Someone has to be there to work with the suppliers on a day-to-day basis to ensure that your instructions are understood by the factories and that problems arising from the factories are communicated back to you quickly and accurately.

In recent years, well-established factories—particularly those with multiple branch operations—have set up to become virtual agents. The best of these suppliers have their own well-staffed merchandising and sales departments. In some instances, these suppliers can do a better job than most agents since, as factories, they have a better technical understanding than a general agent.

Some large companies have set up their own in-house agent divisions. These *buying offices* can have branches in every country where substantial sourcing takes place. Typically, a company that does more than FOB $10 million in a given territory looks to set up its own buying office. The company feels that there are real advantages in having its own dedicated staff whose sole interest is ensuring the customer's satisfaction.

However, even if you are a large importer able to afford your own buying office, you should consider certain advantages offered by retaining an outside company:

- The agent you are about to get rid of has great experience regarding your needs. A new buying office will have to learn these skills.

- Besides the merchandising and quality control departments who work with the factories negotiating price and checking your goods, the buying office will require costly additional support staff including bookkeepers, shipping clerks, messengers and other personnel. While an independent buying office will share these staff expenses among various clients, if you are running your own buying operation, you will have to bear all costs.

In recognition of these realities, many large importers have gone into partnership with their existing agents to set up separate offices within their agent's office. These hybrid offices can offer a win-win solution to both you and your agent. Merchandising and inspection teams belong to you exclusively, while support personnel continues to be provided by the agent on a monthly fee or commission basis. As you have not severed business relations, you can still rely on the complete support of your agent.

Finally, there are some very large importers who simply prefer to work with outside agents altogether. They don't want the overhead of any type of internal operation and, frankly, find it easier to negotiate with outsiders than insiders. After all, you can always fire an outside agent.

What should you pay an agent? Put plainly—more than you think, but probably less than you are paying now.

Unfortunately, many agents collect from both the buyer and the supplier. The agent might quote you 6% of the shipment's value, then turn around and charge the factory another 3% for letter-of-credit opening charge (12 times more than the real opening charges of 0.25%), plus another 2% for administration. Generally speaking, the more specialized your business, the more complex your product, or the further away from major developed areas you work, the higher the agent's costs and, therefore, the higher his commission.

To put things in perspective, if your business is importing a basic product such as coal from a developed country like Australia, then 5% is a high commission. In the fashion garment business, particularly if you are importing from Asia, 7.5%-9.5% would be average if your name is J.C. Penney or Wal-mart. The rest of us are lucky to get away with 10%-12%.

Agents charge customers hidden commissions because they believe that buyers will not pay a commission commensurate with their real costs. Regretfully, it is my experience that their assumptions are correct.

Case Study XXXVII—Wendell's War II: Overpaying Agent's Commission

The following is a true story.

Wendell Wasp pays 5% commission.

Wendell's main product is embellished sweaters produced in Shantou, China. Actually, the term embellished does not fully describe these sweaters. A basic Wendell Wasp sweater would depict the complete Battle of Gettysburg in fine-count embroidery on the front with Pickett's charge, in sequins, running up the left sleeve. More complicated styles might cover the history of France from the Battle of Tours to the death of Charles de Gaulle. This is embellishment in the grand sense of the word.

I was first approached by Wendell who felt his Hong Kong agent was cheating him and wanted me to replace the agent with someone more competitive. It seems that Wendell's business had done very well. From 1991 to 1996, Wendell's volume increased eightfold to $20 million. So successful was his operation that he had been approached by a major American knit operation who wanted to buy his company.

The prospective buyer examined Wendell's books and made an offer. It seems the price offered was far higher then Wendell had expected. Never one to take success lying down, Wendell complained, "How can you stand there and offer such a high price?"

"Very simple," answered the buyer. "You are overpaying for your product. We can buy the same article FOB $3-5 cheaper—and make more profit with your customers."

Wendell's immediate conclusion was, "I must fire my agent."

At tea at the Peninsula Hotel, I tried to make some sense of Wendell's complaint. It isn't often you meet someone in business who says, "I am making too much money and I won't stand for it."

In an effort to understand what was going on in Wendell's mind, I asked some questions: "Yours is a complicated product. Does your agent ship late? Is the quality bad?"

"No," he answered, "I have no problem with quality or delivery. My problem is that my agent is cheating me."

"In the last six years your volume has increased eightfold. Don't you think at least part of the credit should go to your agent?" I continued. "You're now doing $20 million a year. The people offering to buy your company do $400 million, 20 times your volume. Don't you think they should be able to buy at a lower price than you? In any case, what makes you think these people know what they are talking about? I've been in the field longer than them and I couldn't begin to price one of your masterpieces," were my comments.

I thought I was getting through, so I pressed on. "There is one point, however, which you should make clear. Your agent does not work on 5%. More than likely, his total commission is over 20%. You pay 5%, the maker pays 15%. This is a very dangerous situation. You might learn how to cost your product, then go back to your agent and have a very frank meeting with him. Agree to pay your agent 20%, but insist you work together to get proper costings. You have an agent who delivers a difficult product on time and in good quality. You don't want to lose him and he doesn't want to lose you."

I never met Wendell again. I hope he and his agent have developed an honest, mutually profitable relationship. However, somehow I doubt it. Some people just can't allow the next man to make a living.

Transfer Pricing—Duty—Taxes

Agents' commissions are duty-free. Furthermore, since they are part of importers' costs, they are deductible expenses. Most importers work with overseas agents. For these importers, their agents' commissions will continue to be duty-free and deductible as long as the relationship with the agent remains at 'arms-length'.

But, as already pointed out, many larger importers also own their own overseas buying offices. Recently, the U. S. Internal Revenue Service has started to get tough, targeting some of the largest companies. The IRS is questioning whether commissions paid to these buying offices are in fact excessive, and in some cases they have successfully won the right to levy additional tax assessments.

The problem is actually not as simple as the IRS contends. First of all, not all commissions are included in the 'commission'. For example, in a recent case, the IRS brought suit against a major American retailer claiming that the commissions paid to their wholly-owned overseas buying office was 0.5% higher than that paid to an outside agent located in the same city for similar products. But the IRS failed to take into consideration the 3% commission the outside agent charges their suppliers for 'letter-of-credit expenses'. In fact, the outside agent's commission rates were actually higher than those charged by the in-house buying office.

Furthermore, what constitutes a *fair* commission and when does a commission rate become *excessive* are questions open to a large array of answers. Third Horizon Ltd. (THL) has been actively involved in a number of these so-called transfer pricing disputes. In 1993, THL carried out an extensive analysis of garment agents based in Hong Kong.[14] Over 2500 agents, buying offices and trading companies were interviewed. The resulting report lists the commissions charged by well over 1000 companies and clearly demonstrated that commission rates are far from uniform and depend on a variety of factors.

Case Study XXXVIII—Transfer Pricing: A Fair Commission

You are an agent. You have to determine what you should charge your customers. Naturally, being honest, you want to be fair. Your very first customer is Herbie the Mouth. "I am going to make you a millionaire in one season," he promises. "No, don't thank me. You will have to work hard and of course charge me a very reasonable commission rate. You will become my agent for *Donner Party— Outdoor Fun for Everyone*. We sell everything the outdoor person needs."

"You mean products like Goretex outerwear, hiking boots and thermal underwear?"

"All that," Herbie replies, "and much more. Don't forget the glacier picks, yak saddles and yurts."

"Yurts?"

"Absolutely, yurts! You know classic Mongolian felt tents. One of our biggest items. We make them in a top factory in Huhehot, real yurt specialists."

Your hesitations notwithstanding, you and Herbie agree on a 'fair' commission rate. You narrow down the product list to the most important 800 items. You hire the staff, produce the samples and at the end of the first season, you are broke and Herbie is on to his next agent.

What went wrong?

In fact everything. A fair commission is one which allows you to cover the overhead required to service your customers properly, compensates you for your risks and earns you a reasonable return. To arrive at a fair commission you must consider:

1. Complexity of product: A customer whose total business consists of T-shirt blanks is entitled to pay a lower commission than his friend in the overcoat business, simply because blanks require less work than overcoats. Likewise, the customer who buys a single

product pays less than the customer who buys a broad range, simply because you are required to deal with fewer factories and need less staff. Herbie is the worst case scenario—a customer dealing in a large number of unrelated products, each requiring specialized factories and specialized staff on your part.

2.   Supplier quality: A customer buying from full-service factories located in a single industrialized country is entitled to pay less commission than a customer buying from a variety of Third World 0-service factories. Herbie is once again the worst case scenario—a customer who insists on dealing with Louie the Lip in Inner Mongolia.

3.   Customer size: A large customer who places large orders per item is entitled to pay a lower commission than small customers. But large customers who order many different product types can actually do smaller volumes than so-called smaller customers. Herbie is the worst kind of customer—an order for yak saddles will certainly not exceed 50 pieces.

4.   Customer reliability: This final factor is the most important. The customer who causes fewer problems costs less than the customer who causes more problems and is entitled to pay a lower commission. Herbie the Mouth—as befits a man in a class by himself—has to pay the Herbie-the-Mouth premium (as do several real-life major mass-market importers).

What is a fair commission? An agent following up T-shirts produced in Japan is entitled to 5%. The same agent working for Herbie the Mouth's Donner Party must earn 200%—and even at that rate he will not survive long.

Problems of transfer pricing as they relate to the garment industry are particularly complex. For starters, if your agent assists in design work, fabric selection, fabric or trim sourcing, patternmaking or garment inspection, there is a strong possibility that your agent may not be an agent at all—your agent may be a manufacturer. As a manufacturer, the question of fair commissions becomes moot, since manufacturers are legally entitled to charge whatever they can.

Finally, given the increasing scrutiny focused on the commission practices of wholly-owned buying offices, if you as an importer already own your buying office or are planning to set one up, your best move is to run, not walk, to your tax attorney or CPA. Do not seek Cousin Phil's advice or try to work out a solution on your own. You need an experienced professional.

PART II

Part I dealt with Full Value Cost Analysis as a tool to analyze total product costs and, specifically, manufacturing costs. But FVCA is more than an analytical tool. With FVCA, you can learn to buy at the lowest cost, your contractor can also produce at the lowest cost, and his government can develop an industry which can compete on an international basis.

Today's international garment business simply has too many players, too many importers, retailers, suppliers and countries rushing to develop their individual export apparel industries. All garment prices—CMT, FOB, LDP, wholesale and retail—have been declining annually for the past decade. A major shakeout is inevitable. Anyone who cannot offer the greatest value—the best garment at the lowest cost—will be driven out of business.

Whether we like it or not, our industry is at war. Every person in the industry has become a soldier in the Great Garment War. The only relevant question to importers, retailers, suppliers and governments is: When the dust has settled, will I be a winner or will I be dead?

FVCA is a blueprint for survival.

...old-style international garment buying...

Chapter 7
Buying at the Lowest Cost: The Product

Economists say that markets operate with complete knowledge and that business people always try to work in their own best interests. Obviously, they have never talked to anyone in the garment industry.

Holden Schmata
Lectures to MBA graduates

You have now completed 133 pages on the workings of Full Value Cost Analysis. Since this is not an academic treatise, the question you must now be asking is: "What's in it for me?"

The short answer is now that you realize that cheap labor does not automatically bring low CMT, low CMT does not lead to low FOB, and low FOB does not result in low product cost, FVCA may keep you off the streets of Ho Chi Minh City, chasing after the latest cheap-labor-producing country.

But more importantly, FVCA teaches you how to buy at the lowest cost. This section will deal with how you should be looking at your product.

BUYING VS. SOURCING

The international garment industry was built by some remarkable characters like Herbie the Mouth, Wendell Wasp and Cousin Phil, who 40 years ago traveled to Japan, South Korea, Taiwan and Hong Kong, to what was then the ends of the earth, with a sample shirt and a sample pants looking to buy.

In each major city, they would take up residence in what was then the only decent hotel for 500 miles in any direction and day after day be visited by an unending line of mill and factory owners. To each they would show the sample pants and sample shirt, and ask two simple questions: "Can you make this?" and "How much?"

After meeting with and yelling at some 200 makers in all four countries, they would select the one they could trust most—the one who offered to make at the lowest price.

Many of these pioneers were truly great merchants with a unique and intuitive grasp of their product and how best to work in Asia. They left their mark wherever they went. If you doubt me, talk to any elderly Taiwanese or Korean textile industrialist. More likely than not, his English and gestures will be faintly Brooklyn-twinged, an indelible reminder of the customers with whom he started his business.

Yet as exceptional as these original importers were, in the end they remained nothing more than buyers. In today's professional environment, they wouldn't have survived. Today's professionals do not buy—they source. No longer is a shirt or a pair of pants an item. They are now products of materials and processes. Gone are the days where an order was placed with a single supplier or even a single country.

In what is probably the most competitive industry in the world, where survival depends on a continuous search for lower cost and higher quality, the international garment industry has gone global, probably more comprehensively than any other industry to date. Ironically, most academics consider the garment industry as backward. Yet the automobile industry, generally viewed as highly efficient and globally-orientated, requires 40 months to design a new product. A production chain longer than two links is a rarity. Efficiency at that level would bankrupt any Broadway importer in a single season.

In order to build a reliable chain of suppliers, professional sourcing specialists all ask the same three questions:

- What is my product?

- What facilities do I bring to the chain?

- What facilities must I count on the suppliers to provide?

All sourcing begins with your product. Look at it not as a buyer but as a sourcing specialist. Your product is composed of a variety of materials and processes. Look at the flow chart again. There are 91 steps in the manufacturing process. Before the advent of sourcing, when people only 'bought' product, manufacturing was related solely to making stock. They started at Step 87. Successful buyers now start as close to Step 1 as possible.

Find Your Center

The first step to knowing your product is to understand what is special about your particular item. This is the center and every product has one. For men's overcoats, the center is found in the garmentmaking process; for handembroidered sweaters, it is the embellishment. The center may also be outside the garmentmaking process altogether, as in the case of silk blouses where the fiber is the core of the product. As a rule, you always want to source near your center. This is why people sourcing men's overcoats do not consider El Salvador, why silk blouse importers don't rate Brazil highly, and why Duesseldorf is not known for its production of handembroidered sweaters.

As Cousin Phil learned in the great embroidery fiasco, if your center is Schiffly embroidery, your first step is to find a giant machine with 1024 needles. Unfortunately, most professionals still source the way Cousin Phil bought—looking only at direct costs.

Direct Costs

Direct costs are certainly important. But if you source your product strictly on the basis of lowest material and CMT costs, you will wind up producing in some very strange places and paying a very high price.

Take this simple example.

Case Study XXXIX—Yarn-Dyed Cotton Blouses: Direct Costs

You are buying 40-count combed cotton yarn-dyed blouses.

Where is your center?

The center is not the blouse. Finding a blouse factory is about as easy as finding a T-shirt maker.

The center is not the yarn. 40-count combed yarns are not that common but most countries with reasonably well-developed industries produce 40-counts. In fact, the center is the fabric, but more than the fabric itself, something special about your needs. Look at the flow chart. Look at Steps 54-65 concerning *Salesman Samples*. This is the center of your yarn-dyed blouse.

If you cannot get salesman samples in your pattern and colorways, you either have to place stock fabric orders before seeing a garment—a time-tested method of committing suicide—or discard the entire group. The problem is that mills simply do not like producing 100 yards of a colorway. It's not a question of looms. The mill has plenty of looms. It is the other machinery required, some of which may not even be in the mill. To produce your 100 yards, the mill has to go through the entire production process, including yarn-dyeing, warping and sizing. This is a real bother, especially since you need at least three patterns, two colorways each. To produce your yarn-dyed cotton blouses, more than anything else, you need a very friendly mill.

Assume you have two choices—Shanghai or a combination of the U. S. and Mexico.

Shanghai has mills producing good-quality, high-count, yarn-dyed combed cotton. Provided you are a valued customer, the mill will produce 50-100 yards of each colorway for salesman sample fabric. Furthermore, minimum stock fabric orders are only 3,000 yards per pattern. Shanghai Garment Corporation will arrange for a good maker to produce your blouses and put the entire sourcing chain together for FOB $5.75 per blouse, excluding quota.

In the United States, 40-count combed yarn is a niche market, but you can buy the fabric for $2.75 per yard, 60" wide. CMT in Mexico runs about $4.00 per piece.

The direct costs for the same garment made in China and U.S./Mexico work out as follows:

COUNTRY	FABRIC COST	CMT	FOB
China	N/A	N/A	$5.75
U.S./Mexico	$4.13	$4.00	$8.13

The U.S./Mexico blouse costs FOB $2.38 or 41% more than the same blouse produced in China. Based on direct costs, you have no choice—China is the place for your fine cotton blouses.

This is how it works with the traditional costing process. Using FVCA, the results prove very different. One look at the macro costs and the whole picture changes.

Macro Costs

A blouse is a relatively easy garment to produce. Generally, you would have no reason to buy fabric in one place and ship it to another simply in order to find a suitable blousemaker. Likewise, you can rule out working in most of the truly high macro-cost countries. You are not going to find the modern yarn-dyed mill you require in Sudan or North Korea, and, as already discussed, finding suitable makers in these places is also no easy feat.

Furthermore, you can work only in a limited number of countries. First of all, you must go to these places at least once a season as does your designer and your merchandiser. Travel expenses aside, if you work in ten countries, you may find you and your team spending more time in planes than on the ground. At the same time, if you spread yourself too thin, you become important to no one. Unless you are Wal-mart or Jones New York, you must limit the number of countries you work in.

So how do you decide where to work?As the following two case studies illustrate, frequently it is macro costs which affect your ability to buy at lowest cost and your decision over where to place your orders.

Case Study XL—Yarn-Dyed Cotton Blouses: Macro Costs

The macro costs discussed here are duty, quota and overseas freight.

The duty on ladies' woven blouses (6202.30.30) is 16.4%.

The China quota cost for U.S. category 341 is $1.50 per piece.

Calculated on a volume basis, freight costs for woven shirts and blouses are very costly. For seafreight, 40 cubic feet equals one ton. For airfreight, 198 cubic inches equals one pound. Woven shirts and blouses are shipped folded, 8 to 12 pieces to an inner box, with perhaps 6 to 12 boxes to an outer carton. Furthermore, they are often shipped with collars in an upright position. All of this adds considerable volume and, therefore, considerable freight cost.

Mexico is a part of NAFTA. Cotton blouses, provided they are produced from NAFTA yarn and fabric, can be exported to the United States both duty-free and quota-free. Adding these macro cost advantages now makes a considerable difference to your bottom line.

COUNTRY	FOB	QUOTA	DUTY	FREIGHT	CLEARANCE	LDP
China	$5.75	$1.50	$0.94	$0.40	$0.15	$8.74
U.S./Mexico	$8.13	0	0	$0.15	$0.15	$8.43

The cost difference is not great—$8.74 compared to $8.43 or less than 4% more for the Chinese blouse. If you are already working in China, certainly it is not worth relocating to Mexico just to save 4% off the LDP price. Low macro costs in Mexico and the United States (no duty and no quota) are still more or less matched by lower direct costs in China (less expensive fabric and labor).

But there is one further macro-cost advantage in the U.S./Mexico combination—freight delivery time. The Chinese require 90 days for the fabric and garment manufacturing. Shipment time from China by sea is about 35 days. As a result, from the purchase of fabric to stock arrival in the United States, a little over four months is required.

The U.S./Mexico combination can possibly be done in as little as 45 days as American mills usually produce their own fabric collections and often have stock fabric available in stock patterns. In China, all fabric must be indent or specially ordered.

However, this is not the end of the story. Do not assume that just because high-count cotton blouses work out this way that the story will be the same for similar items. Macro costs are not specifically related to the manufacturing process—even though the product itself remains almost completely unchanged, costs can rise or fall substantially.

Take the same item, make a small change, and see the dramatic results.

Case Study XLI—Yarn-Dyed Cotton Shirts: Macro Costs

This is the identical style as described in the two previous case studies—except now the buttons have been shifted from the left to the right. The blouse has become a shirt. Assume that we are talking about boys' sizes with, therefore, identical fabric consumption as the blouses.

In fact, all that has changed are the U.S. Customs classification numbers. Whereas previously U.S. Customs classified the blouse as 6106.10.00 and quota Cat. 341, the shirt has now become 6105.10.00 and quota Cat. 340Z. These minor changes, however, bring great changes to the costs. Duty rate which was 16.4% is now 21%, and the quota cost has increased from $1.50 to $2.50 per piece.

COUNTRY	FOB	QUOTA	DUTY	FREIGHT	CLEARANCE	LDP
China	$5.75	$2.50	$1.21	$0.40	$0.15	$10.01
U.S./Mexico	$8.13	0	0	$0.15	$0.15	$8.43

Where the LDP cost disadvantage of the Chinese blouse was previously $0.31, or 4%, it has now risen to $1.58 or nearly 19%, simply because the buttons and buttonholes were shifted.

The permutations of these cost variations are endless. Not only can changes in gender result in enormous macro-cost differences, so too can changes from woven to knit or from one fiber to another. This final macro-cost case study illustrates what happens to the same product when changed from cotton to synthetic fabric.

Case Study XLII—Yarn-Dyed Synthetic Blouses: Macro Costs

Take the same yarn-dyed blouse, only instead of being made of cotton, it is now in polyester.

Assume that the direct costs remain unchanged from Case Study XXXIX. (The United States does, in fact, enjoy a real advantage over China in synthetic fabrics—although prices are comparable, the selection in the U.S. is much wider.) The most important variable is again U.S. Customs classifications. Where previously U.S. Customs described the blouse as 6106.10.00 and quota Cat. 341, it has now become 6206.40.30 and quota Cat. 641. Duty has likewise changed from 16.4% to 28.6%, and the quota premium from $1.50 to $2.50. While nothing changes in the price for the U.S./Mexico blouse, the LDP cost for the Chinese one continues to rise.

COUNTRY	FOB	QUOTA	DUTY	FREIGHT	CLEARANCE	LDP
China	$5.75	$2.50	$1.65	$0.40	$0.15	$10.45
U.S./Mexico	$8.13	0	0	$0.15	$0.15	$8.43

Where the LDP cost disadvantage of the Chinese cotton blouse was $0.31, or 4%, by changing the fabric to synthetic the difference now rises to $2.02, or nearly 24%.

Macro costs are the single greatest factor affecting total manufacturing costs. Even though American materials are more expensive than Chinese and a Mexican worker's wages are double those of his Chinese counterpart, these direct-cost savings mean little in the face of the macro-cost advantages resulting from NAFTA. Given the examples above, in order to compete on price with U.S./Mexico production, the Chinese FOB would have to be reduced as follows:

Cotton blouse:	-6%
Cotton shirt:	-27%
Synthetic blouse:	-34%

Based on these calculations, even if the FOB cost of the Chinese synthetic blouse were only half that for the Mexican blouse, it would still be too expensive.

Indirect Costs

At this point, knowledgeable professionals may ask: Why pick only China and U.S./Mexico as alternatives? Chinese fabric could have been moved to Sri Lanka where there are good factories, reasonable CMT costs and cheaper quota. Many large groups, for example, The Limited through their Mast Lanka operation, have done quite well there. Another possibility would be Indonesia. Indonesia has some excellent textile mills quite capable of producing 40-count yarn. Indonesia has garment factories, low CMT, as well as abundant and cheap quota.

The answer is high indirect costs. To operate effectively in either Indonesia or Sri Lanka, you need a large presence in the country. Good local agents are hard to find. Companies that do well usually set up their own exclusive local buying offices. Another alternative is to use Korean or Taiwanese agents who work in these countries and who charge high commissions. There are also smaller agents who charge less, but their follow-up is often unreliable.

Furthermore, unless you deal with the very few totally reliable companies, such as Great River in Indonesia or Mast Lanka in Sri Lanka, you will have to buy the fabric yourself. Unfortunately, Great River and Mast Lanka will only work with the largest or most importantcustomers. Owning fabric and working on a CMT basis in either of these countries is about as the same as swallowing a bottle of sulfuric acid. The only result is pain.

These and other indirect-cost considerations must now be addressed. As in most examples drawn from the real world, and unlike macro costs, the indirect-cost advantages between China and Mexico are not clear-cut.

The U.S./Mexico combination has the great advantage of fast turn. Not only is final freight faster from Mexico to the United States than China to the United States, but because of the way the U.S. mills operate, they can offer immediate salesman sample fabric and, in many cases, stock fabric as well. This represents a tremendous timesaving of about 60 days. Although Chinese garment factories will cut and sew much faster than factories in Mexico, this cannot compensate for the much slower fabric delivery time. If fast turn is the priority, the U.S./Mexico option is the obvious choice.

On the other hand, U.S./Mexico can incur other very high indirect costs that, like macro costs, can vary greatly each time the style changes. For example, the 40-count combed cotton yarn-dyed blouse in Case Study

XXXIX may have lower macro costs when produced in U.S./Mexico, but these can be far outweighed by even higher indirect costs. Look at the following illustration.

Case Study XLIII—Yarn-Dyed Cotton Blouses: Indirect Costs

U.S./Mexico suffers from high indirect costs for both fabric and garments.

Lack of facilities on the part of American fabric suppliers often raises their indirect costs. Although high-count yarn-dyed cotton fabric is available in the U.S., it remains very much a niche item. Most mills have little interest in the fabric. As a result, finding a mill running the fabric is a problem in itself. Furthermore, since American mills generally produce their own collections, the choice of existing patterns is limited. What's worse, few mills will produce the customer's patterns and colorways, and those who do will require large minimums. Either you must chose from the limited selection offered by the mill, in which case you receive immediate shipment, or demand your own designs and receive no shipment at all.

The Mexican garmentmakers also lack facilities, which raises their indirect costs. The quality of Mexican garment production is not high; fine cotton yarn-dyed blouses are not easy to produce. The designs are usually stripes or plaids which require matching. If the factory is to ship an acceptable product, it must have competent cutters as well as a well-trained sewing department. Because it is high-count fabric, finishing also presents special problems. Poor pressing will result in permanent shine. Since this is an upmarket product, Mexican levels of quality might not be acceptable. You as the customer will have to play a far greater role with the Mexican factory than with the Chinese.

In the end, for the fine-count yarn-dyed cotton ladies' blouse produced in U.S./Mexico, direct-cost disadvantages are offset by macro-cost advantages, which in turn may be outweighed by even greater indirect costs. You the buyer must decide whether the indirect-cost advantages of fast turn offered by the U.S./Mexican combination are so important as to offset the higher indirect costs of reduced fabric design choice, lower quality standards, and the need for closer follow-up on your part.

High-count yarn-dyed blouses present special indirect-cost problems. See how the situation changes if the same blouse were changed to low-count yarn-dyed fabric.

Case Study XLIV—Low-Count Yarn-Dyed Cotton Blouses: Indirect Costs

Lightweight denim or chambray blouses are available from the same Shanghai Garment Corporation for $4.75 FOB excluding quota.

In the United States, chambray costs about $1.25 per yard, 60" wide. CMT in Mexico runs about $3.50 per blouse.

The relative costs are as follows:

Country	Fabric	CMT	FOB	Quota	Duty	Freight	Clearance	LDP
China	N/A	N/A	$4.50	$1.50	$0.74	$0.40	$0.15	$7.29
U.S./Mexico	$1.88	$3.50	$5.33	0	0	$0.15	$0.15	$5.63

This time while the direct FOB costs still favor the Chinese by $0.83, the macro-cost advantages of U.S./Mexico, $2.49 per blouse, far outweigh any Chinese advantage. The U.S./Mexico option lands the garment with a savings of $1.66 or nearly 30%.

But the real reason why the U.S./Mexico option wins hands down has to do with indirect costs. Low-count yarn-dyed fabric indirect costs are lower in the United States than in China. Unlike high-count yarn-dyed fabric, which is difficult to locate at U.S. mills, 16-count and lower yarn-dyed fabrics are readily available from many sources. You can take your choice from a large number of patterns, many of which are available for immediate delivery.

Furthermore, both U.S. and Asian mills have opened plants in Mexico in recent years to produce chambray and other low-count cotton fabrics, increasing Mexican fabric sourcing possibilities and thereby reducing lead times and freight costs still further. Finally, Mexican garmentmakers will also have lower indirect costs for this order. Sewing and finishing a low-count chambray blouse is much easier than working high-count yarn-dye fabric.

Each small change in product brings major changes in costs. While the effects of macro and indirect costs on basic garments are already substantial, these effects are even more marked as quality standards rise and the items become more difficult to make. Case Studies XXXIX to XLIV all featured basic cotton or synthetic shirts and blouses for J.C. Penney and other moderate-priced stores. At the other end of the spectrum is an Emanuel Ungaro wool blazer.

Case Study XLV—Emanuel Ungaro Wool Blazer: Direct Costs

You are the director of manufacturing at Emanuel Ungaro (USA). You require wool tweed jackets. Jacket production has special needs. Your first consideration is finding a factory capable of making the jackets. Also, there are not many countries with mills capable of producing your fabric. You are willing to ship the fabric from the mill to the factory but since it weighs 14 ounces per yard, you would prefer not to have to ship halfway around the world.

For the quality you require,Bangladesh,India,Indonesia,Pakistan and Sri Lanka are all non-starters. For that matter so is Mexico, at least for the time being. You have four possibilities, each located in a different country. They are as follows:

1. China (in a Hong Kong-owned factory): This looks good. The labor rate here is $0.50 per hour. Productivity is about 75% of Hong Kong, the United States or France, who all work at roughly the same output levels.

2. Hong Kong: The quality is excellent and the factory is reliable. The Hong Kong worker is paid over $4.00 per hour, eight times his China counterpart.

3. France: The fabric is available in France. Why bother airfreighting fabric when Emanuel Ungaro can produce their jackets in a factory in Normandy which makes for top European designers? For the purposes of this case study, we will assume the French worker is paid the same as the U.S. worker below, about $12.50 per hour or 25 times the Chinese sewer.

4. United States: Why go anywhere? The fabric is available in the United States. A legitimate sewer in the U.S., not a slave in a Los Angeles sweatshop, is paid the same as the worker in France.

Logically, the immediate first choice is China, followed by Hong Kong, with France and the United States bringing up the rear. After all, isn't cheap labor the primary reason for importing? Let's look closer.

First consider direct costs calculated traditionally. The fabric is available both in the United States and France. The cost is the same in both countries—$14.00 per yard. The yield is 1.6 yards. In the case of Hong Kong and China, the fabric would have to be brought in by airfreight.

FABRIC COST	CHINA	HONG KONG	FRANCE	U.S.
Fabric FOB	$22.40	$22.40	$22.40	$22.40
Fabric Freight	$ 1.25	$ 1.25	0	0
Total Fabric Cost	$23.65	$23.65	$22.40	$22.40

Now comes the CMT. Let us assume that the jacket takes about 1.25 hours to make, with China requiring 25% more, or about 1.67 hours. In China, trim costs slightly more than elsewhere simply because much of it must be imported. Fortunately, China allows free import of materials for export processing. Finally, note that overhead and profit is generally calculated as a percentage of labor. Using industry averages, China overhead would be about 250% of labor; in Hong Kong 100%; and in France and the United States 33%.

CMT	CHINA	HONG KONG	FRANCE	U.S.
Trim	$ 5.00	$ 4.50	$ 4.50	$ 4.50
Labor	$ 0.83	$ 5.00	$15.63	$15.63
Overhead	$ 2.08	$ 5.00	$ 5.20	$ 5.20
CMT Total	$ 7.91	$14.50	$25.33	$25.33
FOB ex. Comm.	$31.56	$38.15	$47.73	$47.73
Commission	$ 6.31	$ 4.77	$ 2.39	0

The CMT totals are more or less as expected. Even allowing for the higher trim cost, China CMT is just under a third of CMT in the U.S. and France; Hong Kong's CMT is just over half that of the U.S. and France.

Finally, there is agent's commission. Agent's commission for China is 20% of FOB;for Hong Kong, 12.5%. I have also added a 5% commission for France. In the United States you do not need an agent.

The direct costs are also as expected. Herbie the Mouth, Cousin Phil and all the old-time buyers would agree. China with its cheaper labor is still the lowest, followed by Hong Kong where costs are 13% higher, then the United States and France—both high-labor-cost countries—where direct costs are higher by 26% and 32% respectively.

DIRECT COSTS	CHINA	HONG KONG	FRANCE	U.S.
FOB Total	$37.87	$42.92	$50.12	$47.73
COST INDEX	100	113	132	126

So much for the traditional costing methods that we all have been using for the past 50 years. Now, try FVCA. First, include the macro costs and watch the picture change.

Case Study XLVI—Emanuel Ungaro Wool Blazer: Macro Costs

Given the four countries selected, you have little worries regarding logistics, communication, education, political instability or corruption. China should show higher macro costs than France and the U.S. particularly with regard to communication and education, but since all of the work and follow-up will be performed by Hong Kong people, this need not be a significant factor. As with the previous shirt and blouse case studies, the important macro costs discussed here are duty, freight and quota. (Assume each jacket weighs about 1.5 pounds or 681 grams.)

MACRO COSTS	CHINA	HONG KONG	FRANCE	U.S.
QUOTA	$ 8.00	$ 5.00	0	0
FREIGHT	$ 5.00	$ 5.00	$ 0.75	0
DUTY (20% of FOB + $0.683/kg)	$ 8.04	$ 9.05	$10.49	0
CLEARANCE	$ 0.75	$ 0.75	$ 0.75	0
SUBTOTAL	$21.79	$19.80	$11.99	0
FOB COST	$37.87	$42.92	$50.12	$47.73
LDP COST	$59.66	$62.72	$62.11	$47.73
LDP INDEX	100	105	104	80

Suddenly, the picture changes dramatically. With the addition of macro costs, China no longer looks so cheap. In fact, LDP for the U.S. is now 20% lower than in China, France has fallen from 32% to only 4% higher while Hong Kong is only 5% higher.

Furthermore, you have so far ignored the intangible but very real macro costs of reputation. Let's face it—a made-in-China label does not have the same cachet as either a made-in-America or a made-in-France label. A wool jacket labeled made-in-France must be worth at least $50.00 more at wholesale to Emanuel Ungaro than the identical garment marked made-in-China. Saving $3.06 on cost is no saving when, as a result, you lose $50.00 off your selling price.

If all that mattered were direct and macro costs, Emanuel Ungaro would produce his jackets in the United States. However, ultimately he produces in Hong Kong and France. You can understand making in France for the valuable made-in-France label, but why shlep all the way to Hong Kong to pay $62.72 on an item that could be made in the U.S. for only $47.73?

One reason is potential macro-cost savings. If Emanuel Ungaro (USA) wanted to use real Scottish tweed or Italian cashmere, it would find the import duty on fabric (35%+) to be very high indeed. But, in fact, the main reason why Emanuel Ungaro works in Hong Kong and Europe is because American makers have unreasonably high indirect costs.

Case Study XLVII—Emanuel Ungaro Wool Blazer: Indirect Costs

You are still Emanuel Ungaro's director of manufacturing and you are still faced with the same choices about the same wool tweed jackets. The choice is between the Hong Kong maker and the American maker.

- The Hong Kong maker will pay for your fabric; the U.S. one requires you to pay.

- The Hong Kong maker will supply all the trim; the U.S. one expects you to order the trim, pay for the trim, and deliver it to his factory.

- The Hong Kong maker will work on an FOB basis; the U.S. one can work at best CMT and in some cases only CM.

- The Hong Kong maker has a complete pattern department with trained patternmakers, as well as computerized grading and marking facilities. He will check your patterns, make any required corrections based on your approval, and—if you want—grade the patterns and make the markers. The U.S. maker can only produce your goods if you supply the marker.

- The Hong Kong maker has trained sewers and modern machinery capable of producing any type of jacket you require. He also has access to special facilities such as quilting and embroidery. The U.S. maker has problems finding skilled workers and special facilities are your problem.

- The Hong Kong maker is sufficiently capitalized so that if a problem does occur and you put in a claim, he can pay; the U.S. maker has a net worth of about $1.65.

If you were Emanuel Ungaro's director of manufacturing, you too would be working with the maker with low indirect costs—the one located in Hong Kong, not the U.S.

In many senses, an American contractor resembles his counterpart in Indonesia more closely than his counterpart in Hong Kong or Europe. Few American contractors will work on an FOB basis. They cannot order or buy trim and few have pattern or sample facilities. Machinery tends to be outdated. The factories are often dirty with poor lighting or amenities. And these are the more reliable factories.

Below this level are U.S. sweatshops. They resemble factories in Bangladesh, India and Pakistan. There are some advantages to sweatshops in New York and Los Angeles over Lahore and Dhaka. For one, it only takes you a few hours by car to visit your American contractor, not 18 hours by plane. The American contractor probably speaks English a little better than the factory manager in Bangladesh. But other than that, the situation is identical—you would have to supply the same support facilities in Los Angeles as you would in Bangladesh in order to get your order produced.

There are also some major disadvantages. U.S. factories are inflexible. Like Louie the Lip, they make what they make, not what you want. At least the guy in Bangladesh is trying to do better.

It would be wrong to suggest that the entire American industry is backward. There are some important exceptions, particularly in mass-market, basic merchandise. There are some exceptional American T-shirt operations using the most up-to-date machinery and the latest techniques. There are also some excellent factories producing casual wovens, particularly denims, that can compete with any factory in the world. They produce to high levels of quality, have mastered fast turnaround times and benefit from being located in the market where the goods are being sold. Regretfully, these are the exceptions.

For most companies that design, merchandise and sell garments, U.S. domestic production is something to get away from as soon as the company reaches the level where it can produce somewhere else. In the end, Emanuel Ungaro works overseas because few U.S. factories can provide the necessary indirect-cost facilities he needs. Most U.S. factories are 0-service, and Emanuel Ungaro cannot afford to work with 0-service factories.

Chapter 8
Buying at the Lowest Cost: You the Buyer

If after you have done everything possible in your business the maker still produces the wrong garments, then either you are in the wrong business or you have the wrong maker.

Holden Schmata
Lectures to MBA graduates

I have a question: "If there is such a great advantage in reducing macro costs and indirect costs, why does everybody still run to the cheap-labor countries where the macro costs and indirect costs are the highest in the world?"

The answer goes back half a century, to the time Herbie the Mouth and Cousin Phil first went into imports. When they began work, their makers knew nothing at all. If you look at some of the early duplicates these factories produced—turtleneck T-shirts with three sleeves and no turtleneck—you would not believe that anyone could imagine such a garment, let alone actually make one. These early importers all followed one simple rule: *Not only will anything that can go wrong, go wrong, even some things that positively cannot go wrong, will also go wrong.* By following this law, they survived and some even prospered.

These pioneers built failsafe systems that would have brought joy to the heart of Dr. Strangelove. With the exception of the women who actually sat at the sewing machines, they provided everything—patterns, markers, every last bit of trim. They wouldn't trust the maker—and rightly so—to safely supply a single grommet. They put together expensive but experienced staff in the United States who, together with their local agents, checked and double-checked everything. As a result, they could ship a reasonable product even from the depths of hell itself.

The costs were high, but more than offset by cheap labor and, most importantly, there was no other alternative. In 1947, not too many factories in Europe or Asia were still standing and entire industries needed to be rebuilt from ground zero.

In the ensuing five decades, those factories have changed tremendously. Once a factory in Taiwan, Hong Kong or South Korea resembled a scene from *The Lower Depths*, the maker a singlet-clad recent refugee from China who met his customers with a cigarette dangling from his mouth. Today, many of those same factories are air-conditioned and spotless, with the maker more often than not holding a Harvard MBA. These operations have the facilities to produce what the customer requires with the minimum of support.

But while the structures at the factories they are working with have changed, importers remain structured just as they were 50 years ago, operating under the same failsafe systems. Today's importers are equipped to survive in the most primitive conditions; it is in a developed factory that they cannot operate. They still employ gangs of patternmakers and samplemakers located in the United States and armies of inspectors on the ground near the maker. They have created state-of-the-art sourcing systems, yet remain unable to take advantage of the indirect-costs saving that goes with effective sourcing.

INDIRECT COSTS

To survive in today's industry, established importers must reinvent their businesses. They must begin by asking: "What facilities do I bring to the chain and what must I count on the suppliers to provide?"

If you are willing to provide nothing and expect everything to come from the supplier, you will not last long in this industry. If, instead, you answer, "I bring everything while the supplier provides nothing," you are also in real trouble. Your indirect costs are almost certainly prohibitive and, what's worse is, your own people are probably leading you by the nose to countries with some of the highest macro costs in the world.

Go back to the flow chart. Reexamine each step. To manufacture the garment, someone has to carry out each of the 101 steps. That someone has to be either you or the supplier (or your agent). The greater the number of steps you perform, the fewer need be performed by the supplier and the lower down you can go on the factory service scale.

At one extreme, you may be able to provide little more than your sketch, your time and your letter of credit. For this, you will need a full-service factory capable of sourcing fabric and all trim, making your patterns and samples, ensuring that all materials arrive on time and in the right color, quantity, and quality, and finally, capable of producing to your quality standard and level. The full-service factory charges a premium for its facilities. This may still cost less than adding the overhead required to do everything yourself.

If you are able to provide greater facilities, you can work with a normal-service factory whose facilities will complement yours. At the other end of the spectrum, you may be in a position to provide all facilities yourself. All the factory gives you is their preproduction duplicate to ensure that they can actually produce the garment. If you have all the facilities, you can work with a 0-service factory and pay accordingly.

However, don't forget that the demands which the facilities must meet deepen as the buyer moves upscale to higher quality and style. Giorgio Armani requires much greater facilities than Kmart. As a result, even though Giorgio Armani may provide the supplier with more assists than Kmart, he will still require a full-service factory. There are simply that many more steps and that many more facilities required to produce for Giorgio Armani.

This is the real reason that Giorgio Armani will always pay more for his garment than Kmart. For example, both companies sell jeans. Although the actual construction of the jeans is similar, Armani will always pay more for theirs than Kmart because they require more from the factory. The factory must learn just what Armani wants and what facilities they need to meet those special requirements. This learning process takes time. Armani must maintain a cooperative relationship with its suppliers. Armani may want to buy at the lowest cost, but to maintain good working relationships, they must ensure that the supplier actually shows a profit. A bankrupt supplier cannot maintain a relationship.

To take advantage of indirect-cost savings, you must be willing to reexamine your own operation in the United States with an overhead list in one hand and a flow chart in the other. Ask yourself: "What am I doing in my U.S. office that can be done cheaper, faster, or better at the overseas factory?"

Look at the steps:

- 1-10: What does design actually cost me? What will it cost to do part of the work at the supplier? How much of the design work must I do myself and how much can I send to the supplier? How much can I save?

- 11-16: What does it cost me to make the first sample? Can I find a factory that can make my first patterns and the first sample as well, or must I keep the whole U.S.-based team intact? What can I save?

- 28-37: What does it cost me to do all the fabric and trim sourcing myself or even through my agent? Can the factory take on part of the work? Can I trust the maker? Can I reduce my costs in the United States and the commission I pay my agent by having the factory take on this work?

- 54-65: Am I still producing my own salesman samples? Surely, the maker can do this cheaper than I can. How much can I save?

- 68-86: Must I take care of the final corrections and material orders out of the U.S. or even at my agent's? How much can I save by having the factory carry out this work, even if my merchandiser has to fly in for a week to give approval?

Any task you can move from your U.S. office to your overseas supplier saves money twice over. First of all, you save money because your maker is cheaper than you are. He pays his workers less. He has the benefit of scale because he does the same work for many customers, while you have only you for a customer. Also, do not forget that he wants your order and will absorb some of the costs himself. Secondly, and more importantly, any task you give your maker to carry out ceases to be your overhead and becomes part of direct manufacturing costs. You are no longer paying for staff, rent for their offices, nor the electricity bill for their lights; instead, you are now paying so much for each pattern, sample, etc. The more work you do, the more you pay. If you do no work, you pay nothing.

What becomes clear with FVCA is that you should, wherever possible, be trading up to a full-service or normal-service factory. The indirect-cost savings gained are far more important than the direct-costs savings offered by Louie the Lip and his 0-service friends. If you cannot see these savings, it is because you have not included these expenses in your cost sheets. You still believe that your overhead in New York or Los Angeles has nothing to do with the cost of your pants made in El Salvador.

Once you apply the principles of FVCA to your overhead in the United States, the structure of your business, your choice of suppliers and your profit margins will change forever. You will become more competitive and operate on higher margins. Most importantly, because your business will become leaner, you will survive in difficult times and therefore still be around to prosper when—and if—the good times return.

There is yet another important indirect-cost advantage to trading up. The continuous search for cheaper labor has resulted in lowest-common-denominator fashion. To be able to produce in a factory where management systems are rudimentary and workers unskilled, you must take every operation and simplify to a point where it becomes idiot-proof. By the time you have completed the process, you have reached a point where the style becomes totally mediocre. We professionals constantly wonder why consumers have lost interest in clothes, why each year total apparel sales in the United States fall. Perhaps, it is time to look at some of our stuff in the stores and ask honestly: "Would I buy this?"

To produce interesting clothes, you must have a qualified maker with skilled workers. If you make your garments with Louie the Lip, they can only look like Louie-the-Lip garments.

Ethical Sourcing

The final area where you have to consider indirect costs—those costs directly under a factory's control—is ethical sourcing. All companies that engage in garment sourcing insist that their suppliers conform to minimum standards of quality, price and delivery. Ethical sourcing extends this corporate policy to include minimum standards of ethical conduct.

Ethical sourcing has been a policy in some companies for generations. Marks & Spencer has maintained minimum working-condition standards at their suppliers since the company was founded over a century ago. Levi Strauss has also long been a proponent of ethical sourcing, sometimes at the expense of profits. Levi's refusal to work in China until real improvement in various conditions had been demonstrated is an example of Levi's putting their money firmly behind their mouth.

In the past, ethical sourcing concentrated on two broad areas:

- Working Conditions
    - Child labor
    - Prison labor
    - Overtime compensation
    - Sanitary facilities
    - Treatment of women

- Pollution, the environment and ecology
    - Use of chemical products during manufacturing
    - Waste disposal
    - Plant location
    - End product standards

Until recently, ethical sourcing was a concern for individual companies only. No direct relationship between ethical sourcing and garment costs was discerned, except in areas in which importing countries had enacted specific legislation. Examples included the U.S. law prohibiting importation of goods produced in prisons or Germany's ban on merchandise made with certain polluting chemicals.

Ironically, companies who maintained ethical sourcing policies were often penalized. When Levi's moved out of China, they lost not only a low-cost denim fabric and apparel sourcing option, but a promising retail market as well.

Since the early 1990s, however, individual consumers and consumer groups have begun to zoom in on ethical sourcing. With increasing frequency, companies producing goods in countries with poor human rights records, as well as those working with factories with poor working conditions, have been singled out and picketed or otherwise denounced.

The garment industry is particularly susceptible to this type of pressure. Consumers are aware that most garments sold in the United States are imported and primarily produced in Third World countries. The main label in each garment clearly shows the item's country of origin directly below the company's logo. The end consumer buying clothes has a wide choice of alternatives. If the customer does not like you because you are importing your jeans from hell, he or she can stop buying your product and replace it with someone else's without any difficulty at all. In fact, simply by rejecting your label for another, the consumer receives an added perk. It is not very often that you can go to a store, buy a pair of jeans and strike a blow for human dignity at the same time.

If you are an apparel importer, you have to accept that working in countries where police periodically machine-gun students or workers entails higher macro costs. Until now, the only producing country completely affected by protesting consumers has been Burma, a marginal supplier with an unusually vicious government. It has, therefore, been easy for companies to drop Burma.

Similarly, as a garment buyer, you also have to accept the fact that working with some factories also carries higher indirect costs. If the factory looks like a cross between an orphanage and a prison camp, you have a potential problem. If the factory is causing serious pollution, you also have a problem.

The size of the problem you potentially face is also based on who you are. Small importers with their own labels are less at risk than major designer companies that have invested enormous sums to achieve label recognition. Fahrblunget Frocks does not have nearly the same problem as Liz Claiborne.

Ethical sourcing is not easy. Workable standards are difficult to create and even more difficult to maintain. The minute you begin to make a real effort, you start alienating groups. Consumers feel you are not doing enough while producers feel you are making unreasonable requests.

Consider environmental standards. You can throw out entire countries because they are destroying the environment, then you can throw out specific companies because they use products or perform operations that create pollution. But if you start by using absolutely rigid standards, you ultimately end up throwing out every country in the world. We are all guilty of pollution and, arguably, the United States is the guiltiest of all.

At the same time, it is difficult to throw out a garment factory on the grounds of pollution. Garmentmaking does not in itself cause pollution— it is the upstream material processing such as dyeing, printing and the production of the initial chemicals from which synthetic fibers are derived that cause the problem. To what degree can we hold a garment factory in India responsible because the fibermaker located 5,000 miles away in Indonesia polluted air in Sumatra? The garment factory is four steps away from the synthetic feed stock. It had no dealings with the upstream chemical company. Even if you wanted to impose certain standards, such as barring the use of Azo dyestuff, how could you as a garment importer impose the standard and ensure the factories were in compliance? You are a garment importer, not a textile chemist. There is no garment importer in the United States who has the knowledge or facilities to even create reasonable standards.

Imposing working-condition standards also poses difficulties. We can all agree that child labor in Bangladesh is terrible. However, how different is a 12-year-old child working in a jeans factory in Dhaka from a 12-year-old child waking at 5:30 a.m. to work at a family farm in Iowa? We look at the Bangladeshi child as a victim, but his counterpart doing chores in America's heartland is part of the American legend.

How can we even talk about industrial safety, clean working conditions, women's rights in the workplace and child labor when these countries are so poor that a factory, no matter how humble the facilities, is the first step toward real development?

Furthermore, how can a small importer check to ensure that minimum standards are being maintained? The big importer can hire teams of trained personnel to go into their suppliers to check that their standards are being upheld. The small importer simply does not have the capital, the staff, or the knowledge.

Ethical sourcing is difficult to establish and even more difficult to maintain. The precise standards are unclear. No matter what standards you adopt, someone will say you are not doing enough. But however you personally stand, the discussion is important not for its ethical arguments, but rather for how costs are affected. The American consumers who buy the goods you import are concerned. If they believe you are exploiting your workers, collaborating with vicious regimes, or destroying the environment, they will stop buying your T-shirts.

Perhaps there are good and ethical arguments for child labor in poor countries. But frankly, I do not see Michael Eisner, president of Walt Disney, standing up in public to say: "We at Walt Disney, after careful consideration, have decided that exploiting children is a good thing. Henceforth, our T-shirts will be made by Thai and Indonesian children."

I *can* see a Disney spokesperson announcing that their company is 100% against child labor in all its forms and will cease purchasing from any country in which child labor takes place.

To a large degree, ethical sourcing is a public relations exercise. True, there are companies who look at ethical sourcing as a moral imperative. Companies like Levi Strauss and Marks & Spencer established standards long before ethics began affecting retail sales. Now the rest of us must join the ethical sourcing bandwagon because that is what our customers want. And we are all in business to give our customers what they want.

There is nothing wrong with good public relations if the policies are honest. In a populist country like the United States, real change takes place only when people really want change. Changing policy to suit your customer makes good sense. What is dangerous is when companies talk-the-talk but don't walk-the-walk.

Case Study XLVIII—Nike: The Philip Morris of Shoes

Since the advent of the global economy, Nike has been a frontrunner, particularly where international sourcing has been concerned. The history of recent Asian economic development is reflected in Nike's sourcing strategy. Thirty years ago, Nike produced in Japan. Twenty years ago, they switched to Taiwan and South Korea. Ten years ago, they moved again, to southern China and Indonesia. Now they are deeply involved in Vietnam.

Nike has always understood that since they control the facilities that keep indirect costs down, they can concentrate their efforts on direct costs. They unashamedly work where labor is cheapest.

In 1996, several consumer groups in the United States began to picket retailers selling Nike products. These groups argued that Nike was paying workers in Indonesia the equivalent of $0.26 per hour, an extremely low wage.

Recently, these same groups have stepped up their activities, contending that in Vietnam, workers producing Nike products are paid $1.84 per day, below subsistence level for that country. They claim that workers have been losing weight and their health has deteriorated because of Nike's low wages. A supervisor in a factory producing Nike products allegedly forced 56 women to run four kilometers as punishment for wearing incorrect shoes to work. In that incident, a dozen women fainted from heat exhaustion, several requiring hospitalization.[15]

In another reported incident, more than 1,000 Vietnamese workers went on strike because a Korean supervisor hit 15 women in the face with a rubber Nike sole as punishment for minor transgressions. In a third incident, women employed at a Korean-owned Nike sub-contractor were forced to kneel on the floor for 20 minutes, with their hands above their heads, to apologize for lapses in performance.

For a company selling active sportswear and an image of good clean fun, accusations of slave wages and beating up workers was not an image of choice. Faced with this problem, Nike had several options. The truth is always a possibility. Nike might have admitted that they do pay $0.26 per hour in Indonesia and $1.84 per day in Ho Chi Minh City. They could have gone on to show that $0.26 per hour, or $2.60 per 10-hour day, is 45% above average wages for an Indonesian sewer and that, likewise, $1.84 per day is well above average for Vietnam. These are poor wages by U.S. standards, but they are the standards of those countries.

Likewise, they could have admitted the incidents of corporal punishment, taken disciplinary action against not only the local supervisors but executives at corporate headquarters responsible for overseas sourcing, and set up a mechanism for workers to bring complaints to management. These are difficult admissions to make. The truth is often difficult.

A real commitment for improvement on Nike's part would have done much to undo the damage. A compromise solution could have involved not necessarily increasing wages (since low wages is why Nike works in those countries), but the offer of various new facilities. Nike could have sponsored nursery and primary schools for workers' children, scholarships to overseas universities, sports facilities for workers and free medical care. Such a move would have offset the bad publicity.

What Nike did was to employ Mr. Andrew Young, former mayor of Atlanta and former Ambassador to the United Nations, to look into the matter. I am not absolutely certain, but I suspect Mr. Young is not an Indonesia or Vietnam specialist—nor does he have special knowledge of shoe manufacturing. It appears that Mr. Young's only qualifications were that he is a well-known liberal and that he is African-American. If Nike were serious about effecting real change, neither qualification has any value. However, if their goal was purely a public relations exercise, Mr. Young's qualifications were well suited.

Policies which result in actions such as Nike's empty public relations exercise are based on the assumption that the average American is mentally retarded, with an attention span measured in sound bites. The same mistake was made by the major tobacco companies that assumed if they 'stood tough', their problems with large segments of the American public would go away. Ten years later, the tobacco companies are still tough, though not quite standing, as they scramble to settle multi-billion dollar class-action lawsuits. Senior management at the tobacco companies bravely feign confidence that they will not really go to jail. And public perception is that all tobacco company executives are reincarnations of Adolf Hitler.

The public outcry against Nike has reached the point where American university students are demanding that their college teams drop Nike products. Politicians, always ready to join a populist movement, have signed petitions condemning Nike. Web sites spreading anti-Nike material are proliferating and Nike has been regularly spoofed in the *Doonesbury* cartoon series.

Since 1998, Nike's business troubles and earnings falls have been widely reported, while competitors Reebok and Adidas are beginning to nibble away at Nike's once unassailable market leadership.

Is this the corporate image that Nike wants to give to its consumers? Nike should reconsider. They should talk less and *Just Do It*.

Although companies are currently limited in the practical steps they can initiate to implement a realistic and honest policy of ethical sourcing, some steps available to all can already be undertaken.

- Decide if there are countries from which you will not source and list the reasons, stressing why conditions in the designated countries are unsatisfactory.

- Compile a manual of minimum standards for working conditions at all suppliers. Ensure that the standards are precise and can be complied with, and that inspectors can determine whether each specific standard is, in fact, being complied with.

- Compile a manual of minimum environmental standards with which all suppliers must conform. Where standards include the banning of specific dyestuffs and other chemicals, ensure that procedures for fabric testing are in place.

- Where feasible, set up an in-house department that will work in conjunction with your own QC inspection personnel to ensure that all suppliers, as well as subcontractors, are routinely visited. Where an in-house department is not feasible, appoint your local agent responsible for ensuring compliance. Stress that ethical sourcing compliance is a practical necessity and suppliers who fail to meet ethical sourcing standards will be dropped, the same as suppliers who fail to meet standards of quality or reliability.

- Make your standards known to both buyers and end consumers. Show the positive steps you are taking. Become one of the good guys.

Yet even for companies who want to make a genuine effort, serious limitations remain:

- Regardless of the efforts made, no single company can implement a workable ethical sourcing program. Companies just do not have the facilities.

- Their motives will be suspect. When slip-ups do occur, consumers will believe they have occurred due to lack of real commitment and that the entire policy was for show rather than with the intent to really accomplish something.

- In-house training is insufficient to meet needs. For example, few garment companies have in house-chemists capable of identifying and dealing with complex pollution problems.

The only solution would be for companies to work together, perhaps bringing in universities into a wider movement embracing all parties who seriously wish to introduce ethical-sourcing policies. A uniform minimum standard could be set. Professional training could be conducted by specialists trained in each discipline. Designated suppliers could be inspected regularly and the group could grant accreditation. A nonprofit organization affiliated with various universities would be perceived as neutral by the general public. The organization would serve to separate the good guys from the others.

DIRECT COSTS

Arriving at the lowest direct costs is a matter of negotiation. As already discussed, negotiation is not necessarily confrontation. Good negotiators tend to be more cooperative, stressing the long-term relationship over the immediate order. That is why the U.K. retailer Marks & Spencer pays the lowest CMT in the industry (see Case Study XXXIV).

But in the United States, most mass-market retailers and importers act as if they require no relationships. Their buyer/seller philosophy can be summed up in the words of Herbie the Mouth: "If the factory wants to make the goods at our price, quality and delivery date—fine. If they do not, they can drop dead. There are a lot of other factories out there who would give their left arm for an order of 5,000 dozen."

In a sense, they are right. If you are a mass-market importer and you own all the indirect-cost-saving facilities required to manufacture, you can work anywhere and you can pay anything you want. There is always some poor jerk who will accept your order, at any price, provided the quantity is large enough. But the rest of us who don't have orders of a million-dozen per style and who are not willing to provide all the facilities ourselves, we need to find suppliers we can depend on.

If you want a factory to work your way—that is, to supply the facilities you require in the manner you require—you must form a relationship. This would seem so obvious as to not be worth mentioning. Sadly, for most garment customers, a relationship is any meeting that lasts longer than 15 minutes. And a long-term relationship is one that extends to a second meeting.

Our industry, particularly in America, is based on confrontation and the belief that the only way to obtain the right product, at the right price, shipped on time, is through intimidation. Granted, this phenomenon is slowly disappearing as the muggers increasingly become muggees. However, the old guard still exists.

Case Study XLIX—Herbie the Mouth: Losing Through Intimidation

For once in his career, Herbie the Mouth actually had to buy a legitimate product. Because of his universal reputation, Herbie is unable to work in any civilized country on a direct basis. He, therefore, employed an outsider, Holden Schmata, the well-known garment industry consultant, to find a factory to work for him. Holden belonged to the new school and enjoyed an excellent reputation. He would not actually cheat the supplier unless absolutely necessary, which in our industry puts him right up there with Mother Teresa. Holden is welcome everywhere.

His instructions from Herbie were: "I want only the best jacket maker in the world."

Holden did find a good factory located in France. The factory produced for John Galliano and Alexander McQueen and other leading designers. Herbie could not afford the factory's normal CMT price, but by promising consistent business and a long-term relationship, he was able to work out a very good price.

But even without bringing Herbie's name into the relationship, there were doubts on the French side. After all, Holden was American, and French factories generally don't think much of American buyers. It took a year to set up and solidify the relationship, costing Herbie a great deal of money. In the beginning, Holden had to fly to France once a month. Holden's costs alone added over $4 to the cost of each garment shipped in the first season. However, the investment was worth the effort. Orders that had begun with 2,500 units a season soon reached 10,000 units a month.

The quality was exceptional and the delivery on time, which for a French factory is even more exceptional. Holden's work was complete, and Herbie actually paid his fees. Unfortunately, with Holden out of the picture, the relationship lasted for an additional 3 days—not a world record, but certainly worthy of note. This is what happened.

Herbie had this reorder of 70 pieces. He told the factory to produce the reorder. The factory owner refused, telling Herbie that the quantity was below minimum. (The French are also known for being difficult.) Herbie, whose nickname Herbie the Mouth is well deserved, went into his you-can't-do-this-to-me routine, giving the factory a choice of two alternatives: make the reorder or stop doing business with me. The factory in turn gave Herbie a choice of two alternatives, neither of which bears repeating.

Holden Schmata asked Herbie why he ended what had been an exceedingly profitable relationship. After all, the whole fight could have been avoided had Herbie simply asked the factory to accept the small order as a favor and perhaps paid a small premium. Herbie replied: "The only way to treat a factory is to tell them who is boss. Those people in France now know who is boss." This from a man who is now barred not only the factory but from the country as well.

The problem with intimidation is that it works only up to a point. Beyond that point, you lose cooperation or, like Herbie, you get thrown out—the ultimate loss of cooperation.

Mass-market retailers have factory relationships which often don't extend beyond the first order. Some mass-market retailers will occasionally give identical orders to two or more suppliers, knowing that if the style dies at store level, they will cancel at least one of the orders for 'poor quality'. But if you are, for example, a better goods buyer and you want the factory to cooperate, to work your way, you must have a relationship that extends to more than a few orders or even a few programs.

Responsible importers and suppliers are beginning to realize that given the serious problems facing the industry, old-style buyer/seller relationships no longer work. Gradually these are being replaced by strategic relationships where all solutions must be win-win.

Your relationship has to extend over a period of time. Your concern is not whether you are perceived as a tough or soft negotiator—you should be concerned with profit. Both you and your supplier must realize that you have more to gain by combining your interests than maintaining positions of conflict. You must both realize that it is just as hard for you to find a decent factory capable of delivering 50,000 units a month as it is for a good factory to find a decent customer who has 50,000 units a month in orders.

MACRO COSTS

All professionals operate under the same mantra: *Shipping garments is good, not shipping garments is bad.* Sometimes when dealing with a customs official—one who has passed the limits of acceptable corruption and gone into total extortion—we must remind ourselves that what counts is shipping garments and that for professionals, there is no place for ego.

Nevertheless, even the most professional person cannot be totally objective. At some point, each of us reaches a moment where we swear we will never do business in a particular place ever again—in fact, they should all lose every tooth in their mouth except one, and in that one there should be a toothache.

Actually, one high macro-cost country is much like another, and you must be willing to pay that cost if you want to work there. If you are not willing, stay away. Otherwise, terrible things can and do happen.

Case Study L—Solving the Quota Problem: Indonesian-Style

When Holden Schmata first began sourcing, his boss at Schmidlap Enterprises—who was a very good friend of a senior merchandise manager at a large retail chain—was given an order for 100,000 cotton sweaters. The problem is that U.S. quota category 345 for cotton sweaters is very expensive and usually easily available only in countries that do not produce cotton sweaters in the first place.

For this order, Holden decided to buy allegedly made-in-Indonesia sweaters. His good friend Macbeth Wong arranged the whole deal. The goods were to be made in China and shipped to Indonesia, where the made-in-Indonesia labels would be sewn on and the sweaters shipped to the United States with an Indonesian export license, using Indonesian quota.

Everything went well. The goods were produced, transshipped and reshipped to the United States. The sweaters arrived. The quota export license arrived. Unfortunately, the sweaters were marked 'cotton' while the license was marked 'synthetic'. U.S. Customs refused to release the 100,000 sweaters until the license could be amended.

Holden telephoned Macbeth. Macbeth telephoned Indonesia. Indonesia told Macbeth, "No problem." Macbeth told Holden, "No problem."

"Great," said Holden. "When can I have the new license?" "Great," repeated Macbeth. "When can he have the new license?" "When we get the $50,000," replied Indonesia.

"Send $50,000?" cried Macbeth. "What $50,000?" screamed Holden. "I don't know what $50,000!" cried Macbeth. "Just send $50,000."

Holden Schmata took $50,000 in cash and traveled to Indonesia. He and Macbeth went to see the friend who had originally issued the export license.

Unfortunately, as it turned out, the friend was not just corrupt—he was also dishonest. He tried to keep the original bribe for himself. In Indonesia, failing to pay kickbacks on bribes is a very serious offense.

The friend went to jail. The sweaters died in customs. Holden lost his job. And we all know what happened to Macbeth. It was tragic.

Chapter 9
Producing at the Lowest Cost: Factory Structure

To most consultants, increasing productivity boils down to either using workers as machines or using machines as workers. This is called the Schmendrich Theory of factory development.

Holden Schmata
Lectures to MBA graduates

Full Value Cost Analysis is not only a useful tool to customers who want to source production at the lowest cost, but equally valuable to factories that want to reduce costs to become more competitive.

For the factory owner, the first step is to understand just what type of factory you are operating. As previously discussed, factories fall into three categories.

1. The 0-service factory which has the following characteristics:

- Unable to produce more than a limited number of orders at one time; averages five or fewer styles per month;

- Relies on a limited number of customers to fill its capacity, usually under four, and can sometimes work exclusively for a single customer;

- Requires large minimums: 1,000-5,000 dozen per style;

- Usually works CMT only: the customer supplies fabric and often trim as well;

- Requires long lead times relative to the product: a T-shirt factory may require 45 days including fabric; a shirt factory, 60 days after receipt of fabric. Some lead times may be as long as 120-180 days;

- Limited to straight-line assembly-line production. Each garment must be broken down into as many operations as necessary to ensure that each sewer is required to do little more than sew a straight line and that there is a seamless transition from one operation to the next;

- Efficiency remains high only when producing a basic product. Any additions or complexities such as pocket flaps, pleats or darts raises costs disproportionately and causes production delays;

- Cannot deal with changes in order (color or size assortment) or design modifications. Best results are achieved when the factory knows precisely what is required and the customer makes no subsequent changes;

- Customers limited to low-end, mass-market retailers or large active sportswear customers, and importers or agents catering to them;

- Provides no services or assists whatsoever. Enters the manufacturing cycle at Step 87 when all materials and trim have been assembled for stock production;

- Requires constant detailed follow-up. Customer's or agent's inspectors must be present every day throughout the production cycle.

The 0-service factory is inflexible in every way. It is geared to operate using semi-skilled or unskilled workers. The factory enjoys a direct-cost advantage from labor cost alone. In the early stages of a country's industrial development, the wage rates are sufficiently low for the factory to operate, even though the productivity of each worker is also relatively low. Little investment is made in capital equipment. 0-service factories are the rule in countries just beginning to export, such as those in Africa and the less-developed areas of East and South Asia. However, they also occur in developed countries.

2. The normal-service factory which has the following characteristics:

- Able to accept large numbers of orders, between 5-20 per month, depending on size;

- Able to work with several customers, between 2-5 as a rule, although usually commits 50% or more of total production to a single mainstay customer;

- Able to accept smaller minimums; averages 100-1,000 dozen per style.

- Prefers to work on an FOB basis; customer provides special trim only;

- Able to operate with short lead times: 30 days for T-shirts, 45 days for shirts including fabric time;

- Flexible assembly line; sections have fewer operators to allow for smaller orders. In some cases workers are multi-tasked (able to perform several operations on the same garment);

- Can deal with more difficult styles with higher added value. Opening FOB prices are higher but increases incurred by subsequent additions and complexities are relatively minor;

- Can deal with some changes, although last minute changes or changes involving trim will result in surcharges. When customer requests changes, greater follow-up by agent is required;

- Customers consist of a broad range of importers and retailers, from mass-market (for difficult styles) to department stores and designer labels (for casual and basic sportswear);

- Can provide some important services and assists such as pattern grading, basic trim sourcing and salesman sample production;

- Follow-up by customer or agent still required but factory will provide complete cooperation.

The normal-service factory, the backbone of the industry, is serious in its efforts to provide quality and reliability. The customer knows what to expect and usually receives what he requires, provided he does not ask for too much. The normal-service factory operates best when specializing in simple products such as casual pants, shirts and blouses where a full-service factory is not needed or in Third World countries where operating a full-service factory is almost impossible. As a rule, factories offering indirect-cost saving facilities are far more profitable than 0-cost factories that must rely on low labor rates to remain competitive.

3. The full-service factory which has the following characteristics:

- Number of orders produced is limited only by the size of the operation. A large full-service factory is capable of producing over 50-400 styles per month;

- Works with a broad range of customers located in various parts of the world thus assuring steady business throughout the year. Will often restrict the size of any single customer to under 20% of total capacity;

- Flexible minimums, averaging 600+ pieces per style. For any important customer, the full-service factory will accept any order regardless of size, provided the fabric is available;

- Usually insists on working FOB and will on occasion accept orders on an LDP basis. The full service factory knows there is no profit in working CMT;

- Lead times totally flexible. Literally any delivery is possible provided the fabric is in the house and the customer is valued and willing to pay the price;

- Production totally flexible. All operators are multi-tasked, often working in modular teams;

- Productivity relative to lower-service factories rises as styles become more complex or difficult to produce. Basic FOB costs are high but increase little as styles require greater effort;

- Remains flexible when customer requests changes. As long as the fabric is not on the table, all changes are possible, some even after the goods have been spread;

- Customers are normally higher-end, such as better retailers and designer importers. Will often receive orders from reliable mid-priced customers for difficult styles. As a rule, every serious customer tries to maintain an ongoing relationship with at least one full-service factory;

- Provides full services and assists. Once a customer has been accepted, whatever he requires, the factory will supply;

- Requires no follow-up. Agents just get in the way.

The full-service factory is more than a supplier; it is a partner in a strategic relationship. The full-service factory does more than simply provide a good product shipped on time. It has the potential to be involved in every step of the manufacturing cycle, from Step 1 (*Designer attends fabric show*) to Step 101 (*Order ready for shipment*). For the customer who wants the best facilities, the full-service factory is the best choice. For the customer who needs the facilities, the full-service factory is the only choice.

Some professionals and particularly government bureaucrats believe that the different types of factories are simply phases in factory and industry development, and that as an economy develops, 0-service factories progress to normal-service and finally full-service status. This is theoretically true. However, as a factory owner, I would not count on the invisible hand of progress to save my factory. In the real world, 0-service factories do not evolve—they go broke.

If you are operating a 0-service factory, you must face the fact that you cannot survive in the long run. Your only asset is cheap labor, and cheap is a relative term. Your wage rates are about to go up, and new competitors from even lower-wage countries are coming on line every day. Once upon a time, everybody had cheap labor. In 1960, Japan was cheap. In 1970, Hong Kong and Taiwan were cheap. As recently as 1980, South Korea was still somewhat cheap. In 1999, not even the Philippines or the Dominican Republic are cheap. Just because you are located in Sri Lanka where you pay $2.40 per day, don't think you are cheap.

Don't forget a sewer is paid only $1.60 a day in Pakistan, $1.40 in central China, and $1.20 in Bangladesh and Burma. These workers still think they have a good deal and the available labor force is abundant. Going further, there are perhaps another 20 countries where workers are paid under $0.60 per day or $0.06 per hour. Following Asia's recent financial crisis, wages in countries like Indonesia and Thailand which had been rising, when calculated in U.S. dollar equivalents, have now fallen substantially.[16]

Your mass-market customer has his own list of cheap-labor countries which he updates weekly. He knows that you and your 0-service factory are useful only for the last manufacturing steps (87-101). You contribute nothing to the first 85% of the manufacturing process. All he cares about is your ability to keep your direct costs down. If you are located in Costa Rica, Malaysia, the Philippines or Sri Lanka, you are not looking good. If all you have to offer is cheap labor, you really have nothing to offer.

Most 0-service factory managers simply do not understand this reality. Like the old-time buyers, they are adamant that the key to cost reduction, or even maintaining present cost levels, is found somewhere in direct costs, most often in CMT and almost inevitably in labor rates. Their question is always: "How can I keep my wages down?" Their solutions can be as extreme as outlawing labor unions (Malaysia) or sending in the army to shoot striking workers (Indonesia).

Your dilemma is that even if you could control wages, your overheads—which are a far higher percentage of direct costs than wages—are continually rising. Keeping a ceiling on wages will not compensate for the rising cost of electricity, rent, interest and other financial charges as well as your other fixed expenses.

Case Study LI—Wage Rates

You are a Philippine factory manager. You run 500 machines making men's shirts. Your average shirt has an FOB price of $8.00 including quota. You pay your workers the equivalent of $6.60 per day, or $0.66 per hour. A sewer averages 12 shirts per day per machine. Sewing costs are, therefore, $0.55 per shirt.

Just how much would prices go up if wage rates rose by 25%, 50% or 100%? What would prices go down to if wage rates fell by 25%, 50% or if you paid your workers nothing at all?

The first problem is to define just what costs we are talking about. There are, in fact, four separate costs:

1. The FOB price your import customer must pay you;
2. The LDP price the importer must pay in the United States;
3. The wholesale price the store must pay the importer;
4. The retail price the consumer must pay at the store.

Let's examine how changes in labor rates and labor costs affect total costs.

Wage Rate Current	Current	125%	150%	200%	75%	50%	Zero Wages
Wages per day	$ 6.60	$ 8.25	$ 9.90	$13.20	$ 4.95	$ 3.30	0
Sewing cost per unit	$ 0.55	$ 0.69	$ 0.83	$ 1.10	$ 0.41	$ 0.28	0
FOB (including quota)	$ 8.00	$ 8.14	$ 8.27	$ 8.55	$ 7.86	$ 7.73	$ 7.45
Sewing cost as pct of FOB	6.9%	8.5%	10.0%	12.9%	5.2%	3.6%	0.0%
Pct change	1.7%	3.1%	6.0%	-1.7%	-3.3%	-6.9%	
Amount of change	$ 0.14	$ 0.27	$ 0.55	-$ 0.14	-$ 0.27	-$ 0.55	
Landed-duty-paid (LDP)	$10.00	$10.18	$10.35	$10.68	$ 9.84	$ 9.68	$ 9.34
Sewing cost as pct of LDP	5.5%	6.8%	8.0%	10.3%	4.2%	2.8%	0.0%
Wholesale price	$20.00	$20.36	$20.70	$21.36	$19.68	$19.36	$18.68
Sewing cost as pct of wholesale	2.7%	3.4%	4.0%	5.1%	2.1%	1.5%	0.0%

Retail price (based on 55% markup and rounded off)	$44.00	$45.00	$46.00	$47.00	$43.00	$43.00	$41.00
Sewing cost as pct of retail price	1.3%	1.5%	1.8%	2.3%	1.0%	0.6%	0.0%
Retail price change	$ 1.00	$ 2.00	$ 3.00	-$ 1.00	-$1.00	-$ 3.00	
Pct change of retail price	2.3%	4.5%	6.8%	-2.3%	-2.3%	-6.8%	

From the above, it is clear that trying to hold the line on wages alone to reduce FOB cost is a waste of time. The sewer's current contribution to FOB price is only 6.9%. If wages go up 25%, the added costs are only $0.14 or 1.7% of FOB. Likewise, if wages were to go down, the savings would be negligible. Even if the factory paid the worker nothing at all, the total reduction on FOB would still be only 6.9%.

From the viewpoint of the final consumer, the effects of changes in wage rate are also relatively inconsequential—a wage increase of 50% would add only 4.5% to the final retail price while wage cuts of 50% would only lower retail prices by 2.3%. Yet this is the area that 0-service factories look to for controlling costs and where their mass-market customers concentrate most of their efforts as well. Few owners of 0-service factories understand the real dilemma they face. Most live in a state of denial and look at rising wage rates as some kind of temporary problem.

Maintaining the certain but mistaken belief that low wage rates are the key to staying competitive results in costly and incorrect decisions. To many managers and almost all economic planners, rising wages are uncompetitive, so the best solution is to bring in sophisticated machinery—either to increase workers' productivity or to replace workers altogether. Intelligent managers who hold MBAs from top U.S. universities are so caught up focusing on cheap labor that they can no longer work out a basic amortization calculation, as illustrated by the following case study.

Case Study LII—Amortizing the New Machine: Sri Lanka

You are a factory owner and you have now moved to Sri Lanka, where you are still running 500 machines making men's shirts. You pay your workers $1.80 per day or $0.18 per hour. A sewer averages 10 shirts per day per machine. Sewing costs are, therefore, $0.18 per shirt.

You have decided to cut labor costs by bringing in computerized sewing machinery which will definitely increase productivity. There is a limit to how much more can be produced by the introduction of a new sewing machine: no sewing machine alone will double productivity. For the sake of this example, we will suspend reality and assume that there exists a machine so efficient that it will allow you to cut your workforce by 50%. This machine costs only $2,000 each which, for a new computerized specialty machine, is a very low figure indeed. (Perhaps you are buying secondhand, reconditioned machinery).

We will assume that you can borrow long-term funds at 15% per annum. You want to amortize the machine in five years. Based on this information, you calculate that your monthly installment will be $47.58 per machine to repay $2,000 borrowed for 60 months at 15% interest per annum.

SEWING COSTS PER 1000 SHIRTS (100 = 10 shirts per machine per day)					
Productivity index	100	125	150	175	200
Number of machines required	100	80	67	57	50
Wages per day	$ 1.80	$ 1.80	$ 1.80	$ 1.80	$ 1.80
Total daily workers wages	$ 180.00	$ 144.00	$ 120.60	$ 102.60	$ 90.00
Wages/month (25 days)	$4,500.00	$3,600.00	$3,000.00	$2,571.43	$2,250.00
Wage savings per month		$ 900.00	$1,500.00	$1,928.57	$2,250.00
Cost of amortization		$3,806.40	$3,172.00	$2,718.86	$2,379.00
Loss per month		$2,906.40	$1,672.00	$ 790.29	$ 129.00

In the end, even assuming the existence of a $2,000 machine that will double productivity, you will lose $129 per month.

The high interest rates in Third World countries also do not help, but they are a secondary consideration. The main problem is that the lower the wage rate, the less value capital investment as a means of reducing costs becomes.

As long as the Indonesian, Philippine or Sri Lankan factory owner looks to direct costs as a means of lowering total costs, he has no solution to his long-term problems. There is little the 0-service factory owner can do to reduce direct costs. By international standards, he is currently already paying nothing to his workers. He cannot pay them less. He cannot lower costs by bringing in machinery. His workers are his machines and those machines are so cheap that he simply cannot amortize any real capital expenditure.

Contrast your factory in Sri Lanka with your factory in Italy. Here you have very skilled but highly paid workers who earn $16.45 per hour compared to $0.20. Here an investment in the most advanced machinery helps your bottom line. Not only is it worthwhile to bring in better sewing equipment, but it is also advisable to reorganize and possibly reconstruct the entire factory to ensure the greatest possible productivity.

Case Study LIII—Amortizing the New Machine: Italy

Now you are living in beautiful Italy where you are still running your 500-machine factory making the same men's shirts.

You pay your workers $16.45 per hour, over 90 times what you paid a worker in Sri Lanka. A sewer averages better than 12 shirts a day, somewhat better than Sri Lanka. The sewing cost is, therefore, $10.97 per shirt.

Definitely, it is time to invest in capital equipment. You have a variety of choices.

You can simply bring in new and better sewing machines. This is the cheapest method and, as in Sri Lanka, will double productivity.

You can also completely reorganize each department bringing in new machinery throughout. This will, of course, cost more but will increase productivity even further.

Finally, you can rebuild the entire factory, bringing all new machinery, systems and total automation. This is possible, but very costly. The question is: How much can you spend?

SEWING COSTS PER 1000 SHIRTS (100 = 12 shirts per machine per day)					
Productivity index	100	125	150	175	200
Machines required	100	80	67	57	50
Daily wage	$131.60	$131.60	$131.60	$131.60	$131.60
Total daily wages	$ 13,160	$ 10,528	$ 8,773	$ 7,520	$ 6,580
Total monthly wage (21 days)	$276,360	$221,088	$184,240	$157,920	$138,180
Wage saving/month	N/A	$55,272	$ 92,120	$118,440	$138,180
Investment $34,500 per worker		$55,272 (loan of $2.76mn for 60 months at 7.5% interest)			
Investment $68,656 per worker			$92,120 (loan of $4.6mn for 60 months at 7.5% interest)		
Investment $103,508 per worker				$118,440 (loan of $5.9mn for 60 months at 7.5% interest)	
Investment $138,000 per worker					$138,180 (loan of $6.9mn for 60 mos. at 7.5% interest)

Unlike the previous Sri Lankan scenario where the factory cannot afford a $2,000 investment even if productivity doubles, the Italian factory can afford to invest over $34,000 per worker just to obtain a 25% productivity increase and a whopping $138,000 per worker if productivity could be doubled. This is why Italian factories are high-tech while Sri Lankan factories are not.

While these figures may appear extreme, there are indeed areas in garment production where such increases in productivity are possible and the investment justified. The Italian garment industry benefits from many advantages, including low macro costs since the country is an EU member, and low indirect costs, thanks to its great expertise in fashion and garment production. By reducing direct costs, Italian factories are now able to compete quite effectively with those in any other exporting country in a variety of products. For a customer in Western Europe, it is cheaper to buy a basic sweater produced in Italy than one produced in China. The same is true for synthetic shirts, blouses and particularly true for high-value-added garments such as jackets and coats.

At the other extreme, in the final analysis, the 0-service factory can operate successfully only in the poorest of countries. As soon as the country begins developing, overheads rise, wage rates rise and inflation rates rise. The 0-service factory becomes increasingly uncompetitive and the low-end, mass-market customer begins to look elsewhere for the next cheap-labor country.

Some factory owners and managers in Asia, Latin America and elsewhere see the problem, but most perceive themselves as victims caught in a trap. They all offer variations of the same reply:

- "I have nothing to offer my customer except cheap labor and cheap CMT price."

- "I cannot change to a better quality customer because I lack the facilities the better customer requires."

- "My present mass-market customer does not want those facilities and certainly will not pay for them."

- "If I try to develop these facilities, my costs will rise and I risk losing my present customers before I have a chance to reach a level where I can attract the better ones."

There is something to be said for these arguments. To change from a 0-service factory to a full-service factory is not a gradual, evolutionary process. It requires an entirely new factory structure, employing better qualified workers, technicians and managers. It is both costly and risky. You might fail. However, if you do not change, you will certainly go broke. When you compare the risk of failure with the certainty of failure, taking risks becomes attractive.

PRODUCTIVITY AND INDIRECT COSTS

The problems raised in the Sri Lankan and Philippine case studies seem to contradict everything ever written on the subject of manufacturing development. We have all been taught that the secret to running a successful factory is to achieve greater efficiency through increased productivity.

Productivity is a measure of output relative to input. In a factory, it is the value of garments produced relative to the value of the inputs required to produce those garments, in this case, labor, capital and material. You can, as commonly accepted, get higher productivity by increasing the number of units produced. You can bring in better machinery and more efficient production techniques. But consider that because value is measured in dollars, there is another dimension by which productivity can be increased—by producing higher-value-added goods. The question then becomes, which is more suitable for the garment industry, and then, what sector of the garment industry are you talking about?

If you are talking about the part of the garment industry that deals only with cheap mass-market importers and retailers, there is little room for value-added production. You can switch from cheap blouses to cheap dresses, but your customer will be unwilling to pay more for the added work. They will underpay you for the cheap but value-added dress, just as they underpaid you for the cheap no value-added blouse. Your only hope is to raise productivity by increasing efficiency, that is, to produce more units with less input. Unfortunately, as already demonstrated, here too there is no real solution. If you are now paying your workers $0.25 an hour, you can neither reduce wages further nor can you make any capital investment to produce more garments with fewer workers.

Giving workers further training would help. However, the change in efficiency will be minor relative to what you the factory owner are now being paid for your work—unless worker training is part of a fundamental change in the factory structure. In fact, as we will discuss later, worker training is very important to making your factory profitable. But the advantages will be lost if you continue to work with mass-market importers and retailers.

Escaping from the mass-market customer by trading up to a better customer who pays more is, however, a viable solution. Value-added can entail either more expensive materials or a better-made product or producing for a customer who pays more for the same product. This last point is unique to the fashion industry. A Giorgio Armani blouse has greater value than a Kmart blouse simply because the label reads Giorgio Armani. Yet in many cases, the difference between one company's product and another's is not that easy to define, even though the difference in retail price might be considerable. Often the fabric is quite similar, even identical, as are the sewing techniques. After all, an oxford shirt is an oxford shirt. Unless you have your shirts custom-made, they are all very much alike. Brooks Brothers may use real mother-of-pearl buttons, while Target uses polyester buttons. The Brooks Brothers oxford may be from Europe, while Target uses Chinese oxford. Furthermore, Chinese oxford is actually quite good. The Brooks Brothers sewing would be single-needle throughout, while Target might use some double-needle machinery. Even here, single-needle sewing is now available from most high-speed factories and Target's sewing may well be identical to Brooks Brothers.

Having said the above, there *are* differences. The consumer may not see them, but they can feel them. I am not suggesting that an Oscar de la Renta little throwaway dress at $2,500 is worth $2,500. That is up to the customer. I am saying that Oscar de la Renta's dress at $2,500 is a better product than a similar dress available at Saks for $400. There are differences. And if you want to produce for better people, your product and your factory has to reflect those differences, as shown in the following case study.

Case Study LIV—The Silk Blouse

What is the real difference between an Ellen Tracy silk crepe de Chine blouse and one from Kmart? Let me say at once that there is a difference. Ellen Tracy produces one of the best quality blouses available in the United States and have done so for decades. Kmart produces just what you would expect from Kmart.

However, they both use the same fabrics. Almost all silk crepe de Chine blouses use Chinese fabric. Chinese silk crepe de Chine is a commodity that is available in a variety of qualities, all of which are differentiated by weight. Everyone uses the same stuff.

Nor is there a difference in the machinery. Both factories would utilize the same sewing machines. In fact, the Kmart factory might even have slightly more sophisticated machines than the factory producing for Ellen Tracy.

An Ellen Tracy blouse is not more complicated than a Kmart blouse to make. In terms of fabric and the machinery required to make the garments, the blouses are about the same. Yet they are different. The Ellen Tracy blouse requires twice the work of the Kmart one and each operation requires highly-skilled professionals. A factory without these skills could no more produce for Ellen Tracy than construct a mechanical horse that flies.

Just take one series of operations as an illustration. Silk by its very nature is damaged, characterized by slubs, uneven threads and discolorations. Both the Kmart and the Ellen Tracy factory will inspect all silk fabric on a machine before cutting. In both cases, the piece of fabric is considered acceptable if it has fewer than a given number of damages. In fact, Kmart precutting inspection may be more exacting than the inspection for Ellen Tracy.

Ellen Tracy's maker, however, carries out two additional steps. Step I is to inspect all fabric a second time when it is laid out on the cutting table. Because cutting tables are very long (minimum 15 yards) and very well lit, the cutters can see more on the table than the inspectors can on a machine. Any major damage is either cut away or marked with a circle in indelible ink to be replaced later on. After cutting, the pieces for each garment are bundled separately (Kmart bundles contain pieces for a dozen garments). Each bundle is opened and inspected once again. Pieces with circle marks are brought back to the cutting table for new panels.

Step II begins at this point. Every piece of every garment is reexamined for minor damages. This requires a great deal of judgment on the part of the factory inspectors because not only the nature of the damage is important, but also its location. A fabric flaw that appears at the hem may be passable, while an almost insignificant flaw would require a new panel if it occurred anywhere in the front or upper 17 inches of the back.

Finally, the factory producing for Ellen Tracy must deal with special problems inherent to silk fabric. Every piece of silk crepe de Chine has a different shade. Factories working for Ellen Tracy have to save a few yards from every piece for panel recuts in the event of additional fabric damages which occur or are found in later operations. The remaining balance of leftover fabric can be cut into additional garments only after final inspection. At that time garments are cut individually, similar to a tailor shop.

These are the differences for cutting alone. For each additional operation, factories working for Ellen Tracy must carry out other steps above and beyond those performed by the Kmart factory.

A factory in Indonesia or Pakistan producing Kmart blouses would say that any factory required to perform this amount of additional work would go broke. Yet these operations are required by Ellen Tracy and other importers of better-quality goods.

What is more important is that better customers will pay extra for this work. A factory in China producing a crepe de Chine blouse for Kmart is paid under $0.90 for cutting and making. It would be unfair to tell you what Ellen Tracy pays to have one of their blouses produced, but it is safe to say that it is over five times what Kmart pays.

Trading up to Ellen Tracy production creates a real change in the value of productivity even though the output in units actually goes down. The factory can produce about 10 Kmart blouses per machine a day compared with only 7.5 for Ellen Tracy. However, with Ellen Tracy, output value increases by a ratio of 5:1. The Kmart maker produces for $9.00 per machine per day. The Ellen Tracy maker produces $37.50 per machine for the same period—a productivity increase of 416%. Why would anyone want to work for Kmart if they could build a factory for Ellen Tracy?

Admittedly, few factories have the skills required to work for an Ellen Tracy-type customer. In fact, many of Ellen Tracy's suppliers literally grew up with the brand, producing to Ellen Tracy standards simply because they assisted in developing those standards.

Nevertheless, there does exist a wide range of customers between Ellen Tracy and the mass market, each with increasingly higher standards. If you now operate a 0-service factory, you are still at the very bottom. If your factory is to survive, it must develop the tools required to move upward. There is no survival at the bottom.

174

MACRO COSTS

If your factory is located in Indonesia, you unfortunately cannot reduce the macro costs of being in Indonesia. You cannot provide greater infrastructure, reduce bureaucratic inefficiency, eliminate corruption, increase education, lower interest rates, reorganize the tax system, or any of the other tasks so desperately needed to reduce macro costs. This can be done only by government. Despite these limitations, however, factories *can* lower their macro costs. Here we are talking not about structural changes but rather new strategies, and these ideas will be covered in the next chapter (see Case Study LXI—Breaking into NAFTA).

INDIRECT COSTS

This is the area in which you have the greatest control and where improvements in your factory will bring real change to your cost structure. Just as we have shown for apparel importers, you the factory owner cannot take steps to reduce indirect costs unless you first include indirect costs in your cost structure.

To run a successful factory today, you must first understand the nature of the modern manufacturing process. You must look at yourself and your factory in a broader context. You must learn to step back and take on a wider and more long-term perspective. You must look past Steps 87-101 in the flow chart and consider which of the other 86 operations you can perform and what additional facilities you must develop to offer the customer.

Remember that unlike in the days when Herbie the Mouth ran the industry, importers no longer buy—today they source. Instead of one-stop-shopping, where the buyer places his orders on the basis of the factory with the lowest FOB price, sourcing specialists now work with a chain of suppliers, each adding material or process until the garment is complete. To succeed in this global economy, the factory must integrate itself in that chain.

Horizontal Integration

Horizontal integration occurs when the mill continues its original operation, but extends its area of responsibility. Printers can provide computer-assisted design (CAD) services or even design prints for their customers. Spinners can employ systems to ensure a better mix of raw material for an improved quality product. Garment manufacturers can provide pattern and samplemaking facilities. The list is almost endless.

The benefit of horizontal integration is in the resulting synergies. Your profit comes not because your buyer pays more for his garment—in fact, on a full-value-cost basis the garment probably costs him less. You increase profits because you make extra money on every indirect-cost-saving facility you provide to your customer.

Each additional facility brings greater profit simply because it reduces the customer's costs. Note, however, that to be of value, the indirect-cost-saving facility must be at least to some degree special. No customer is going to pay you a premium because you have access to good quality hangtags or cartons. Even Louie the Lip will provide reasonable hangtags. If the service is widely available, it has little value to the customer.

Each additional indirect-cost facility also places your factory in a higher bracket. The more facilities offered, the fewer the competitors that can match you. The ability to provide better facilities, better product, smaller minimums and more professional work brings better customers and more profit.

But if you want to run a profitable factory that offers high-value facilities, the first area that needs restructuring is *you*.

Management

The vast majority of 0-service factories are owner-managed. Most are family businesses and management styles tend to be autocratic. Owner/managers typically operate under the motto: "This is my company. There is a right way, a wrong way and my way. Here we do things my way. If you don't like it, you can get out."

This attitude is why 0-service factories cannot attract competent managers. Why would an educated and experienced professional want to work in a company where policy is based on the boss's social, cultural and business prejudices and where the only way they will sit on the corporate board is on the lap of the boss's daughter?

If you recognize yourself and your factory here, consider the following: Your management style will be reflected in your factory floor. Nowhere is this truer than in the garment industry, and nowhere in the garment industry is this more certain than in a factory. A factory is a closed-door environment where people spend more time than in their own homes. In most countries, a worker will spend a minimum of ten hours a day, six days a week at the factory. You as the manager can create any environment you want. If your factory resembles a Third World prison, it is because you see your workers as prisoners who will not do a day's work unless forced to—and yourself as a warden placed there to ensure that every last worker gives an honest day's work for an honest day's pay—whatever that means.

If your factory is filled with pieces of brand-new, state-of-the-art equipment still resting in their original cases because no one in the company knows how to set them up, much less operate them, it is because you believe that machinery brings progress—whatever that means.

If your factory employs 10-year-old children to sew T-shirts, if your people work in squalor, if your supervisors maintain discipline by beating workers, and if you believe this is necessary to operate at a profit, it is because that is how you perceive your factory. Furthermore, if you run your factory based on these ideas, you are not just a poor manager, you are also crazy. Just as the executives at the importing and retailing companies who buy from you in the belief that these conditions are unfortunate but necessary if their company is to remain competitive are not only incompetent, but also certifiable.

Every time you walk into a factory and see strange things happening, you can be sure it is the result of strange management. The belief that management policy is universally based on the desire to increase profit is a myth. Some total lunatics are running around operating factories.

Case Study LV—Pakistan and the Air-Conditioned Factory

A factory in Karachi produces shirts. Management is worried that as their direct costs rise, they will not be able to hold on to their customers who are mass-market importers. They approach higher-quality buyers, but either cannot interest them in the factory product or lose the new customer after the first order. They hire Holden Schmata to advise them. The first problem Holden discovers is that the factory is filthy. This is understandable, since the factory is located in Karachi and Karachi is a filthy city. Holden suggests management seal the windows and air condition the entire factory.

Air conditioning, he explains, will not only improve cleanliness, but will solve many other problems as well, which in turn will greatly increase the overall efficiency and profitability of the company. In fact, a garment factory—particularly one located in a hot climate—must be air conditioned if it is to compete effectively. Without air conditioning, the limitations are so great that the factory can never advance from the most basic level of development. Consider the following proven facts:

- Worker productivity falls 20%-30% when temperature exceeds 30°C.

- When humidity rises above 90%, many operations cannot be carried out effectively.

- Many fabrics, including wool, silk and some synthetics, are hygroscopic or moisture-absorbing. For a factory producing coats, jackets, pants or skirts, fabric types change with each season, for example, cotton for spring, wool for fall. Without air conditioning, the factory simply cannot produce much of the required work.

"This will not work," states the factory owner. "The cost of air conditioners is too great for a poor factory like ours."

Holden explains that air conditioning is not expensive, especially if the only imported component you buy is the compressor with the rest, including the costly ducting, usually produced from local materials and labor.

"This will not work," states the factory owner. "Even at the lower cost, the factory could never recoup the outlay."

Holden explains that the increase in productivity alone will pay for the entire investment in the first year of operation. "How can you not make this investment—a 100% annual return on investment is too good to pass up."

"This will not work," states the factory owner. "Local workers are not used to air conditioning. They will all become sick."

Holden explains that the air conditioner has a thermostat. "You can control the temperature to operate at a moderate level."

"This will not work," states the factory owner. "You do not understand the character of the people in my country. Here air conditioning is for office people, for senior executives. If you give workers air-conditioned surroundings, they will say, 'Thank you very much' and then go on to demand more and more until I am driven out of business. Well, I will not be driven out of business and I will not give the workers air conditioning, even if I make twice the return."

Here is an educated factory owner, with an MBA, who has yet to emerge into the fifteenth century and who would rather go broke than improve working conditions. He is not alone. He has many colleagues in the developed world who share the same beliefs.

Sociologists would suggest this attitude is a classic case of *cultural determinism*. Management is no longer looking at what will lower costs and increase profits—they are looking at their own cultural ethos. I prefer the more blunt approach. In the admittedly narrow world of running a garment factory, anyone who suggests that a legitimate capital investment amortizable in one year should be turned down just because the workers might also benefit is crazy. That person has no more business running a factory than a man in a sanitarium wearing a tricorn hat has at being appointed chairman of the Joint Chiefs of Staff.

The failure of management to keep its attention directed to profit and loss is a fundamental problem of indirect-cost structure. The case of the air conditioner simply brings the existing problem to the surface. A factory cannot remain competitive unless management is willing to shift its ideas. If you are running a factory and you cannot bring yourself to change your outlook, your best strategy is to seek other employment before you bankrupt the entire operation.

Communication

After management, the most important facility is communication. The factory first enters the flow chart at Step 17—*Information collected sent to factory*. Step 18—*Customer information received*—is not just a one-step process; it is the most recurring process. This is the process by which factory staff communicates the customer's requirements to the other departments and also communicates any data sent from those departments to the customer. When working with 0-service factories, the customer takes this operation away from the factory and gives it to his local agent. In fact, it can be said that with a 0-service factory, the most important functions of the agent are to ensure that the customer's instructions reach the factory, that those instructions are understood by the factory, and that the factory can fulfill those instructions.

For a normal-service factory, communication becomes a three-part conversation, with the customer giving some instructions to the agent and some to the factory, albeit through the agent. The factory for its part communicates with the agent and with the customer, also through the agent. Finally, for a full-service factory, the agent's role becomes simply a conduit through which customer and factory communicate directly.

There are many problems associated with the customer's ability to communicate with the factory:

- There can be language difficulties. The factory staff may not understand what the customer is saying because their English is poor. This results in mistranslation;

- There can be technical difficulties. The factory staff may not understand what the customer is saying because their knowledge of garments is poor. This, too, results in mistranslation;

- There can be cultural difficulties. The factory staff may not understand what the customer is saying because their knowledge of the customer's company and country is poor. This results in the most serious mistranslation of all.

The same problems occur when the factory communicates back to the customer. If the factory cannot provide the required facilities, in the end the customer will rely on his agent. At least the agent understands English, understands garments and understands precisely what the customer wants.

Assuming the Agent's Role

As your factory develops its ability to communicate, not only do indirect costs fall because there is now greater understanding between you and your customer, but there is also a direct-cost advantage—you and your customer no longer need rely on the agent. When you operate a 0-service or even a normal-service factory, your customer has no choice. He must employ an agent who is necessary to provide the facilities you lack. However, the agent brings his own problems and difficulties.

One difficulty in using an agent is that the agent often has his own ax to grind. He makes his living because the customer cannot communicate with the factory directly. He has a vested interest in keeping the factory and the customer apart. The less the factory is able to communicate with the customer, the more important is the agent's role and the greater is his commission.

Another difficulty is that most agents really do not have the technical knowledge they profess to have. In fact, since the factory has to actually produce the goods, the factory usually has more technical knowledge than the agent. However, since the agent has the ear of the customer, the agent usually takes credit for success while pushing blame on the factory in the event of problems. When things go well and the customer receives the right merchandise on time, it is due to the agent's hard work. However, when problems occur, it is always the fault of the stupid factory. The factory can never win, because the factory cannot talk to the customer. The customer may not even know who the factory is. In the end, the customer must believe his agent, since he has no relationships apart from his agent.

Finally, even the best agents cause obstruction. Each time information is filtered through another party there is one more chance that delays and errors will occur. Imagine a party game where a group of children are seated in a row. The first child whispers something to the next child, who in turn whispers the message to the next. Eventually, the last child repeats the message aloud. The fun is hearing how the text has changed. Now imagine playing the same game, only this time halfway through the row the child shifts from English to Chinese. Also, instead of the message, "Joanie wears pink panties," the text is four pages of specifications and technical instructions. Frankly, the chances of all the information moving uncontaminated through the agent is exceedingly small.

If the factory is to develop, you must start dealing directly with the customer, which means limiting the role of the agent. This way the factory and the customer each have access to the other. There is better understanding and the possibility of error is reduced. The factory is able to give real input to the customer which may improve quality, reduce costs or allow for more trouble-free production.

Most importantly, by undertaking direct communication, the role of the agent becomes less important. Agents' commissions cease to be a direct cost and become indirect costs. The customer looks to pay the agent a lower commission because he needs the agent less. Since agents charge open or hidden commissions as high as 30%-100% of FOB, there is real savings to be gained here. Ultimately, the customer saves money and can afford to pay the factory more.

The greatest problem facing a factory wishing to work directly with the customer is finding or training suitable staff. You would need a person who has the following qualifications:

• Fluent and colloquial English, or whatever is the language of the customer. Good English is not enough. You are trying to convince the customer that you can deal direct. His impression is based on what he hears and, if what he hears has poor syntax or grammar or a heavy accent, he will unconsciously assume he is dealing with amateurs and still needs his agent to communicate;

- Strong technical knowledge. The person communicating must know garments. That person should be a trained patternmaker, preferably someone with sample room background;

- Knowledge of the customer's country and company;

- Native to the country where the factory is located.

Unfortunately, the ideal merchandiser simply does not exist. Most often, a candidate will have good communication skills but will lack technical knowledge and experience. Successful full-service factories solve this problem by splitting the job function in two—an outside person who talks to the customer, and one or more insiders who talk to the factory. Customers often have no inkling of how their orders are really handled.

In a typical scenario, the *outsider* is a young woman in her late twenties or early thirties, usually upper-class, who might well have been educated overseas and wants to become part of the fashion industry. She is attractive, well-dressed, and, ideally, reasonably well-traveled. She looks and talks the part. To most Western customers, she looks very good. The only thing she lacks is anything to say.

The words are actually supplied by the *insider*, who is one of the most technically qualified persons in the entire operation. The insider must understand written English reasonably well, but more importantly, must understand all aspects of garment production. In many full-service factories, the *insider* doubles as the head of the sample department. She is the one who looks at the garments and does the real work. In large factories, the insider is actually head of a coordinating department where the costings and schedules are worked out. Sample orders and production orders are typed here.

Described simply, a customer's faxes come first to the outsider who sends them directly to the insider, who translates them and passes the customer's instructions to the relevant factory department Replies to customers' queries or factory requests for information originate only from the insider, who in turn passes them to the outsider who then sends out the faxes under her own name. In a well-run, full-service factory, no customer ever visits the coordination department and no one ever sees the *insider*. The customer believes that the *outsider* is one of the smartest young women he has ever met, and in many cases actually offers her a job in the belief that he has discovered the one person in the entire country with real knowledge of the industry.

Worker Training

The use of in-house training to increase workers' skills is one of the most important indirect-cost facilities open to any factory. Worker training begins with the recognition that your workers are not simple tools, but rather capital assets worthy of additional investment and that the return on this investment is very high indeed. Managers of full-service factories recognize that one of the best ways to keep direct costs down is to increase their workers' skills.

The greatest disincentive to worker training is management's attitude that they are inevitably training operators for their competitors. "Every time I train a worker, another factory steals them by offering more money. For once, let my competitors do the training and let me do the stealing."

In fact, these complaints are well founded. But what other scenario would you expect? We're talking about people, not machines, however you treat them. Once the worker has developed skills from whatever source, their value rises, and they are aware that they are now worth more. If you want to keep a skilled worker, you have to pay the going wage. If it is of any consolation, you are in the same position having invested $300 to train your factory worker as a New York banker who spends $80,000 to send his worker back to university for an MBA. If you don't pay the going wage, you will both lose your investment.

Case Study LVI—The Major American Bank

Large U.S. companies often sponsor their employees to pursue advanced degree study, particularly in business. In theory, this policy makes considerable sense. MBA candidates perform better academically if they have several years of practical experience before entering an MBA program. Companies realize they need middle management with both specific knowledge of their industry and academic qualifications. Both requirements can be met more efficiently if the best of their employees are sent for further study. The costs are quite high—about $80,000 per employee. However, amortized over ten or more years, the time during which the employee is expected to continue with the company after graduation, the advantages far outweigh the costs.

A large New York-based bank has such a program. Departments are asked to recommend qualified individuals. Candidates go through a selection process with those chosen sent to the leading business schools. Two years later, they rejoin their company and, with alarming frequency, quit after another year to go work somewhere else.

You may ask, "What sort of ungrateful wretch takes an $80,000 education from his boss and a year later whistles goodbye?"

You can also ask, "What sort of simple-minded manager allows this to happen?"

The problem is one of placement. Before going back for an MBA, the young executive would have earned $45,000-$55,000 a year. Salaries for MBA graduates from first-class universities start at $100,000 a year. There is no chance the person would want to return to their old job. However, given that employment in large companies is frequently carried out at the department level, the department head who first recommended the executive might not have an open position at the appropriate level. Therefore, in a very real sense, the new MBA is often forced to look for a new job after graduation. Naturally, he or she will first look in the company which sent them back to school. However, if they cannot find a suitable job in-house, they will look elsewhere. Let's face it—loyalty means a lot, but it does not stand up to a 40% cut in pay.

We may laugh at the Chinese state company which takes a recent Harvard Ph.D. graduate and sticks him in a bookkeeping department with an abacus. However, at least the state company found their Ph.D. a job. How much sillier is the Wall Street bank which tells their graduate returning with a newly acquired Columbia MBA, "Sorry, we have no place for you. Why not try our competitor?"

Professional Staff

While increasing basic worker skills is vital to an evolving factory, the real margins in productivity and profit gains come from trained technical and managerial staff. In the United States, a trained patternmaker is paid at least $75,000, while a sewer in Hong Kong is paid $10,200—less than 15%. A Hong Kong patternmaker earns roughly $20,000. Thus the annual product cost savings for employing one Hong Kong patternmaker—a minimum of $55,000—is worth five Hong Kong sewers. In every country in Asia, with the exception of Japan, the development of a skilled professional is worth many times more than any conceivable savings from a semi-skilled worker's wages. The less developed the country, the greater the advantage in training skilled professionals.

For Third World countries such as Vietnam, Burma and Bangladesh, the potential savings derived from training professionals is so great that the rate of wages paid to semiskilled workers becomes irrelevant to garment costings. A factory of nearly 400 workers in Bangladesh could raise wages by 50% for all its workers and still spend less than the product savings represented by employing one local patternmaker.[17]

Similar calculations hold true for merchandisers, designers, quality assurance specialists, traffic managers, and all of the other high-priced professionals with which importers must now provide themselves. By meeting their efforts and training factory managers, finance, costing and other specialists, you, the factory owner, will derive greater cost-effectiveness than by increasing basic worker efficiency.

In the final analysis, you cannot make the transition from 0-service factory to full-service factory without training to provide both skilled workers and qualified technical and management staff. The better customer simply cannot work with a factory that lacks either. Real productivity comes from working with the better customer, not producing more garments for the mass-market importer.

Working Conditions

Working conditions are the one area of indirect costs ultimately under the control of the factories and mills. Ensuring that factory conditions are acceptable to customers is the responsibility of the producing companies themselves.

It is commonly believed that the pressure to improve working conditions originates from Western governments—a form of disguised protectionism. This misconception is extremely dangerous to both factories and government ministries who uphold it. What is true is that some Western governments, including that of the United States, are trying to politicize problems of working conditions in Third World countries, no doubt driven by labor unions and other protectionist groups in their home countries. Attempts to bring the issue of working conditions before the WTO are certainly politically motivated.

If only governments were involved, the debate would not be serious. Governments may talk a great deal about morality but seldom, if ever, will actually use it to create policy. For you, while the politicians and various interest groups haggle, the immediate problem boils down to dollars and cents. Stated plainly, poor working conditions will raise your indirect costs to a level where no reasonable customer can afford to place orders in your factory.

Child Labor, Sanitary Conditions, Women's Rights

More and more U.S. consumers do not want to buy garments produced by children. They do not want to buy garments made in factories where people are forced to work in substandard conditions without proper lighting, ventilation or sanitary facilities.

This concern has been taken up by importers and retailers who, having invested tens and sometimes hundreds of millions of dollars to build a label's reputation, do not want to see that investment lost because some factory in Asia does not want to invest a few hundred dollars to install a toilet.

The problem is serious and will become more serious in the near future. Don't make the mistake of thinking that the problem will disappear, that in the end, American and European consumers won't be willing pay more in order to buy garments produced in satisfactory working conditions. That is simple self-delusion. The consumer will not need to pay more because actually, no added costs need be involved. It is just as easy to buy a T-shirt produced in reasonable conditions as one produced in poor conditions. Everybody in the world is currently producing T-shirts, jeans and other basic garments. Child labor, poor lighting and filth are not cost-effective for factory owners. They are simply the physical evidence of second-rate management.

On a practical level, buyer demands for better working conditions can be classified into three general groups:

1. Areas of particular importance for which real solutions must be found, including child labor, poor treatment of women in the workplace, unsanitary conditions and employment of prison labor. These are core complaints. Factories must meet real standards in these areas if they are to work with good customers.

2. Areas of importance where there are no clear-cut guidelines, including overtime work and minimum wages. Low wages and long hours are clearly areas of concern to consumers in the industrialized countries. Their perception of overseas garment factories are tinged by the memory of the sweatshops that were endemic to their own countries at the beginning of the twentieth century and which still exist in parts of the United States. The problem is to clearly define and create procedures to ensure improvements are carried out. A 60-hour week is unheard of in Europe and the United States where workers average 35-40 hours. Yet for most developing countries, ten-hour days and six-day weeks are the norm, often not considered overtime. To the American consumer, wages of $0.26 an hour are appalling. In Indonesia, $0.26 an hour is well above average. Nike has been attacked by consumer groups who accused the company of paying workers in Vietnam $1.84 per day. It was claimed that workers were losing weight because they were unable to buy sufficient food at the present wage rate. This is nonsense—$1.84 per day might be an appalling wage in Milwaukee but in Ho Chi Minh City, where wages average $1.00 per day, it is an excellent wage indeed. In these gray areas, legitimate factories and their customers must cooperate to create reasonable minimum standards and enforce them. If possible, the standards should be publicized.

3. Areas of minimal importance but which have the active support of politicians and vested interest groups in the industrialized West, most notably the right to form labor unions. Labor unions and the right of Asian workers to organize for collective bargaining are completely political issues. There is no question that the United States and the EU, pushed by unions in their home countries, would like to incorporate the right of workers to organize into the WTO agreements. However, unlike other problems discussed above, importers are not under any consumer pressure to request change. Labor unions no longer enjoy the same popular support among consumers in the industrialized West as in the past. Consumers are more concerned about child labor and equal opportunity for women, which they consider to be more serious problems.

Pollution

Pollution issues fall soundly in the political arena, particularly with regard to exports to Germany and other countries in Western Europe, where single-issue pro-environment Green parties enjoy broad support.

As a result of their efforts, there is an increasingly long list of chemicals, notably dyestuff, which can no longer be used in textile and garment production. Factories and mills are required to ensure that chemicals on the banned list have not been used, and tests must be carried out to verify that products do not contain these materials.

Since these inspection procedures must be carried out by the factory, they constitute a serious indirect cost. Any merchandise arriving in Europe which is found to contain banned substances will not be permitted entry; factories and mills would be held accountable for the resulting loss.

It is unfortunately true that, at least to some degree, protectionist forces in Europe are using ecological concerns as a tool to restrict imports. Regretfully, there is little that you can do.

Human Rights

Of all the issues affecting factories, this is the most difficult, simply because as a factory manager you have no control over human rights in your country. The matter is one concerning government policy and, therefore, a macro-cost factor. Unfortunately, whether or not you control them, human rights violations in your country almost inevitably affect your business. There are two steps that you can take now to improve your situation:

- Work with your government to bring about improvements in human rights. It is not necessary for you to put on a red bandanna and go to the hills to join your local branch of the People's Revolution. Most improvements in human rights are brought about by those working within the system. A poor human rights record is bad for business. At the same time, you might let it be known that you are one of the good guys. If carried out judiciously, a little public relations will cause you no harm with your government and might pay dividends in the future. It will certainly go down well with your customers.

- Ensure that disputes involving your company do not escalate into confrontation between poor, exploited workers and police and army personnel armed with Russian Kalashnikovs—or worse—American M-16 rifles.

Case Study LVII—The Medan Riots

In April 1994, tens of thousands of garment workers rioted in Medan, Indonesia.

Some Western experts stated authoritatively that the riots were the result of striking workers and outsiders from the Indonesian Workers Welfare Union trying to unionize local factories. Other specialists put the cause as planned demonstrations for higher wages. Workers in Medan were looking to obtain parity with garmentworkers elsewhere in Indonesia. They were striking to receive the minimum wage of $1.47 per day.

There is no question that the IWWU, which is not a recognized union, was present during the events that followed; its leader Pak Pahan was arrested in Medan. There is also no doubt that workers in Medan were not being paid minimum wage.

In fact, the strike and ensuing riots were caused by a Moslem holiday. Indonesia being a Moslem country, Moslem holidays are normally paid holidays. The factory owners, being Chinese, felt that since that particular day was not an official holiday, paid leave was not required. The factory owners did not pay and the workers went on strike.

The strikes turned to riots. Two Chinese factory owners were lynched and a Chinese woman allegedly raped. The army came in to mediate. Shots were fired—although the government was later unable to determine who fired the first shot. The strike was broken and the workers were forced back to their machines. The government then told the Medan factory owners to give their workers holiday pay and ordered that, in future, the holiday was to be a paid holiday.

The Medan riots illustrate a classic lose-lose situation. In retrospect, if the Medan factory owners had been trying to work out the most counterproductive policy possible and had employed outside specialists to advise them, chances are they could not have found a more effective policy. In one fell swoop, they managed to turn a demonstration for holiday pay into an ethnic riot. In the process, they alienated their workers, their own government and their customers—and still had to pay the holiday bonus in the end.

The Indonesian government's reaction wasn't much better. They, too, trapped themselves in the lose-lose situation. For a few days, Indonesia was once again presented to the world as a place where workers are routinely shot down by the military. Cancelled out by the dramatic pictures of bleeding workers was the fact that the Indonesian government did, in the end, ensure that worker bonuses were paid and wages increased in accordance with the law.

Too often factories treat human rights the same way they treat problems of pollution. They plead either that the problem is so pervasive that there is nothing they can do or, worse, argue that they can do whatever they want because anyway the acid rain will fall on someone else's head. Neither is true. What is true is that you as a factory owner are an important and valued part of your society. The results of a poor human rights record will be higher macro costs for those working in your country, eventually leading to a loss of customers. It is not necessary for you to martyr yourself for the cause of human rights. Nor do you have to resort to acts of violence. But you can work within the system and achieve positive results.

In the final analysis, in all areas involving working conditions and human rights, the goal of the factory is to reduce costs. Pollution and working conditions raise indirect costs just as human rights violations

...Do not fall into the trap of empty pollution guidelines compliance!...

raise macro costs. To keep these costs low, you must work together with your customer in an honest fashion. Furthermore, you must ensure that presented guidelines can and will be implemented. There will be pressure on factories to accept guidelines that everyone knows will never be enforced. The agent gives you a pretty piece of paper which you sign. He marks you down in his book as one of the good guys, winks, and walks away. You tear up the paper or give it to your daughter to play with. And nothing is done. Don't fall into that trap. These problems are real and will not go away simply because you sign a piece of paper.

DIRECT COSTS

In general, 0-service factories must rely on low direct costs to remain competitive, while normal-service and full-service factories can take advantage of the indirect-cost savings they can offer their customers. But whatever your service level, direct costs are important to all factories. If you had the greatest full-service factory in the world, offering your customers every indirect-cost saving imaginable, they would still push for lower direct costs. Fortunately, as your factory develops better facilities, opportunities arise to reduce direct costs in almost every area—material costs, labor costs, overheads and agents' commission.

Material Costs

Louie the Lip may spend six hours in his 0-service factory adjusting a marker to save three inches on a dozen garments. Modern factories (as well as their customers) all have computerized marking facilities that will work out a better yield in less than an hour. The days when the factory could *steal* a quarter-of-a-yard by taking smaller seam allowances are long gone. Today's customers are too professional, too experienced, and just too smart.

For the full-service factory, saving money on material comes from ensuring that every inch of fabric is cut. This is not an easy task. First of all, better customers, who use costly materials, will order several styles in the same fabric. From the moment the customer sends his initial breakdown, he is changing assortments every day (see Case Study XX—Merchandising to the Last Drop). He wants fewer sizes 4, 6, and 8 and more 12, 14 and 16. The fabric has arrived in the factory and your customer is still asking to drop navy color in Jacket Style 1 but to add more orange in Jacket Style 2. The fabric is physically on the cutting table and your customer now wants to add back sizes 4 and 6. Each change in assortment changes the material requirements—not just for fabric but for all items from buttons and zippers to labels and polybags. If you want to stay in business, you must make sure that your customer uses up every inch of fabric and pays for every zipper and button. If he wants fewer orange jackets in Style 1, that's fine. Just make sure that he gives you a new assortment for orange in another style. Make sure he pays for those orange buttons that can no longer be used for Style 1. Flexibility and the ability for your customer to constantly change his assortments is one of the most important indirect-cost-saving facilities you can offer—as long as you hold your customer responsible.

A second problem results from damaged garments. A 0-service factory dealing with a low-end customer will first try to ship the buyer any damaged garments. Later, when he is caught, he will hang the damages in stock. The 0-service factory lacks the facilities to repair damages and, in any case, the low cost of each individual garment makes the exercise pointless. But a full-service factory cannot ship damages to his customer unless a prior arrangement has been made; neither can he afford to hang expensive garments in stock.

The full-service factory must have the facilities to repair garments. Damaged panels must be removed and replaced with recut panels. This work is costly and time-consuming. Fabric must be set aside before cutting and saved for recut panels. A cutter is necessary to cut the panels and a sewer to take out the damaged sections and replace them with the new panels. In order to save these damaged garments, the factory must have its own in-house tailor shop.

A third problem revolves around the conflicting pressures on the cutting department itself. You, the factory owner, look to the cutting department to minimize fabric loss. You want to recut damaged panels and later cut all remaining fabric into additional stock garments. However, the rest of the factory looks at the cutting department as the vehicle which supplies the sewing machines with an uninterrupted stream of work. Every day the cutting department must produce a minimum of cut garments if the machines are to have work. Your goals, unfortunately, come into conflict with the needs of the rest of the factory. When that occurs, all attempts to maximize material usage is thrown out of the window in order to satisfy the needs of the sewing floor.

In small factories, these conflicting goals are never reconciled. As a result, a 50-machine factory inevitably wastes fabric. Larger factories and particularly factory groups are structured specifically to solve this problem by centralizing all cutting in an area apart from the sewing sections. Centralized cutting enables the factory to organize cutting priorities so that all sewing departments have constant work, while additional and separate facilities are simultaneously responsible for maximizing fabric usage.

Labor Costs

0-service factories keep labor costs down by not paying their workers, or at least paying them as little as possible. If the workers complain, they are fired. If the workers complain further, there is always the army. Whatever happens, there is no loss to the factory. In a 0-service factory, workers are at best semi-skilled. They can easily be discarded and just as easily replaced.

The 0-service factory operates in straight assembly-line mode. Workers are trained to become a simple tool, performing a single step over and over again. The factory buys an entire worker, but throws away 95%, retaining only that part which operates the screwdriver. Because the rest of the worker is never utilized, the 0-service factory is inflexible. Any difficulty results in substantial loss of productivity. Some common examples of difficulties include:

- Any complex operation that cannot be broken down into a series of simple steps;

- Small orders, where the work runs out before the section comes up to speed;

- Any last-minute changes by the customer;

- Late arrival of material or trim.

Unfortunately, such problems are the very nature of the garment business—the better the customer, the more problems he will bring. In fact, the core of what makes the customer a better customer is that he is paying the factory more money so that the factory can deal with these problems.

The full-service factory also divides work into sections. However, here the garment is not broken down to simple, one-operation steps. Workers must be sufficiently skilled to perform multiple tasks. Where a worker in a 0-service factory sits robotically performing a single operation, the full-service factory worker looks beyond her own operation, for example, taking note of and compensating for errors made in a previous operation. Because the worker has these skills, production can make use of techniques not available to the 0-service factory. An operator capable of working in a full-service factory is a capital asset. Worker training is a capital investment, and the return on that investment is very high indeed.

You cannot operate a quality factory with semi-skilled workers. 0-service factories are simply incapable of working with better customers. However, workers skilled in multiple-tasking permit you to solve the problems presented by better clients. The skilled worker may be paid more but he certainly provides a greater margin of profit.

Overheads

The most difficult of all direct-cost calculations is overhead. Most factory managers know what they pay for rent, electricity, salaries, interest and other finance expenses. They can add these together and arrive at a total overhead figure. The problem occurs when they try to allocate their overhead expenses on a per-unit basis. Most simply divide their total overhead into the total units produced, allocating the same overhead for every customer, every style and every unit. This blind practice is precisely why clients like Herbie the Mouth and Cousin Phil continue to make a living.

Overhead is a measure of how long it takes a garment to pass through the factory. The more time required for the manufacturing process, the greater the overhead. For normal-service and full-service factories, this manufacturing time must include preproduction as well as production stages.

Three factors affect overhead:

- The style: A factory produces twelve skirts per day per machine, but only six jackets. The overhead for a jacket, therefore, equals twice the overhead for a skirt. More complicated styles require more overhead than simpler styles.

- The size of the order: The time required for preproduction is the same, regardless of the size of the order. Patterns must be made, corrected and graded. Duplicates must be produced and approved by the customer. Fabric and trim must be ordered. Whether the order is for 1,000 dozen or 100 units, the same work must be carried out and the same total overhead must be spent. As a result, the preproduction overhead-per-unit for an order of 100 pieces is actually 120 times the per-unit cost for an order of 1,000 dozen. Furthermore, the order size also affects the overhead calculation for the production phase. The larger the order, the more time the sewers spend overall producing that order and the better their speed and efficiency. As a result, the last garment batch is produced much faster and with fewer errors than the first. The overhead-per-unit falls even further.

- Quality of customer: It costs more to produce a garment for Herbie the Mouth than for Talbots, because Herbie the Mouth inevitably causes trouble. Talbots' only demand is for a decent garment shipped on time. Any trouble arising from a Talbots' order is more than likely the factory's fault. But Herbie the Mouth decided the size of his claim even before he placed his order. Herbie the Mouth and Talbots each have a rating for how difficult a customer they are. That rating must be included in your overhead calculation.

Intelligent factory managers periodically review their overhead allocation practices. Customers with increasing quantities per style are given an overhead reduction while those with falling quantities are asked to pay more. Similarly, those customers who are easier to work with are given an overhead break while those who cause trouble are obliged to pay more. In this way, cooperative customers providing profitable orders are rewarded and encouraged for their behavior while the not-so-good customers are penalized.

Agent's Commission

If a customer wants to work with Louie the Lip, his agent literally has to take up permanent residence in the factory. For this, the agent charges a commission. The more difficult the factory, the higher the agent's costs and the greater the agent's commission.

If the customer moves up to a normal-service factory, his agent is required to do less work. He has lower costs and is theoretically entitled to a lower commission. At the very top, a customer who works with a full-service factory may find that an agent actually hinders smooth communications and workflow. In this case, the customer would do well to forgo using an agent completely and to avoid paying any commission at all.

The better the customer, the more he requires factories that can provide indirect-cost-saving facilities and the less he needs an agent. Most customers pay their agent a minimum of 10% commission. This adds up to a considerable sum of money. If you run a factory that is sufficiently reliable with quality standards and levels equal to or above your customer's requirements, he can save 10% on every order he places with you. This is a major direct-cost savings.

Conclusions

To survive in the coming period, you must create service facilities in your factory that make working with you attractive. Without these facilities, you will be relegated to working only with mass-market retailers and importers who will stay with you only until someone else down the block or in the next county, country or continent offers them a price savings of five cents per unit or even per dozen.

By adding facilities, you can trade up to a better quality customer and thereby survive. But, as we have already warned, creating a normal-service factory, let alone a full-service one, from a 0-service factory is not an easy task. You will have to change every aspect of your operation, starting with yourself. The sole justification for making these changes is the certain knowledge that without them you will simply not survive.

These added facilities will also permit you to map out new strategies for adding profit to your existing operation. In the next chapter, we will outline some workable strategies.

Chapter 10
Producing at the Lowest Cost: Factory Strategies

When circumstances turn against you, a strategy of 'more of the same' works only if your goal is to make room for new companies.

Holden Schmata

All strategies begin at the same point. To make a profit from any service or facility, you must first have a customer for that service or facility. Each new facility adds a new department; each new department adds overhead costs. For a particular facility to make sense, it must add greater value than cost. Part of this value comes from the fact that better customers require these facilities, without which you cannot attract these better customers to your factory in the first place. The better customer is the source of real increases in productivity—the value of output less input for the goods you are selling. In fact, however, the real value comes from the added profit these facilities bring. The better customer will pay a premium for these facilities. In some cases, the premium can double the factory's net profit on the order.

The advantage of horizontal integration can be put this way:

New Facilities = New Services = New Profit

Your first step as you take on this strategy is to find a new type of customer.

STRATEGIC RELATIONSHIPS

To make the transition from a 0-service factory to full-service factory requires not only considerable financial investment, but also access to trained professionals. Both are vital if the factory is to make a successful transition.

You want to guarantee that the facilities you are creating, the staff and workers you are training, and the machinery you are purchasing will be translated into better orders and more profit. Preferably, you would like to know in advance just who will provide those orders. At the same time, since the facilities required for indirect-costs reduction are for the most part technical, you must ask yourself: Where is this technology to come from? Who is going to teach my staff, upgrade worker skills, and provide the systems fundamental to operating a modern full-service factory?

The traditional buyer/seller relationship where the customer might place orders if your most recent price quotations look good is not a prudent basis for the investment you have to make. The traditional buyer will not assist in providing the technology you require. He has no interest in doing so.

You need an edge. That edge is a *strategic relationship*. In today's competitive environment, both buyers and sellers face similar problems. You need a reliable customer who can supply you with steady business on a long-term basis. You need a customer who will work with you to develop your factory. Luckily for you, the customer is in the same situation. He has to find reliable factories that will form a part of his sourcing chain, to take his orders on a continuous basis every season and produce his goods to his standard. The right customer seeks to train the factory to his standards because otherwise he will never get his product.

So parallel are the aims of both parties that if you have chosen the correct company for a strategic relationship, your counterpart will act almost as a partner. The best of these companies will go to great lengths to encourage and assist you and your factory to develop the in-depth facilities and skills required to make the leap to a full-service factory.

The right buyer/partner will not only assist you in upgrading management and technical skills, but basic worker skills as well. It is in their interests as well to introduce modern production systems and techniques and to expand the facilities available at your factory so that you can provide a more competitive product to a better customer.

A strategic relationship is like a marriage. If successful, it brings joy and happiness. If it fails, the alimony can kill you. Before considering any strategic relationship, you must decide: Whom do I want as a partner? There are two important factors to consider:

- Reliability

- Ability

Of these, *reliability* is the more important. All partnerships are based on mutual profit and mutual trust. When the partners are located thousands of miles apart, trust becomes paramount to the success of the operation and, unfortunately, more difficult to maintain. Each side must have confidence that the other is performing as agreed and that mutual profit is truly mutual and has been divided fairly.

The greatest care must be taken to ensure that a prospective strategic partner is reliable. Regretfully, many of the largest importers are unsuitable for strategic relationships because they are also unsuitable for *any* long-term relationship. The best illustration of this type of partner is the Taiwanese joint venture, so-named because most Taiwanese joint ventures are structured this way.

Case Study LVIII—The Taiwanese Joint Venture

A Taiwanese company sets up a factory together with a local organization. The basis of the joint venture is that the Taiwanese side will supply technical assistance and a part of the machinery together

196

with all the orders. The local side supplies the plant, most of the machinery and the workers.

The Taiwanese company solicits orders from its customers and places them with the joint-venture factory. However, before passing the order, the Taiwanese partner first takes out a healthy sales commission. Furthermore, since the factory works on a CM basis only, the Taiwanese partner also takes out the cost of all fabric and trim, together with a further purchasing commission. There is also a commission to cover the cost of administration and finance. In fact, for every task carried out by the Taiwanese partner, there will be a commission charge, even sometimes where no tasks have been carried out at all.

In the end, there is little left over to cover manufacturing costs, let alone allow the factory to show a profit. Since their share of profits has been taken even before the letter of credit is opened to the joint-venture factory, the Taiwanese investors have little interest in a share of factory profits or even if the factory has any profits to share. Should the factory complain, the Taiwanese company will argue that rising macro costs have made the joint venture less profitable than first projected. As the overseas investor has no real interest in any type of equity participation, this type of joint venture is tailor-made for countries where foreign ownership is restricted.

In a viable strategic relationship investment, equity and product control must be balanced, both in relation to the ratio of investment contribution as well as in terms of the responsibilities and risks incurred by both parties. Strategic relationships in which the foreign side does all the work and shoulders all the risk, while the role of the local partner is limited to navigating the company through the muddy waters of the local 'government system', are equally shortsighted. Only those foreign companies that can envision substantial enough profits will participate, and they will normally demand special relationships with special guarantees. Companies which must rely on the more normal forms of profit will go elsewhere to countries with lower macro costs.

Frequently, a prospective partner will have already established similar strategic relationships elsewhere. You would be well advised to investigate these other relationships. Companies with strategic relationships that have existed for many years generally play by the rules and make reasonable partners. Conversely, companies with a history of repeated short-term relationships generally do not make good partners, even though the reasons for each breakdown may appear to be plausible.

Clearly, each side must also have the *ability* to fulfill his role in the partnership. For the buying side, this includes not only the ability to place sufficient orders to make the project feasible. The proposed partner must also be capable of providing the assists required for the producing side to develop the facilities needed to join the sourcing chain. This is not a simple requirement. Very often the partner himself does not have the technical skills required.

The producing side must also have the ability to fulfill its role. It is easy to talk about developing facilities and finding or training qualified personnel. However, in Third World countries, upgrading facilities is no mean feat. In most places, trained technicians do not exist nor do the means of training them. In fact, where standards are low, they remain low because few see the need to raise them, and even fewer are willing to pay the price required to do so.

When looking to build a strategic relationship, the first decision must be to select the type of company required. Your partner need not be the actual importer. A qualified partner can be found in any part of the industry, for example:

- Trading company or agent;

- Buyer, such as an importer or retailer;

- Producer, such as a factory or mill.

There are advantages and disadvantages with each. The trading company will have access to many buyers, but may try to keep them hidden from you. The importer or retailer will offer a more open relationship, but will only represent a single buyer. Furthermore, neither the trading company nor the importer may have the expertise required to train your staff and upgrade your facilities. On the other hand, a strategic relationship with a factory will provide both access to many buyers as well as technical expertise. However, since both partners would then be producers, conflict of interest issues might arise.

More important than the type of company is the company itself. In the end, before entering into any long-term strategic relationship, you must ask yourself three questions:

- Are these people reliable?

- Do they have the ability to deliver what they have promised?

- Can I live with them for a long period of time?

Only a company for which you can give an unqualified *YES* to all three questions is the right partner for you.

Successful strategic relationships are based on an implicit understanding that both sides are interdependent and that the profit derived by one side must be matched by equal profit for the other. This premise leads to the next step in your strategic relationship efforts, how to lower costs with mutual benefits for both you and your buyer.

INDIRECT-COST STRATEGIES

Most potential strategies involve facilities aimed at lowering indirect costs. The factory tries to provide a service that the customer requires and is now buying elsewhere at a higher price. In the garment manufacturing process, horizontal integration can occur anywhere in the flow chart, from design (Steps 1-10) to the end of preproduction (Step 86). Let's look at design first.

Design

Manufacturing begins with design. Few factories are equipped to offer their own collection or produce a collection on demand for a customer. The costs to the factory would be too high and the results probably unacceptable to the customer. However, if the factory can make a more modest investment, important savings can be gained.

Consider the advent of private-label merchandise. For the past twenty years, in an effort to lower costs, retailers have been reducing their purchases of labeled garments in favor of private label. There is a substantial difference between buying apparel from Schmidlap Importers with the Schmidlap label and buying directly from the factory with a private-store label. In order to buy directly, the store had to design their own styles, produce their own patterns and probably make their own sample collections. This costs money. In the end, Schmidlap and their fellow importers came to their store customers with a deal. Schmidlap would produce a private-label collection for the store. The store would place their order for production. Schmidlap would take care of the overseas production and ship the entire order directly to the store. The store would pay Schmidlap by letter of credit.

Eventually, instead of designing a collection, Schmidlap would design a group of ranges. In some cases, the store would look at the garments in each range, decide which ranges they liked, and Schmidlap designers would modify or add styles to the range to suit the store buyer. In other cases, the buyer would bring her own style (purchased in Europe) and ask Schmidlap to make that for the store. In every case, any styles sold were exclusive to the buyer.

Schmidlap would have a guaranteed sale with a letter of credit. Their store customer had exclusive merchandise at a very reduced price. The price differences were considerable. This is private-label business.

Case Study LIX—Schmidlap's Private Label

Because overseas suppliers had no design facilities and little suitable patternmaking facilities, private-label business became the exclusive property of Schmidlap and their colleagues, while the factory position remained unchanged.

The costing of private label is particularly important to understand. The initial costs are always identical.

EXPENSE	Schmidlap with Schmidlap Label	Schmidlap Private Label	Store Direct with Overseas Label
FOB	$10.00	$10.00	$10.00
Duty (20%)	$ 2.00	$ 2.00	$ 2.00
Freight	$ 1.00	$ 1.00	$ 1.00
Clearance	$ 0.25	$ 0.25	$ 0.25
Agent Comm. (10%)	$ 1.00	$ 1.00	$ 1.00
LDP	$14.25	$14.25	$14.25

The markup (the percentage of selling price that is profit) is what changes: Schmidlap with their own label will want a 50% markup—that is, 50% of Schmidlap's price as profit. For private label, they will work on a 25% markup. Naturally, if the store could work directly with the overseas factory, they would pay no markup at all.

SCHMIDLAP PROFIT	SCHMIDLAP LABEL	SCHMIDLAP PRIVATE LABEL	STORE DIRECT
Profit	$14.25	$ 4.75	$ 0.00
Markup pct	50%	25%	0%
Wholesale price	$28.50	$19.00	$14.25

For the stores, the differences are critical—not only for their profit margins, but in their ability to provide customers with merchandise at competitive prices.

STORE POSITION	SCHMIDLAP LABEL	SCHMIDLAP PRIVATE LABEL	STORE DIRECT
Retail price	$57.00	$42.75	$42.75
Store profit	$28.50	$28.50	$28.50
Store markup pct	50%	56%	67%

By changing to private label, the store still has the benefit of Schmidlap's expertise, but at a much lower cost. Their markup rises 6% while, at the same time, they provide their customers with a 25% reduction in retail price.

Everyone benefited from private label. U.S. private-label specialists have prospered and grown. However, it is now time to ask: Just how important is Schmidlap to the process? How much of this process could be taken over by the overseas maker? What would be the added costs? Schmidlap provides some design work and some patternmaking. In return, they earn 25% of the wholesale price after allowing for overseas agent's commission. Couldn't the store and the maker, working together, do away with Schmidlap altogether?

200

In our example, the maker's FOB price is $10.00. A normal maker—if very successful—could hope to earn 5% net profit, or $0.50 per item. Schmidlap is paid $4.75 for their effort.

Consider this—instead of $10.00, the maker is paid $11.00, an increase of 10%, which effectively triples their $0.50 profit. In return, the maker must provide good patternmaking as well as someone capable of taking samples provided by the store and modifying them to suit the buyers' demands. This is not true design work, which may be far beyond the capability of most factories. Rather it is 'styling', which is not that difficult—and often all that Schmidlap does anyway. Such a service represents real indirect-cost savings to the customer. He pays an additional $1.00 per item in direct costs, plus $0.18 in duty—a total of $1.18. In return, the customer saves $4.75 in indirect costs—an amount equal to 47.5% of the FOB price.

Above the mutual added profit for both factory and retailer, there is a further advantage here—enhanced direct relationships. As long as the maker works through Schmidlap, the retailer and the actual supplier have no real relationship. When orders are shipped on time and with good quality, Schmidlap is responsible. When goods are late or quality problems appear, the maker is responsible. It is always in Schmidlap's interest to magnify problems and denigrate the maker's abilities, for the more difficult it appears to be to work with the factory, the more important becomes Schmidlap's role.

From the maker's point of view, there is nothing to be gained by establishing a long-term relationship with Schmidlap. In fact, with Schmidlap there are no long-term relationships. If problems occur, Schmidlap will drop the maker just to show the maker is to blame. Even when the orders go well, Schmidlap will drop the maker if they find another who will work for ten cents less per dozen.

Meanwhile, the goals of the store buyers are different. They are generally looking for problem-free, long-term relationships. When problems appear, they want suppliers who will take responsibility. For the maker working directly with the store, it pays to act responsibly. As long as the store is in business the following season, it will continue to buy if the maker does his part. As far as Schmidlap is concerned, the maker should have no idea at all about the business status of the final retail store customer.

From Step 1 to final Step 101, opportunities exist for the factory to create new facilities which will provide new services and new sources of profit. In fact, opportunities exist even after Step 101, past the entire manufacturing process.

The manufacturing process ends when the completed order has been loaded on a ship or placed in the forwarder's warehouse at the airport, ready to be shipped to the customer's home country. At that point, the factory's work is completed. The customer, however, must then carry out additional steps. If the goods have been shipped by air, it is the responsibility of the customer to ensure that the garments are, in fact, loaded aboard an airplane and not off-loaded until they have reached the final destination. If transshipments such as sea/air, sea/rail, or sea/truck are required, the customer must ensure that all logistics go smoothly. At the final destination, the customer must arrange customs clearance and pay duty. In the event of a problem with duty or quota, the customer may face serious delay and real loss. The customer may ultimately recover any losses from the factory, but this is by no means certain—particularly since on an FOB basis, the factory is paid immediately after the goods are placed aboard the ship or handed over to the airline.

The great disadvantage for importers of this system is that while his customer will cancel if the goods are not in the store by a specified date, the supplier is on time as long as the merchandise is on the boat or plane on the correct date. Between the overseas shipping date and the store delivery date, the importer is completely liable even though he has zero control over events.

Although they have plenty of other problems, companies which buy domestically do not run this high level of risk. Optimally, the importer would like to maintain the advantages of buying merchandise overseas but with the much reduced risks of the domestic buyer. Instead of opening his letter of credit FOB Jakarta, he could now open the same letter of credit FOB New York. The supplier ships on LDP terms.

Case Study LX—Shipping LDP

Offering your customer LDP shipments is one of the best ways to increase profits with little increase in costs. Everyone benefits.

The buyer reduces his risk and, at the same time, can close his traffic department whose main job was tracking shipments from the time they leave the overseas factory to arrival at the port of entry, as well as ensuring rapid customs clearance. A traffic manager costs $75,000 per year. Even a small department can carry an overhead of twice that amount.

Some trading companies and agents currently work on an LDP basis. In many cases, overseas buying offices wholly-owned by large U.S. retailers or importers also work LDP. For them, the primary motivation is not reducing risk but rather reducing expenses. The home office in the United States transfers their costs to the overseas office which not only performs the same follow-up less expensively, but also converts an overhead expense to a direct product expense. Furthermore, by working LDP, the buyer converts a whole series of costs—freight, insurance, clearance and trucking—to a single item, thus simplifying their entire billing procedures. The retailer normally pays their office the same commission percentage; only the base changes from FOB to LDP.

Smaller importers who do not have their own buying offices seldom enjoy this option. For them, the only choices are either to continue buying FOB or working with a trading company who will charge them on an LDP basis. This LDP price contains a hidden premium for the service, a premium which is almost always exorbitant.

To a factory working on an FOB basis and netting 5% profit, the change to LDP terms brings great profit for little added expense or risk, provided the customer is reliable. Mass-market retailers and sharpshooting importers incapable of forming a long-term relationship are unsuitable LDP customers. The risks for both sides would be intolerable.

But for a responsible factory capable of shipping an acceptable product on time, working with a customer interested in maintaining a long-term relationship, LDP offers greater profit and substantially reduced indirect costs to both sides. The steps the factory must follow in order to be able to ship LDP are not difficult. A well-trained shipping clerk can carry out the entire procedure. If the goods are shipped by sea, there is nothing to be done until the ship arrives. If the goods are shipped by air, the airline will automatically track the airwaybill for you on request. A reliable shipping forwarder and customs broker will do the rest. In the event of problems at customs, the factory stands a better chance of solving the problems through the customs broker than the customer. If changes in documentation are required, the factory can move quickly and has greater understanding than the customer.

The actual added costs to both sides are negligible and are simply added to the final LDP price. Even if the factory still works on the same net 5% (which is, incidentally, far less than a buying office would charge their parent), the additional profit is considerable. Using the same FOB $5.75 yarn-dyed blouse described in previous case studies, the calculations would now work out as follows:

ITEM	FOB	FOB LESS 5%	QUOTA	DUTY	FRT	CLR	ADDED EXP	5% NET	LDP
Blouse	$5.75	$5.46	$1.50	$0.92	$0.40	$0.15	$0.10	$0.45	$8.97

Working with a 5% mark-up, the actual FOB cost to the factory is $5.46, to which quota, duty (now adjusted for the lowered FOB cost), freight, clearance and the cost of the extra LDP work must be added, giving a pre-profit LDP price of $8.53. Adding a 5% mark-up, the final LDP price is now $8.97.

The customer pays 5% more for his LDP price, a difference of about $0.45 per unit. On the other hand, he saves $150,000 in overhead. Therefore, for any quantities up to 300,000 units annually he shows a direct profit and, after that volume, he still enjoys the advantages receiving LDP goods gives over FOB. Most importantly, the customer has shifted responsibility to the supplier. In the event of late arrival, he does not have to argue, plead or compromise—he simply does not pay. He has placed himself in the same secure position as his domestic competitor. He no longer cares that the merchandise is being produced in central China—he is buying FOB New York.

For the factory, their profit rises. Their overhead expense rises by $0.10 per unit which is passed on to the customer. Net profit rises by 54%; where previously the factory earned $0.29 (5% of $5.75), it now earns $0.45 (5% of $8.97).

MACRO-COST STRATEGIES

Factory strategies abound and are not restricted to indirect-cost-saving facilities. It is even possible for a full-service factory to overcome macro-cost disadvantages. Because macro costs are the greatest costs of all, in order to prosper, factories must develop strategies to deal with the disadvantages of being located in high-cost countries. Provided a factory has the facilities, they can overcome even the highest macro costs.

Consider the following: As the world continues to break up into mutually-exclusive trading blocs, those factories not included in any blocs face rising macro costs relative to the insiders. As we have previously shown, these macro-cost differences are so high that no indirect or direct-cost advantage can compensate. To factories in Asia, whose main customers are located in the United States and Western Europe, NAFTA and the EU are by far the greatest challenges they face.

Case Study LXI—Breaking into NAFTA

You own a Hong Kong company with factories in China, producing ladies' better-quality blouses, dresses and sportswear. Your customers include some of the best label names in America. Your quality is excellent. You have an impeccable reputation for on-time delivery. Your prices are competitive. You offer some of the best patternmaking and samplemaking facilities in the world. Your customers respect and rely on you. Yet you are facing disaster.

In the next five years, you will be driven out of business. You will not be able to compete with Mexican factories. Right now, your customers do not want to work in Mexico. The quality is terrible there. Deliveries are inevitably late. Factories are unreliable. Yet, you know that their quality and delivery will improve. Eventually, Mexican factories will learn to be reliable and, at that point, their lower macro costs will destroy your company. The Mexican factory pays no duty, requires no quota, and it can ship by sea or truck with goods arriving in the United States before your air shipment. Consider the following blouse costings.

COUNTRY	FABRIC	CMT	QUOTA	DUTY	FRT	CLR	LDP
China	$3.00	$2.00	$2.00	$1.43	$0.75	$0.15	$9.33
Mexico	$3.00	$3.00	0	0	$0.25	$0.15	$6.38

There is no way around the arithmetic. Even with a CMT 50% higher than yours, the Mexican factory is $2.95 (32%) cheaper at FOB. Even if your workers were paid nothing, you could not compete. Either you go out of business or you have to join NAFTA.

How do you join NAFTA? Actually, it is not difficult. You set up a factory in Mexico. You have factories in China which are controlled from Hong Kong. What is the big deal setting up in Mexico? In fact, if you set up in Mexico, you would have all the advantages.

- You have the customers. Few American importers of better-quality garments would trust a Mexican factory to deliver decent goods on time. However, the customers would trust you.

- You have the ability to set up a factory to produce quality merchandise. You have already done the same thing in China. The customers would still come to Hong Kong to place their orders. They could decide for themselves whether to buy from China or Mexico. Since, under NAFTA regulations both yarn and fabric have to be of NAFTA origin to qualify for duty-free and quota-free status, they could buy from Mexico if the fabric is available in North America. Furthermore, unlike dealing with a purely Mexican operation where the customer has to decide to work in Mexico before he even begins designing the collection, working with you, the customer can delay his decision with the knowledge that should the fabric be unavailable in North America, he can always produce his garments in your Chinese factory.

- You have the indirect-cost-savings facilities. It would take a Mexican factory a generation and millions of dollars to replicate your staff of trained technicians and managers. You have the people and the system. You can still run the preproduction in Hong Kong, buy the fabric and the trim through your Hong Kong operation, and make the patterns and duplicates in Hong Kong. The Mexican factory would simply operate on a CM basis.

In fact, if you really make the effort, no Mexican factory will be able to compete with you. As an added bonus, the Mexican government will offer you tax incentives, special union contracts and even plant and machinery subsidies.

Overcoming high macro costs by setting up branch factories is a viable strategy *if you have the indirect-cost facilities*. If you have strategic relationships, your customers will follow you and be grateful for the opportunity you are giving them. If you have the experience setting up quality factories outside your home country, Mexico should pose no greater problems than Indonesia or Vietnam. If you have the trained staff, your people can train Mexican technicians. However, if yours is a 0-service factory, no strategies are available.

Conclusions—To the META System

Either you look at your factory as a process where skilled operators, technicians and managers interact with other capital tools to manufacture garments or it is just a room full of machines. If you can look at your factory as a process, you perceive it as an ever-changing dynamic structure, built to recognize and meet challenges as they occur.

As a factory ceases to be 0-service and evolves to develop facilities to reduce indirect costs, its management creates systems to deal with the day-to-day problems of producing garments. For example, if fabric and trim are to be in place in time to cut the garments and maintain production schedules, the factory requires a plan. Likewise, each operation must be accounted for and each to function effectively. These needs are met by system.

System is necessary to keep the factory going. But traditionally, system has dealt only with the present and a static structure. In a today's rapidly evolving world, you need a dynamic system—capable of seeing new opportunities, understanding what facilities you must build to take advantage of those opportunities, and creating strategies to profit from both the new opportunities and your new facilities.

There is no formula capable of carrying out these changes. META-system—the system to create system—is what you can bring to your factory. As long as you remain flexible and open to change, as long as you understand that your factory is a cooperative structure, the factory will develop to meet each new challenge.

Chapter 11
Developing a Competitive Industry: Creating Capital Assets

The definition of a developed country: A place where people can afford to worry about the danger of cheap labor imports

Holden Schmata
Lecture to the International Monetary Fund

Buyers can reduce direct costs through negotiation and factories can reduce indirect costs by providing greater facilities, but neither buyer nor factory can do anything to reduce macro costs. Yet as FVCA shows, macro costs constitute the single most important factor determining where a buyer will place his orders. Only governments can change macro-cost factors. The next two chapters will address those levels of change and how countries can best meet the oncoming challenges.

At a time when international production capacity far outstrips worldwide demand for imported garments, low macro costs constitute the difference between a competitive flourishing industry and a bankrupt one. The coming period will be critical for all those in the global apparel industry. As we have seen, all factors appear especially negative for most Third World countries.

- Garment demand from developed countries is falling and will continue to slide;

- Garment production facilities are increasing worldwide as more countries use garment exports as a first step in industrial development;

- Trading blocs are redirecting garment purchases to bloc members and favored suppliers.

Then there is the controversial issue of international trade liberalization. Regretfully, instead of making world trade more equitable, liberalization looks like a one-way street—the Third World liberalizes while the industrialized West benefits. Given current policies in the United States and Western Europe, there is every possibility that Third World tariffs will be forced down while those in the industrialized countries will remain unchanged, and that Third World non-tariff barriers will disappear while U.S. and EU quotas remain—despite the promises made at the Uruguay Round of WTO negotiation. To the textile and garment industries in Third World countries, the results of such 'trade liberalization' would be catastrophic. Put simply, the second and third-line garment producers in Asia, Africa, and Central and South America will receive a double-barrel shotgun blast that will utterly decimate their industries.

Garment Exports

Trade liberalization as it appears to be evolving will not bring Third World garment exporters unlimited access to markets in the developed world; current quotas on garment exports will almost certainly stay in place. Not only are textile and garment manufacturers in the developed countries fighting to retain them, but, ironically, their counterparts in the first and even second-line Third World garment exporting countries stand firmly behind them. American manufacturers fear unrestrained Third World imports; second-line Third World manufacturers in large quota-holding countries such as Bangladesh, India, Indonesia, Pakistan and Turkey fear China even more. Without quota restraints, they believe China will take over the entire garment-export market. Retaining current quotas provides guaranteed, albeit limited, markets for their goods in the United States and the EU.

To some degree, their fears are justified. The vast proportion of garments produced by Third World factories are of indifferent quality. Factories are limited in the types of garments they can make and deliveries are often erratic. In fact, the only advantages many of these countries have are cheap labor and large quotas. Wages in countries like Bangladesh, India, Indonesia, Pakistan and Sri Lanka are lower than those in Chinese export factories. China quota is limited and, when exhausted, Western importers have to go elsewhere.

The future looks particularly bleak for Asian countries which previously relied heavily on their export-apparel industries. The figures speak for themselves. For the past three years, Asia's total share of garment exports to both the United States and the EU has been falling—including from Hong Kong and China. Five years ago, Asia accounted for 80% of clothing imports to the United States. Today, Asia's total share has been cut in half, while Mexico has risen from nowhere to single-handedly become America's largest overseas garment supplier.

Trade liberalization is attacking from both sides. In recent years, garment exporters in industrialized countries have been pressing for Third World countries to reduce duties on garment imports. Until the 1980s, U.S. and European manufacturers had little interest in garment exports. That changed as much of the Third World became a seemingly insatiable market for imported branded goods. Despite Asia's recent financial hiccups, the market for branded apparel clearly exists. U.S. companies like Donna Karan, Tommy Hilfiger, Ralph Lauren and Calvin Klein see real profit in their overseas retail outlets. Why should they lose money because of excessive duties, particularly when the U.S. negative balance of trade in garments is the worst of all major commodities?

It's not just high-end labels trying to get into the Third World. As Mexico becomes increasingly competitive, U.S. manufacturers of moderate-priced garments working there will be able to produce ever more competitively. And even these moderate-priced labels are beginning to look for retail markets worldwide.

Finally, there is growing pressure from regional blocs of developing countries to enhance intra-bloc trade through tariff reduction. In Asia, APEC has agreed to phase out tariffs for all but the poorest member countries from 2010, with the balance following in 2020.

The loss of tariff and other import restrictions will wreak havoc in the domestic markets of Third World countries. In the past, especially during Asia's boom years, a domestic supplier in a Third World country faced virtually no competition whatsoever. He was able to sell his product at almost any price. Go into any budget-priced department store in Jakarta, Bangkok or Bombay and you would be appalled. Look at a pair of jeans or a sport shirt—it is usually badly designed and poorly stitched. The price, however, is often higher than what you would pay for a pair of Levi's in the United States. In a free market, these goods for local consumption could not survive.

It's anybody's guess how long Asia's retail markets will take to return to relative health. But given the scenarios discussed above, the garment producer who previously thrived on the highly profitable domestic market will find his business woefully reduced. Likewise, the weaver, whose inflated profit was largely equal to the 30%-120% duty charged to his overseas competitor will be out of business and he will be taking his upstream yarn supplier together with his downstream fabric printer, dyer and finisher with him.

In the coming period, the domestic market in each country will be simultaneously faced by two assaults:

- Present suppliers to local wholesalers and retailers will have to contend with foreign competition for their existing customers. Trade liberalization will disrupt the local retail market. Even if they wanted to, local retail customers would not be able to maintain past loyalties, and larger retailers and wholesalers will have to find more cost-effective product just to survive themselves. They, too, will look overseas to buy, because that is where their new competition sources their goods.

- New retail companies will open who have only limited interest in buying from local suppliers. The major international mass-market retailers will set up their own retail outlets in every Third World country with a viable local market. Given the increased competition in their home markets coupled with diminishing demand, these retail giants look at the Third World as the single fastest growing retail market in the world. Marks & Spencer, Wal-Mart and Kmart have all entered Asia and, despite the slowdown, recognize that sooner or later, Asia's markets will recover. These companies source internationally with sophisticated sourcing chains set up all over the world. Although many are trying to keep retail prices competitive by sourcing locally, local suppliers would be naive to expect any special treatment from international retailers if their products and services are not up to international standards.

This is the scenario facing the garment industry in all developing countries. As international competition heightens and trade liberalization brings more foreign goods into local markets, countries with high macro costs simply will not be able to compete. Governments must take steps to reduce macro costs if they want overseas buyers to continue to place orders or make direct investments.

Third World governments have yet to fully recognize just how much choice American and Western European garment importers and retailers have over where to buy their goods. Buying a T-shirt is not the same as buying a precious or rare commodity. I have yet to find a country so poor and so underdeveloped that it did not have a single T-shirt factory. Nor, unlike other industries, do garment people necessarily flock to a place because it has raw materials. Everybody in the fabric business buys wool from Australia, but few apparel buyers actually place orders there. Garment people produce where garment costs are low.

If a government wishes to develop a successful export garment industry, it must create an environment that will encourage industrial development. A coordinated policy must be outlined which will:

- Attract foreign buyers;

- Promote investment by local companies;

- Encourage foreign companies to set up factories.

Unfortunately, instead of opening up to global realities, isolationist attitudes remain very much widespread in Third World governments. A thesis favored by Asia's second-generation wannabe nations—led by Indonesia, Malaysia and Thailand—is known as the *Asian Value Concept*. (Note that this so-called *Asian Value Concept* has as much to do with true Asian values as french-fried potatoes has with authentic Gallic cuisine.) Asian-value proponents start with the assumption that the single most important responsibility of government is to ensure a reasonable standard of living for its citizens and that, therefore, rapid economic development is of the highest priority. They believe that attaining this goal requires disciplined hard work on the part of all citizens, who must sacrifice at least some of their individual rights and freedoms so that society as a whole can benefit.

Asian-value adherents look at the people in the West—particularly Americans—as undisciplined, lazy and selfish. They see America's preoccupation with individual rights as symptomatic of the belligerent and contentious nature of its citizens, and they believe that these characteristics will ultimately cause Western economies to stagnate and be overtaken by Asian societies who, unlike America, are able to subordinate their selfish instincts to a common good.

However you view the importance of personal freedoms, theoretically the Asian-value philosophy appears to be a marvelous tool with which to develop not only a garment industry but the entire economy as well. Imagine, government has all the power it needs to build a competitive industry. Certainly, Indonesia, South Korea, the Philippines and Thailand all enjoyed rapid economic development in the past two decades. All had very competitive export-garment industries—until their economies collectively imploded in late 1997. The very Asian-value system which was supposed to bring lasting prosperity and stability brought them down.

> **Case Study LXII—Developing Your Own Garment Industry: Asian-Style**
>
> Picture a country so desperate to develop a successful export-garment industry that it changes its name to Garmentia. You have been hired for the job with the title Big Garmento. What steps do you take to encourage overseas customers to buy your garments, local garment companies to expand, and foreign companies to set up local factories?
>
> This is what happens under Asian Value Concept:
>
> - To build a competitive industry, the key is to keep wages down. At first, this shouldn't be difficult—your fellow citizens are poor and you have the added benefit of high unemployment. Later on, you can create specific policies to ensure wages do not rise. For example, either avoid setting minimum-wage laws or make it clear to factory owners that any such laws will not be enforced. You can outlaw labor unions or, better yet, set up your own national labor union, which every worker must join, dedicated to limiting wage increases. Finally, if all else fails, there is always the police, the courts and, as a last resort, the army. Of course these are temporary measures, necessary only until development is achieved.
>
> - To find the capital necessary for development, take the money saved by your citizens. Ensure that all local banks use their deposits to provide loans to the correct companies as defined by you. Better yet, start your own banks, together with your friends. That way, you can be sure the right people are getting the loans.
>
> - Finding foreign capital is not difficult. There is always an over-abundance of hot money sloshing around the world. All you have to do is provide a safe home with a relatively high return. With the right policy, the steps are easy. First, peg your currency (the Garment Button) to the U.S. dollar simply by declaring that henceforth the government of Garmentia will support the local currency at the pegged rate. Don't worry that this is a totally impossible scenario—within a week every international banker will accept your word. Then you raise interest on bank deposits to a rate of 1000 points over U.S. 30-year treasury bonds. That's it. All you have to do now is stand aside and allow the money to pour in. Since your currency is fixed to the U.S. dollar, foreigners will deposit their money in your banks, earn a high yield, and because the Garment Button is fixed, they will be certain that they can always withdraw their money in U.S. dollars at the original rate.

- Finding additional loans for your local companies is even easier. In fact, by pegging the Garment Button to the U.S. dollar and raising interest rates, you have already implemented all the policy required. Your local companies need not even pay your higher rate of interest—they can go straight to European, Japanese and American banks and borrow U.S. dollars at their lower rates. Since international bankers believe everything foreign government officials say, and your currency is already convertible to the U.S. dollar at a fixed rate, they see little currency risk.

Now things look really good. Between the foreign money in your banks and large amounts borrowed overseas by your local companies, you have far more money than you really need for investment in garments. You can throw some of the excess money into loans—particularly to your friends—which previously were not considered prudent. The balance you put into the stock market and property markets which are showing much bigger returns than any garment factory.

This is industrial development with Asian values. Everybody benefits—naturally some benefit more than others.

COUNTRY	PRE-1997 CRISIS	POST-1997 CRASH
INDONESIA	2,400 rupiah	17,000 rupiah
S. KOREA	800 won	2,000 won
THAILAND	25 baht	50 baht
MALAYSIA	2·45 ringgit	4·8 ringgit

In fact, the problem with development through so-called Asian values is that ultimately no one benefited—with the exception of Big Garmento and his friends.

Targeting preferred companies for special loans gave them more capital than they could absorb. Some of the money was wasted on poor investments; the bulk was put into the stock and property markets. As these markets rose, so did the paper profits of the preferred companies which, in turn, encouraged them to borrow even more money—mostly overseas in U.S. dollars—to buy even more property and more stocks, which in turn increased of the value of the markets even further, which permitted even more borrowing ... until the balloon burst.

Pegging exchange rates and raising interest rates brought in large amounts of hot money which the local banks, unable to find viable projects for capital investment, poured into the already red-hot stock and property markets. The money rolled in—until the day a few people became worried about a few banks in Bangkok—and the world came to an end. Then the money flooded out even faster than it had come in—first from Thailand, then Indonesia, the Philippines, Malaysia, and finally from South Korea. First stock markets collapsed. Then property markets collapsed and then the foreign investors pulled their money out, causing the currencies to collapse—which just goes to show that currencies remain pegged only up to the second when people cease to believe they are pegged.

Thailand spent $20 billion in less than two weeks trying to defend their baht. The Indonesian rupiah lost 70% of its value in a month. The local companies, who had borrowed U.S. dollars at low rates, discovered that since their revenue was in local currency, they now owed two to four times the amount borrowed and were all effectively bankrupt. The South Korean, Indonesian, Malaysian and Thai banks, who had followed government instructions and taken their depositors' savings and loaned them out to preferred borrowers, found these loans all unrecoverable. They too were bankrupt. It was a near clean sweep—almost every major bank and publicly-traded company in Indonesia, South Korea and Thailand was broke.

Garment exporters were especially hard hit. Many economists suggested that the fall of the Indonesian rupiah by 70% would bring about an export boom, since local wages would also fall by 70% in U.S. dollar terms, thus making Indonesian garments more competitive. That the export boom failed to materialize surprised no one except the economists, who know little about garments.

Nobody moved production to Indonesia for a simple reason. The problem in Indonesia was never high labor costs. The problem in Indonesia was that even before the economic crisis of 1997 very little worked. After the crisis, nothing worked. Factories, even if they had orders, could not pay for materials. Even if they had the money, no international bank would honor a letter of credit drawn on an Indonesian bank. The only alternative would be for the buyer to supply the fabric, which under the circumstances required greater faith than most people could muster. Most importantly, as we have shown in earlier portions of this book, is that Indonesian labor costs do not really matter. Prior to the collapse, the direct-labor cost of a man's shirt produced in Indonesia was about 12 cents. When the currency fell by 70%, the direct-labor cost dropped to a 3.6 cents. Any garment professional who moved production to Indonesia to save 8.4 cents should have his head examined.

In the end, the Asian countries—Indonesia, South Korea, Malaysia and Thailand—which tried to achieve development by using so-called Asian values, by restricting labor prices, falsely pegging their currencies, forcing local banks to give preferential loans to selected companies, or encouraging inflows of hot money, were eaten alive. Those Asian countries—Hong Kong, Singapore and Taiwan—whatever their social philosophies, which did not follow Asian values as a means of development, although harmed by the knock-on effects of the problems with their neighbors, survived relatively unscathed.

The problem is not only with the idea of development through Asian values. It lies with any belief that there exists somewhere a grand plan for economic development. There is no grand plan, and any attempt to impose a plan inevitably leads to economic distortions.

An economy develops the same way an industry develops. If a government wishes to achieve economic development, it must first determine what companies require—that they themselves cannot provide—and then try to provide these things. If you are a government and you want a viable garment industry, you have to ensure that garment costs are low. More than any other factor, low garment costs come from low macro costs.

There are five main areas of macro costs of equally paramount importance: education, infrastructure, government policy, human rights and the politics of trade. Serious problems in any single area can raise macro costs to a point where importers will be forced to go elsewhere.

EDUCATION

In-house training by factories is an important step forward, particularly with regard to increasing worker and clerical skills. If the factory has overseas tie-ups, assistance from foreign partners is also invaluable. But, in the end, neither effort can achieve much in a country with poor educational facilities.

So important is education that the true measure of economic development is the degree to which a country can offer an education to each of its citizens and the subsequent ability to offer employment opportunities commensurate with each person's education. A garment factory may not require the skills of a law firm, a hospital, or even a computer software developer. But a garment factory does require educated managers and technicians. Today, senior management in large factories must have postgraduate education either in engineering or business; middle management and technical staff must have either undergraduate degrees or have completed rigorous training at polytechnic schools. The importance of formal education is becoming so evident in the garment industry that many polytechnics have now achieved university status and offer specialized postgraduate degrees in garment marketing, production, merchandising and design.

No factory is large enough to have its own in-house university. It is the responsibility of government to provide facilities for tertiary education. The absence of a pool of educated people immediately marks a country as unacceptable for either investment or any long-term strategic relationship. Before managers and technical staff can be taught the finer points of customer requirements, they must be qualified to learn.

Lack of educated technicians and managers is the greatest bar to further development in Third World countries. In many countries, not only are there insufficient facilities for tertiary education, those that do exist are misused. In South Asia, over half of all university graduates have degrees in history, economics or other social sciences. In these same countries, 40% of all university graduates are unemployed. Universities must provide professionals with practical skills and government must supply the universities

Poor tertiary educational facilities are not unique to developing countries—even leading garment and fashion centers in the industrialized West risk losing their preeminent positions if their educational facilities do not keep up with the latest developments in an increasingly dynamic industry.

Case Study LXIII—Italian Design

Italy is possibly the fashion design center of the world today. In recent years, Italian design houses have captured the title long held by France. It isn't only the big name design houses that have generated this excitement, but also a myriad of smaller but no less commercial companies who employ extremely professional designers and sales teams.

The paradox is that just as Italian design has reached such high levels of acclaim, more American and British—and fewer Italians—are being hired in Italy to head design teams. Part of the reason appears to be fact that the U.S. and the U.K. have produced some truly talented people who are more appreciated in Milan than New York or London.

Another factor could also be the very high standards of U.S. and U.K. design schools and their ability to change with the times. Design has always been a technically-orientated profession. While design students of past generations had to learn techniques of sketching, draping, knitstitch and patternmaking, modern students must also add computer literacy and be conversant with the latest computer-assisted design (CAD) systems.

Today, a single designer with the latest CAD system can design a knit jacquard, work out three colorways and a garment to go with the knit, provide a photograph of the completed garment in each colorway, and give knitters computerized instructions to produce the jacquard—in less than a morning.

Computers have revolutionized design. Simply by seeing a picture, designers can reject unsuitable styles or make changes to improve styles without the need to produce fabric, cut patterns or make samples. Thousands of dollars can be saved each season. Companies looking to reduce costs and design time see CAD systems as the way of the future. Any company producing fast turn goods must design with CAD systems.

Any designer graduating from London's Royal College of Art or Saint Martin's, Parson's or FIT in New York, or RISD in Providence has worked with the latest CAD technology. Surprisingly, Italian schools seldom teach these techniques at all. Instead, their graduates must rely on traditional teaching methods which, however fundamental to garmentmaking, will not answer the highly commercial demands which today's design houses must also face.

Italy currently stands at the forefront of fashion design, but it will not keep that position unless Italian schools provide the education required to support that industry. In this regard, Italy is no different than India, Indonesia or the Ivory Coast.

The ability to provide education is only half the challenge. Equally important, and just as problematic, is the ability to make judicious use of whatever educated resources do exist. In some countries, certain fields may simply churn out an excess of graduates. For example, India appears to be graduating enough skilled computer programmers for the entire developed world.

There are other problems facing educated people in developing countries. Graduates with valuable skills are often underemployed or rejected for political reasons. Chinese organizations will sponsor young employees for study in Western universities, frequently up to master's and doctorate degree level. However, on return to the organization, the new graduates are often shunted into meaningless clerical positions. Senior management's rationale is that the 'young' graduates, often in their mid-thirties, must gain experience before they can be promoted. In fact, while the official Chinese Communist Party line now supports a Western-influenced socialist market economy, the older managers fear that the younger generation will replace them, probably uncovering corrupt and inefficient practices in the process.

...the 'young' returnee Chinese MBA in his new position...

Politics notwithstanding, a garment factory must have access to trained and qualified professionals and technicians. These are the people who will create and run the facilities required to reduce indirect costs. Without these facilities, the better customer will not come because he cannot work. The personnel required must be educated. This is the role of government.

For an industry to develop and for a nation to develop, the first task of government is to provide the opportunity for education.

INFRASTRUCTURE

For a garment industry to be competitive, factories must operate in an environment with proper infrastructure. Proper infrastructure means enormous costs. In Asia alone, one trillion dollars will be needed for infrastructure projects during the next decade if development is to continue at any reasonable pace. These amounts are far above the resources of the single governments concerned. Furthermore, whenever large sums of money are involved, certain political dimensions will inevitably come into play, interfering with any investment flows.

There are three main areas where improvements must be made:

Electricity Generation

The garment industry does not consume vast amounts of power. However, where insufficient electrical power exists, the garment industry suffers along with everybody else. For many years, Chinese factories were allowed electricity only six days a week. Brownouts have been and remain commonplace in many parts of India, the Philippines and Thailand.

Most factories in developing countries must run their own power generators, but these back-up generators are stop-gap measures at best. Air conditioning and modern pressing machinery require relatively large amounts of power and are, therefore, not readily available to factories supplying their own electricity. Furthermore, generating your own electrical power raises direct costs. For factories in India or the Philippines which already have high indirect costs, the added direct costs of in-house electrical power generation often represent the final nail in the coffin of their export-apparel dreams.

Endemic power shortages are often the first consideration of foreign companies looking at joint-venture or other investment opportunities. Since the early 1990s, several Asian governments, recognizing their lack of necessary funds or expertise, began permitting foreign companies to construct large-scale power generating projects. In several countries, notably the Philippines and China, these projects have been working out reasonably well. However, several problems remain.

For one, socialist governments have found it psychologically difficult to permit private ownership, especially by foreign corporations, of utilities. This has been a particular problem in India where despite the very high price of electricity and the efforts of foreign companies over a number of years to negotiate projects, final agreements have been few and far between.

Case Study LXIV—Indian Electricity Story

This is a story with a happy ending—so far.

India has the highest-priced electricity in the world—for those who pay. About 25% of the total power produced is stolen, and almost 50% is given away free as part of political deals. By 1991, the country had a chronic 8% shortage of electrical power, reaching 18% during peak periods. The estimated cost of adding 30,000 megawatts was $30 billion. There was simply no way for the country to meet its minimum demands on its own.

In 1992, the Indian government finally opened the market to foreign companies. Top Indian bureaucrats traveled the world over to drum up interest.

In January 1993, Enron Oil and Gas Company of Houston received approval from the Indian government to set up a wholly-owned, 2015-megawatt coastal power station at Dabhol in western Maharashtra State. Construction was to begin at once, with the first of three stages expected to be generating substantial amounts of electricity by 1995.

That's when the Indian-style bureaucratic problems began. Only weeks after the project won environmental clearance, a new set of rules was put into effect, essentially forcing the company to return to step one. In August 1994, some 18 months later, Enron again received final approval to begin work on the power station. Construction was scheduled to commence immediately.

Once again, the Indian government and bureaucracy went into action. After a series of consultations, on September 2, 1995, the project was unilaterally canceled by the government. The Bharatiya Janata Party (BJP), having won control of Maharashtra State in the meantime, simply decided that the project's terms were too profitable for Enron. The more extreme Shiv Sena party, in coalition with the BJP, declared the project in opposition to the tenet of *Swadeshi*, promulgated by Gandhi, whereby everything that India needs should be produced by Indians. Along with the local companies who had previously lost the contract to Enron, they insisted the entire bidding process be repeated, that *Swadeshi* be taken into consideration in the new round of bids, and that the winning contractor should not be permitted excessive profits.

These are all fine statements. Profits should not be excessive and should be commensurate with risk. Self-sufficiency is a worthy goal.

Certainly electrical power stations should be environmentally friendly. However, in India, the real fight is seldom over the environment, self-sufficiency, or even excessive profits. The real fight is over political power—who controls it and who can use it. In India, power is measured by the ability to stop all movement. That is what happened on September 2, 1995.

Fortunately, the story does have a happy turn. In February 1997, only four years after Enron first received final approval, the project was reinstated. Enron feels it has learned and profited from their experience in India's rough-and-tumble investment waters. In fact, they even set up a new center offering advice to other companies planning to work in India on how to deal with the government and bureaucracy—naturally, the help comes for a fee.

Unfortunately, the so-far happy events of February 1997 marked only the end of Chapter 1 of the Great Indian Adventure Story. Even now, a new Chapter 2 is unfolding and in true Indian style, the story may prove to be yet another overly intricate plot leading to nowhere in the end.

The issue of what constitutes 'reasonable' returns is a major hurdle which Third World countries must overcome if they are to encourage foreign companies to invest in electricity and other infrastructure projects. On the one hand, power generation in developing countries has traditionally been held by local monopolies and has provided a guaranteed profit—albeit at relatively low rates of return—to the investor. But constructing electrical power stations requires billions of dollars of up-front investments in countries considered to be high risk. These conditions necessitate higher returns on investment. In the resulting stalemate, governments worry they will be cheated by foreigners, while foreign companies fear they will not be able to recoup their investment costs.

The whole situation has become so highly politicized that many Third World governments can no longer see the forest for the trees. They are so afraid of being cheated that they forget that it is not only electricity generation at stake, but all the other industries who cannot expand without increased power supplies.

Transportation

The garment industry demands relatively short lead times—30 to 45 days is considered reasonable. Anything longer limits the type of customer and type of garment that can be ordered. Factories do everything in their power to produce and ship faster. Where transportation networks are insufficient to meet their needs, delays pile up and the industry cannot function. It makes no sense for a factory to struggle to shave a few days off their production time, when the turnaround time for a vessel can be measured in weeks. What's more, factories get hit by transportation bottlenecks both ways: materials are delayed coming in and finished garments are delayed going out.

As with power generation, some countries are allowing foreign companies to make investments in the transportation sector. Thailand has approved projects by foreign companies to build private toll roads. Remarkably, China, communism's last bastion, has allowed investment in both road and seaport facilities and leads the region in foreign-invested infrastructure projects. Unfortunately, many of these transportation schemes have been even more difficult to get off the ground than power projects. To many governments, foreign-controlled private toll roads are simply beyond the pale of their wildest imaginations.

Telecommunications

This is the third and most difficult area for infrastructure investment. The apparel and fashion industries deal with a limitless number of details. At every stage, instructions must be provided, queried, explained and confirmed. Companies large and small depend on faxes, and increasingly e-mail, to operate efficiently. Many importers speak daily with their overseas agents and sometimes their factories. To survive in the garment business you need accurate answers fast. If you cannot communicate, there is no sense trying to work with a factory at all. Your merchandisers and coordinators depend on good communications to help you keep indirect costs down. However, if it takes three days to get a fax through, often the case in Pakistan and Bangladesh, or if at the end of the month the telephone and fax bill exceeds $10,000, as happens in Indonesia and India, work simply becomes too difficult.

Unfortunately, telecommunications combines all the worst elements of politics and investment. The problems of just getting a telephone in some developing countries are so great that everyone has their own horror story. Surely, it is faster to wait your turn to emigrate to the United States than to get a telephone in Bombay—the line is shorter and moves faster.

All countries, without exception, subsidize the cost of local telephone calls with high overseas rates. In many countries, these subsidies can make calling overseas prohibitively expensive. Nor can the high costs be entirely avoided by calling from the U.S. to the overseas factory. Since U.S. long-distance providers must kick back an agreed amount to the foreign telephone company anyway, the cost of telephoning countries like Indonesia and India from the United States is still quite high.

E-mail is often not a solution since you cannot have e-mail without a telephone, and getting the telephone is the big problem. Many countries are trying to overcome the shortage of fixed-line telephone facilities by using mobile phones. This simply shifts the problem. Portable telephones overcome the need for substantial investments in fiber-optic cable but operating costs are much higher. As a result, while you may find it easier to get a phone in the first place, the cost of each connection will make an even bigger hole in your pocket.

Most governments theoretically understand that lack of infrastructure inhibits not only foreign investment but all economic development. They also recognize that infrastructure investment is the government's responsibility. Unfortunately, politics has its own priorities and the subject of foreign investment in infrastructure brings out the worst in governments. At the end of the day, however, each government must decide whether it wants its industries to remain internationally competitive, or whether they will simply be sacrificed in the name of ideological purity or opportunities for the chosen few.

As the first industry for developing nations rushing to join the export bandwagon, the garment industry is particularly vulnerable. The widespread perception is that regardless of how few resources are available, there is a place at the bottom rung for everybody. Unfortunately, that bottom rung is very crowded. Today, if you don't move upward, the newest entrant may push you off the ladder altogether. If government is not willing to make the necessary investments in education and infrastructure, the industry simply will not survive.

Chapter 12
Developing a Competitive Industry: Maintaining Capital Assets

An old Jewish man has a conversation with The Almighty. "Is it true," he asks,"that we are the chosen people?" "Yes," replies The Almighty, "you are my chosen people." To which the old man says, "Then next time, please choose someone else."

Holden Schmata
Lecture to U.N. Conference on
Targeting Industries for Economic Development

Third World countries remain underdeveloped because they lack the capital assets required for development—education, infrastructure, stable government, efficient bureaucracy, an equitable and sound legal system. They also lack the funds necessary to rapidly create these assets. However, these observations explain only why the development process may be slow. They do not explain why, in the half-century since 1945, so few countries have undergone real economic development, while many Third World countries have failed to develop at all.

Let's face it. The countries of South Asia—Bangladesh, India, Sri Lanka and Pakistan—are just about as poor today as they were 30 years ago. The standard of living in sub-Saharan Africa has not risen since the end of the colonial era. The answer cannot be simply lack of funds—these countries have access to both foreign aid and cheap loans. In fact, they have received massive financial aid from the industrialized West and Japan. Surely, 50 years of financial assistance should have brought higher per-capita income growth to these countries.

Over the years, social scientists have offered many reasons and solutions for this stubborn inability on the part of certain areas to develop. In the 1950s and 1960s, economists devised a theory of development through massive projects. The idea originated way back in the nineteenth century when economic development was measured by coal, iron and steel production. Clearly, it was thought, the great powers—the United States, Great Britain, Germany and even the former Soviet Union—had developed through investment in heavy industry.

The theory called for large-scale investments by Third World governments, of course financed by the great powers, the World Bank and the United Nations. Local state monopolies were created in every Third World country to eliminate ostensibly harmful competition. Large international cartels for commodities such as tin, rubber, coffee, and finally oil were created to ensure steadily rising prices for Third World products. Unfortunately, without exception, each monopoly and cartel ended in spectacular failure. The large state companies went broke as did the cartels. OPEC, the largest and seemingly most successful cartel of the 1970s, may wind up as the greatest failure of all, despite the sharp price increases of 1999-2000.

After the economists, came the political scientists. The late 1960s and 1970s was the era of the anti-colonialists who offered the theory of Western guilt. Third World countries could not progress because their previous colonial masters had prevented indigenous political, social and economic institutions from developing. The fault lay with the Western European powers and the United States. What is remarkable is that everybody agreed—including Western Europe and the United States. Although the Cold War was raging, the United States, the former Soviet Union and China all contributed vast sums to Third World governments with no strings attached. After all, strings would have been just another form of neo-colonialism. The Third World government leaders took the money, and spent most of it on palaces and other useless glitzy projects, or armies to keep themselves in power. What little remained was invested—usually in Swiss banks.

In the 1980s, the sociologists took center stage. For them, the problem was clearly overpopulation. Countries could not develop because all funds were spent just to feed their growing citizenry. Only population control would pave the way for meaningful development programs. Failure to control population would bring universal catastrophe. In the name of social development, the Indian and Chinese governments instituted massive sterilization programs—with largely coercive means.

In the end, the entire population control program had no effect on Indian economic development whatsoever. In China, the one-child-per-family policy resulted in a marked increase in female infanticide and a demographic distortion—too many men, not enough women—that the Chinese government will have to cope with for the next 40 years. In fact, voluntary population control worked only in the developed countries who, ironically, now face serious problems of aging populations and insufficient working-age people contributing funds to pay for the older generation's retirement benefits.

In fact, each theory was in its own way both correct and equally irrelevant. As the economists of the 1950s contended, there are indeed areas, such as education and infrastructure, where some state control is necessary. Supra-national organizations—such as the IMF, the World Bank, and various trade blocs—can also play important roles.

The political scientists were also partially right. The colonial powers left the Third World without indigenous organizations to cope with the problems of development. Most of these countries lacked trained bureaucracies, strong banking systems and quality universities.

The sociologists also have a point. Economic development is very difficult where population growth is excessive.

Nevertheless, none of these theories answers the fundamental question: Why did some countries develop while others failed? The answer does not lie in the degree of government interference. Japan, with a totally government-controlled economy, grew in the post-war era from a bombed-out shell to become the second largest economic power in the world. At the same time, the economies of the countries of central Africa, with the same degree of government interference, collapsed. Nor is it determined by a colonial past. Singapore and Burma both had the same British colonial past; when the British left, both had educated populations and growing economies. Yet Singaporeans today enjoy one of the most developed economies on the world, while the Burmese have been flushed down the toilet. Finally, the difference is not simply overpopulation. Certainly South Asia's overpopulation has wreaked havoc on their economies, but at the same time the most densely populated territory in the world is Hong Kong, where people enjoy a standard of living higher than in most countries of Western Europe. China, with the world's largest population, has over the past two decades enjoyed Asia's highest growth rate.

Since the early 1990s, a new theory has come along—let's call it the responsible governments theory—which may not only explain why countries develop but also what steps can be taken to enhance development. Advocates believe the following:

- Development requires creation and preservation of capital assets.

- The state's role should be limited to education, infrastructure and other important assets where all governments must play a role.

- Governments should encourage development by local and foreign investment rather than controlled development.

- The direct control and allocation of funds by government officials inevitably leads to economic mismanagement, poor investment allocation and corruption.

- Corruption is the single greatest hindrance to economic development.

South Asian and sub-Saharan African government officials were not born corrupt. Corruption results from a fundamental flaw inherent to all interventionist development policies. If you give a poorly paid bureaucrat a billion dollars to spend, he will inevitably become rich in the process. If, to ensure his honesty, you put a supervisor over the bureaucrat, the supervisor will also become rich, as will his supervisor, all the way up until the entire billion dollars is gone.

Supporters of the new development theory, including Western governments, the World Bank and the IMF, are now placing restrictions on loans or grants to countries where corruption is rife. Countries like Kenya and Nigeria are being told that they must either reform or do without.

Analysis of the events leading up to the collapse of the Indonesian economy and the overthrow of the Suharto regime were instrumental in bringing about this new perspective in development policy. Here is a country with rich natural resources and a hardworking population, which up to late 1997 enjoyed a rate of foreign investment second only to China in Asia. Today the Indonesian economy has been virtually destroyed, its currency massively depreciated. Almost all its major corporations and banks are insolvent. This catastrophe was undeniably and completely caused by the Indonesian government's corruption and mismanagement. Dr. Suharto, his family and their cronies literally looted the entire country. Government monopolies in Indonesia's most profitable commodities such as plywood, oil and cigarettes were created with the sole purpose of bringing wealth to a small group of insiders at the expense of the remaining 200 million population.

What is special about Indonesia is that the IMF, and the World Bank both refused to assist the Indonesian government until and unless real government reform takes place. Unfortunately B.J. Habibie—Dr. Suharto's successor—did not restore confidence. After all what can you expect from the man who bought the East German Navy and referred to his boss as SGS, Super-Genius-Suharto. Fortunately, Indonesia's newly elected president, Mr. Wahid, currently appears to be moving in the right direction.

While the Indonesian debacle has finally brought change to the way many professionals look at industrial development, even now, some interventionists persist in fighting a rearguard action. A great debate rages among some politicians, bureaucrats and academics still trapped in the nineteenth century. The subject concerns industrial policy: Should governments single out specific industries for special assistance? Proponents argue that special efforts should be made to encourage investment and development of certain key industries.

On behalf of the worldwide garment industry, my reply to the politicians, bureaucrats and academics worldwide is: Please pick someone else. Do not encourage us. Do not do us any favors. Just do not make it any more difficult than it already is for garment people to do business. Between crazy buyers, lousy factories, importers going broke all the time and changing fashions, we have enough troubles already.

What the international garment industry needs from governments of exporting countries is common sense, not fancy ideas. Fundamentally, ours is a fairly simple industry with a simple set of ideas.

- Shipping garments is good.

- Not shipping garments is bad.

- Anything that helps us ship garments should be encouraged, and anything which stops us from shipping garments should be discouraged.

Granted, this is not much of a mission statement, but at least it rings true. To work in overseas factories, we need certain facilities that only the factory can provide. If the factory will not provide these facilities, we have to go elsewhere. Beyond the factory facilities, there are other facilities which the factory cannot provide that you the governments must provide. If we cannot find sufficiently educated people, if the roads are terrible, or we cannot send faxes, we cannot ship our garments. Since all we care about is shipping garments—we cannot work in your country.

Beyond the infrastructure and the education, we only want to be treated fairly. Taxes and import duties are a part of doing business everywhere and those in the garment industry, both manufacturers and importers, should pay their fair share. But if taxes and duties are too high, then the cost of shipping garments may become too high. Just as importantly, taxes, duties and other fees must be equal across the board. If I have to pay more than the next person because the next person has some special deal going, then I have two choices—I can either negotiate the same better deal or I can go someplace else. In most cases, going elsewhere is a very easy move. As a customer, there is nothing to keep me in your country—except low costs. If your costs rise, there is no reason for me to stay there at all.

Even if I have an existing investment in a local garment factory, there is little to keep me in your country. A garment factory is not a steel mill nor is it a hardwood forest. In most places a garment factory is only a room full of relatively cheap machinery. If costs rise, it is easy for me to leave the machinery and go someplace else. I have done it before.

A good and fair business environment is a crucial capital asset for any country hoping to develop an international garment industry. Any move that harms that environment, that favors one group over another, destroys irreplaceable capital assets just as surely as destroying a machine or blowing up an office building. Government must at all costs protect these assets.

More than anything else, we need a level playing field.

One final point: A good legal system will go a long way towards the establishment of a level playing field.. But a level playing field does not happen simply by enacting laws. An unfair set of laws or a good set of laws unfairly enforced quickly creates an environment where investment and economic development wither. Bad law is worse than no law.

It is possible to buy garments successfully or even build a profitable garment factory in a country without law. Anyone who has worked in China has dealt in a country with virtually no law. Although the Beijing government is making a serious effort to create a true legal system, no garment professional would dare make an issue about a contract with a Chinese corporation. Certainly, any foreigner who takes a Chinese corporation to court must have a death wish. In China, when things go wrong, you smile and negotiate. Law is not a prerequisite for honest dealings, and dishonest people frequently operate quite effectively in countries with very sophisticated legal systems—often by taking full advantage of the very laws created to protect their victims.

The problem is not *law versus no law*. The problem occurs when there are two sets of laws or where laws are enforced for some and not for others, and where courts, rather than offering remedy for injustice, become weapons of insider elites to maintain power. In this environment, business simply cannot operate.

In the final analysis, if you are a government that wishes to achieve economic development through foreign investment and foreign trade, the best policy is to do nothing. Simply provide the infrastructure and social overhead capital that only government can provide and leave the rest to the professionals. They need neither special favors, special help nor special consideration.

As the level of competition increases, it becomes more difficult for both importers and suppliers to succeed in the international garment industry. Each year more factories in more countries enter the already overcrowded market. In many cases, developing countries such as China, India, Indonesia, Pakistan, Sri Lanka and Turkey look to the textile and garment industries for important contributions to export growth. Some—including Bangladesh, Pakistan, Sri Lanka and Tunisia—have centered their entire development plans on exports from these related sectors.[18]

As the number of producers increases, so does the rate of attrition. There simply are not enough customers to go around. In order to survive, some suppliers are forced to lower their prices until they go broke. Each year governments who had hoped to create profitable textile and garment-export industries as important tools of development find their industries unable to compete. In an increasingly competitive environment, the chances of success continue to shrink.

Who will be the winners and who will be the losers?

The old generation of garment exporters had a simple answer. Since they assumed the key to being competitive was low wages, it followed that the countries who paid their workers the least would be the winners. Then as wages in these countries rise, they will be replaced by others offering even lower wages. There is some evidence to back this stance. Fifty years ago, when Japan was a low-wage country emerging from the ruins of World War II, it was a major garment exporter. As wages rose, garment exports fell. By 1995, Japan's garment exports totaled only $530 million, while its garment imports were nearly $19 billion.[19]

South Korea and Taiwan, who in the 1960s replaced Japan as Asia's leading low-cost garment exporters, have now become uncompetitive. As late as 1990, South Korea exported $7.9 billion worth of garments, accounting for 12.1% of total exports. By 1995, that figure had slid below $5 billion, accounting for only 4% of total Korean exports. During the same period, Taiwanese exports fell from $4 billion to $3.3 billion, and while in 1990 garments accounted for 5.9% of total Taiwanese exports, by 1995 that percentage had dropped to 2.9%.

More recently, a third generation of cheap-labor countries have appeared. Bangladesh, China, India, Indonesia and Sri Lanka have become the countries of choice. The old-school garment professionals would argue that eventually this third generation, too, will be faced by rising wages and replaced by yet a fourth generation.

The problem with this scenario is that it just does not coincide with the facts. Of the ten largest garment exporters, five are actually high-wage industrialized countries.[20] Only one, China, can be classified as Third World. In fact, countries such as Bangladesh, Indonesia and Sri Lanka are only relatively minor players in the international garment industry.

Even China does not fit the traditional model. China is presently the largest garment exporter in the world. Average apparel industry wages in China are less than $0.20 per hour, comparable to Sri Lanka (but higher than Bangladesh, India, Indonesia and Pakistan). However, since export textile and garment industries are located in the more developed areas, average wages paid to these workers (as of 1995) were nearly three times higher, in fact, $0.58 per hour. If wage rates alone determined the ability of an industry to compete, then customers should now be fleeing China for Bangladesh, Burma and Pakistan. This simply is not happening. Chinese garment-export volumes are 6.5 times those of India, 15 times those of Pakistan, and 20 times those of Bangladesh. Clearly there are more factors involved in determining who survives than wage rates.

Full Value Cost Analysis has shown us a different picture. The international garment industry is simply not moving down to increasingly poorer countries, nor will it do so in the future.

Part III deals with four major garment-exporting areas and, using FVCA tools, projects their future. The four areas are:

WINNERS	LOSERS
EUROPEAN UNION	UNITED STATES
HONG KONG/CHINA	INDONESIA

...European Union international trade policy...

Chapter 13
The European Union

If you ask most Asian textile and garment producers or U.S. garment importers whose industry is the least competitive and the most vulnerable to cheap labor imports, the general consensus would be Western Europe. Many analysts predict that within ten years the only European industrial sewing machines in existence will be in museums—the entire industry will have collapsed under the weight of cheap-labor imports. This is actually one of the great myths of our times, perpetuated to a large degree by the French, German and Italian makers themselves. With tears in their eyes, they plead incessantly for greater and greater import restraints to permit what little still remains of their once great textile and garment industries to continue, if only for a few more years, to eke out a modest living.

This is nonsense. The EU is the largest and most developed trading bloc in the world. It has an aggregate GDP equal to that of the United States and external trade larger than that of the United States, even excluding intra-EU trade.

Nowhere is this more evident than in textiles and garments.[21] Already dominating nearly two-thirds of the world's trade in the two sectors, the EU notably exercises almost complete control over the imports it allows to enter the EU bloc. In 1995, 68.5% of all textile and 43.4% of all garment imports within the EU were exports from other members of the EU. After adding goods produced locally for domestic consumption, over 90% of all textiles and 70% of all garments consumed in the EU were produced in the EU. Furthermore, given the large portion of textile exports to Eastern Europe and North Africa, much of the extra-EU imports would have used EU-originated fabric.

The textile and garment-export industries are two of the EU's greatest success stories. It is here that the EU has been able to achieve low macro costs, coupled with low indirect and direct costs, to achieve what is probably the most competitive industry in existence anywhere in the world today. The sector's sustained preeminence is attributable to several historical advantages:

- The area has been the world's most important textile and garment design center for over a thousand years.

- The skill level of its workers and technicians is of the highest order. Western Europe has a tradition of skilled craftsmen, also dating back to medieval times.

- The quality of its machinery is unequaled. The industrial revolution began in Western Europe with new textile technology and that engineering innovation continues today.

- Western Europe has a stable, well-established domestic market for fashionable, better quality garments, unlike Asia.

Western Europe's leading position in the international textile and garment industries would have been even more dominant today had it not abdicated its position in the early post-World War II period. In 1945, the countries that today form the EU had all but been destroyed by the war. Their industrial plants lay in ruins. The people were penniless, unable to create effective domestic demand for textiles and garments. Over the following decade, Europe worked towards rebuilding their industries as they had existed before the war.

Recreating the past is almost always an error. For the European textile and garment industries, this strategy proved catastrophic. The world had changed since 1939. Prior to the war, Western Europe had enjoyed a complete monopoly on design innovation—new fabrics and new styles were always European. Also, pre-war Asia had also been a major importer of European textiles.

European mill owners forgot that during the war new fibers such as nylon had been developed in the United States. They underestimated the readiness of American mills and garment factories to meet the demands of U.S. consumers once rationing controls had been lifted. They failed to recognize that Asian countries, just becoming independent and rebuilding their own economies, looked at garments and textiles as ideal industries for development. Even Europe's historical fashion edge provided little support. American mills with their new synthetics and more efficient machinery already monopolized their own domestic textile market. American garment manufacturers discovered that it was far more profitable to copy European fashion ideas than to buy the European-made garments themselves.

By the time the European mills and garment factories discovered how the world had evolved, most were bankrupt. Far from regaining their traditional overseas markets in Asia, the newly developing industries in Hong Kong, Japan, South Korea and Taiwan were able to produce both textiles and garments at lower costs and sell in Europe at lower prices than the European manufacturers. At the same time, the United States ceased to be a profitable market for European-made textiles and garments.

By the late 1950s, a great shakeout of the European textile and garment industries had taken place. Those still around after the dust had settled, particularly Continental European manufacturers, began to work out strategies for survival and eventual return to profitability. Rather than turn away from their traditional values of high-quality standards, design innovation and reasonable minimums, they chose to make these indirect-cost advantages central to their strategies.

The textile mills—particularly in Belgium, Germany, Italy, Luxembourg, the Netherlands and to some degree, France—made major investments in new capital equipment. (As a result of this sustained investment from their textile mill colleagues, the European textile machine industry is today a thriving and highly profitable sector. Throughout Asia, from China to South Korea and even Japan, textile mills and fabric converters use European equipment.) Slowly the mills began to recover.

Progress in the garment industry did not keep pace with textiles. As recently as 1980, British, French and Italian garment factories generally used obsolete machinery, and all had reputations for inflexibility and late delivery. Quality standards were always high, but what good is high quality if the factory refuses to make what the customer wants and then ships late?

This scenario has now changed dramatically. Today, four of the world's top ten textile exporters and four of the top ten garment exporters are EU countries. Furthermore, the EU encompasses both high and low-end producers. Britain, France, Germany, Italy and the Netherlands all have viable high-end industries while Greece, Portugal and Spain export low-end merchandise. Some countries such as Italy are able to produce both high-end and low-end garments within its own borders. High-quality production centers around Florence and Milan, while Bari in southern Italy produces cheaper export goods.

MACRO COSTS

Much of the EU garment industry's success is attributable to its low macro costs, a reflection of important factors such as excellent education, infrastructure and logistics, availability of materials and sub-materials, lack of corruption, label cachet, and the existence of trade restraints.

Education

European colleges and polytechnics provide the highest standards of garment industry-related education. This is true not only for design and marketing, but in the technical aspects of production as well. In countries such as Britain and Germany, students studying garment design are taught the latest computer-assisted design using the most up-to-date machinery. Students interested in patternmaking or factory management are likewise exposed to the latest computer-assisted manufacturing techniques and equipment.

Not only do European governments support technical education, but their industry also takes an active role. This contrasts with the United States where garmentmakers still place minimal value on formal education. In Germany, for example, leading garment producers provide senior staff to teach in polytechnic schools. This way students are ensured practical education from those who actively work in the field, while the company contributing the instructors can now call its head of production *Herr Professor*.

More than any other factor, education provides the edge that keeps the European industry ahead of its Third World competitors.

Infrastructure and Logistics

In Europe, you pick up your telephone, dial a number and speak to your party. You take the whole operation for granted. In countries like Bangladesh, India, Indonesia and Pakistan, the fact that you have a telephone to pick up is in itself remarkable. That it works and that you can actually talk to someone on the other end is exceptional. The fact that the cost of your telephone service in these countries may be many times that of Europe is simply one more fact of life for working in the Third World. The light switch that actually turns on the lights, the fax machine that actually faxes, the *autostrada* (*autobahn* or thruway) that actually goes where you want to go—these are all things that Europeans take for granted but which most Third World garment-exporting nations still lack.

It is less expensive and much faster to truck wool tweed fabric from Glasgow, Scotland, to southern Italy than fabric produced in Jakarta, Indonesia, to Medan, Indonesia. To obtain the same level of infrastructure that currently exists in Western Europe, Asia will need to spend over *a trillion dollars* in the next generation and some countries have hardly begun. Many European buyers can't wait and will prefer to work closer to home.

Materials and Sub-materials

Everything is available in the EU. All the support industries and products required to operate are in place and readily obtainable. Special fabrics, yarns and trim, are all a telephone call away with 24-hour delivery to your door. Because what you need is available when you need it, your factory in Germany or Italy can make more informed decisions later in the production cycle, keep minimal inventories and provide customers with wider choice and faster delivery.

China has a developing wool industry. You can buy wool/acrylic yarn in one quality (60/40) in a choice of two counts (48/2 and 56/2) in many colors, provided you are willing to wait 90 days for delivery and open your letter of credit 120 days in advance.

In contrast, Germany has a developed wool industry. You can buy wool/acrylic yarn in six compositions and ten counts in a choice of about a thousand colors with 3-day delivery and 60-day credit terms. If you, a sweater manufacturer, deal with German yarn suppliers, you can sell first, then produce. In China, you have to be a good guesser because you will have to buy your yarn before you have had an opportunity to sell anything at all.

Costings are relative. The EU's strong levels of education, infrastructure and well-developed support industries provide their apparel manufacturers with lower macro costs. The fact that German choice for wool/acrylic yarn is wider, that delivery is faster and payment terms more favorable, offers undeniable macro-cost advantages for working with Germany over China.

Corruption

Compared to Third World garment-exporting nations, EU countries are relatively corruption-free. Corruption does exist in Europe, especially in multi-billion dollar arms acquisitions or the illegal drug trade. However, when you the garmentmaker import fabric from Europe, you pay customs *duty*—you do not pay the customs *officer*. You pay your electricity bill— not the man who comes to read the meter.

The absence of corruption goes a long way towards leveling the playing field. In Europe, an outsider can survive. An American company can succeed on its own in London, Paris or Milan. If the same company set up in Karachi, Jakarta or Bombay, it would not survive for a week without a local partner who knows the ways in, out and around the local system.

EU companies enjoy lower macro costs not only because they do not pay bribes. They have lower costs overall because the system simply operates more smoothly without corruption. If orders are late, the fault lies with the factory that controls the production process, not with a government agency that used its power to stop all operations because some bureaucrat felt he was not receiving his fair cut.

Label Cachet

Which would you prefer—a garment marked *Made in Pakistan* or a garment marked *Made in France*? Hong Kong produces garments as well made as any from Italy, but I would pay more for the garment marked *Made in Italy*. This may not be fair, but it is a reality. EU countries enjoy a macro-cost advantage simply because their country names and European location connote long-standing quality with consumers. Importers, in turn, use this country-of-origin advantage as a selling point.

Trade Restraints

Of all the important macro-cost advantages enjoyed by EU members, the most significant is political. All trade blocs are by nature exclusionary. The mirror of the advantages enjoyed by members is disadvantages imposed on all nonmembers. EU members export garments duty-free; nonmembers pay an average of 20%. Members ship free of non-tariff restrictions; nonmember imports are strictly controlled by quota. When all else fails, the EU arbitrarily imposes dumping duties on outside exporters.

Most trading blocs try to protect their members. Few do so with the single-minded determination of the European Union. A measure of the EU's ability to exclude garment imports from outside the bloc will be demonstrated in 2004, when the World Trade Organization is scheduled to phase out all textile and garment quotas. Regardless of the WTO's good intentions and all their efforts, I can assure you that on January 1,

2005, yet another new quota year will begin. The motto of the bloc should be: *The EU takes care of its own, all others can drop dead.*

INDIRECT COSTS

A modern Italian or German garment factory is a capital-intensive operation. Many garment products for which Asian factories wrongly assume they enjoy an absolute advantage can, in fact, be produced in Italy or Germany at far lower direct costs. Some of these items are basic and intarsia sweaters, all types of lined coats and jackets and tailored pants. In fact, the only areas in which Asia has a clear, direct-cost advantage are handknit or ornamented sweaters, cotton blouses, down jackets and coats, straw handbags, silk garments of all types, and some cashmere sweaters.

However, it is not in the *direct* costs where the European mills and factories enjoy their greatest advantage. The secret of the European industry's success is in its *indirect-cost* advantages, including:

- Strong research and development;

- Continuous upgrading of worker skills;

- Understanding the customer's needs;

- Good management.

Research and Development

Europe's dominance in innovative textile research and development takes physical form twice a year, when thousands of European textile and yarn companies present their latest collections in massively staged shows. These shows are nothing like the glamourous *haute couture* fashion shows of Paris, New York and Milan featured so prominently in *Vogue and Women's Wear Daily*. These are industry shows, such as the well-established *Premiere Vision* in Paris, where mills show their newest fabrics. This is real business.

Apparel designers from the world over plan their collections around the latest fabric ideas presented at these shows. Suppliers who want their fabrics to be included in the new season must participate. Asian mills are locked out. For the most part, Asian mills do no collections anyway—their forte is copying. However, the timing of the European fabric and yarn shows is such that it is almost impossible to copy the fabrics fast enough to produce stock garments in time for the upcoming season. If an international manufacturer wants the latest fashion fabrics and yarn, he must nearly always buy from European mills and produce his garments in Europe.

When discussing research and development in the textile and garment industries, most people look first to the textile sector, pointing to evidence such as newly discovered yarn polymers or the latest in high-speed looms and computerized finishing equipment. While these are indeed important, R&D plays an even greater role in garments. While an outsider might not associate garments with R&D at all, the garment industry arguably invented its own form of continuous R&D. It is called fashion.

Worker Skills

Worker skills are highly prized in Europe, a simple reality that still escapes many Third World factory managers. Once again, sophisticated worker skills are immediately associated with the capital-intensive textiles sector. For example, most industry professionals recognize that the quality of Chinese silk finished in China, even with Italian or German machinery, cannot compare with the same Chinese fabric finished in France, Germany or Italy.

What most people do not realize is that worker skills are even more important in European garment production than textiles. The look and fit of even a moderately-priced European garment is special. Asian sewers take the fashion out of a garment —Europeans put the fashion back in. To a Chinese sewer, a dress or a jacket is just a product. The sewer follows the instructions and specifications, ensures that seam allowances and machine tension are correct, and sews the garment without any regard to what they are making. To a European worker, the garment is something to wear. In Europe, the sewer will have an opinion about the style and will understand what the designer wants. The result is not only better 'fashion'—it generally ensures that mistakes in a European factory will not end in complete disaster.

In a competitive environment, satisfaction of customer needs is vital to survival. Sadly, many Third World producers operate with the attitude: "This is what I make. Take it or leave it." When profitable domestic sales are rising, failure to satisfy less profitable export customers may not be costly. But when market conditions change, the inability to adapt may mean the difference between survival and going out of business. This was the error made by many European companies themselves in the 1950s, and the survivors have learned from their mistake. The best illustration of this lesson concerns minimums. Third World producers regularly demand minimums of as high as 2,500 dozen per style or 10,000 yards per pattern. The European factory works with virtually no minimums at all.

European mills and factories have chosen to satisfy their customers. Despite the sobering realities of Asia's recent financial turmoil, few Asian manufacturers have yet to do the same.

DIRECT COSTS

A garment sewer in Italy is paid over $16 an hour, including benefits. The same worker in Vietnam is paid $0.16 an hour. A sewer in Germany is paid between $22 and $29 an hour, depending on which part of Germany and whose study you looking at. The same worker in Sri Lanka is paid $0.26. What direct-cost advantage can there be in a factory where wages are a hundred times greater than wages in a competitor's factory?

239

In fact, given the recent advances in garmentmaking technology and provided a company is willing to make substantial investments, EU direct costs for many products compare quite well with direct costs in China and other low-labor-cost exporting countries.

The textile sector's capital-intensive nature is well established. Modern spinning, weaving, knitting, dyeing and printing mills require large amounts of capital. Each new job in the Italian spinning industry requires an additional investment in new machinery in excess of $300,000. In a modern textile mill, labor rates are by far secondary cost considerations. Furthermore, additional labor resources cannot replace modern machinery either in achieving higher product quality or lowering product cost. For example, China may have a monopoly on raw cashmere and plenty of low-cost, relatively skilled workers, but cashmere yarns and fabric produced in China are in every way inferior to those produced in Italy's high-tech mills.

In recent years, many EU garment producers have also made substantial capital investments. Today, not only are most sweater yarns better and cheaper in Europe than in Asia, the EU has also regained its preeminent position as a novelty sweater producer. Computerized knitting machines can produce jacquards, intarsias and specialty stitches to a higher-quality standard and at a lower cost than even the cheapest Asian makers. Those same efficiency levels have also been attained in a wide range of other garment products, from lingerie to jackets and coats.

Thanks to these cost and product advantages, the countries of the EU have been able to maintain their lead within the EU at the expense of Asia. From 1993 to 1995, intra-EU share of total world apparel imports was stable, falling only from 43.8% to 43.4%. During the same period, world market share of Asian apparel imports fell from 30.5% to 28.5%.

In order to further solidify intra-European trade, certain preferred export countries—Central and Eastern Europe, Turkey and French-speaking North Africa—are being encouraged to increase sales to the EU over traditional Asian exporters.

EU PREFERRED EXPORTERS

In addition to intra-EU trade, there are two other trading blocs of importance to Europe:

- Asia

- Eastern Europe-Turkey-North Africa.

In 1995, these two blocs, together with intra-EU trade, constituted 87.3% of EU textile imports and 88.7% of garment imports.

The preceding section clearly explains why intra-EU trade constitutes such a large percentage of the EU's textile and garment imports. Asia's position as a major post-World War II garment and textile manufacturing center also explains its strong role. But the existence of the third bloc is a little harder to understand.

- Why is Eastern Europe-North Africa-Turkey a bloc?

- Why is the Eastern Europe-North Africa-Turkey bloc so important to EU trade?

- Why is the market share for this bloc growing so rapidly,[22] particularly when market share for both Asia and intra-EU trade is actually slightly declining?

The answer to all three questions is the same: macro-cost advantages. The European Union is more than simply a customs union—it is also very much a political union. In some circumstances, political considerations are more important to trade than comparative trade advantages. These political considerations affect macro costs, nowhere more than in Eastern Europe, Turkey and North Africa.

Eastern Europe

In the twentieth century, Western Europe nations fought two devastating wars whose immediate causes were of Eastern European origin. Up to the end of the Cold War, there existed the real possibility that there could be a third, even more horrendous, war. Western European leaders believe that stability, prosperity and democratic institutions are closely interrelated: one does not exist without the other. The same leaders also consider a stable, prosperous and democratic Eastern Europe to be one of their primary responsibilities.

To Western European government leaders, the German hyperinflation beginning in 1923, the collapse of the Kreditanstalt Bank in 1931, the collapse of the Weimar Republic, the rise of the Nazi Party, and World War II are all part and parcel of an inextricably linked chain of events. Loss of prosperity brought instability. The loss of stability brought the rise of totalitarian regimes, which in turn resulted in a catastrophic war and the destruction of Western Europe.

Compared to the Battle of Armageddon, the sacrifice of some T-shirts and jeans, a few million yards of twill fabric or pounds of texturized yarn, is negligible. To help the newly formed Eastern European democracies to achieve prosperity and stability, the EU will provide credits, tariff advantages,[23] and any other assistance it can. This is just a fact of life.

Turkey

If Eastern Europe is the memory of past catastrophes, fundamentalist Islamic countries is the nightmare of the future. To most European governments, the end of the Cold War simply substituted one imminent

...European governments fear the spread of Fundamentalist Islam...

disaster with another. As the threat of Soviet expansion dissipated, it was replaced with the spread of Fundamentalist Islam. Over twelve centuries after the Battle of Tours, European governments once again cringe at the specter of alien horsemen brandishing their swords across the river.

While you may question the logic of their fears, you must accept its existence. In the eyes of most European government leaders, Islam is Colonel Qaddafi, the Mullahs of Iran and Saddam Hussein. Nor is this fear limited to Europe. A plane explodes off Long Island or a federal government building is blown up in Oklahoma City and the immediate U.S. government reaction is: "Islamic Fundamentalists did this." It matters little that the latter turned out to be the work of home-grown right-wing lunatics while the former was most likely an accident.

For European leaders, a single buffer exists in the region: secular Islamic Turkey.

European governments look at the current rise of Fundamentalist Islam the same way they look at the past rise of totalitarian governments. Poverty results in instability. Instability results in a decline of democratic institutions. The decline of democratic institutions brings the rise of Fundamentalist Islam. Again, Europe will assist Turkey in whatever ways necessary if it keeps the fundamentalist hordes at bay.

To attract Turkish support and keep it loyal to the Western way of life, T-shirts have also become a weapon of war. Many countries supported NATO in its defense of Kuwait during the Gulf War. However, for its support, Turkey received an added thank you from Europe's longstanding American allies: its allocations for the perennially exhausted quota categories 338/9 and 638/9 (cotton and MMF knit shirts) were doubled.

North Africa

In 1994, Tunisia exported $1.84 billion worth of garments worldwide. Of this amount, $1.68 billion was exported to the EU. For the same period, Morocco exported $739 million worldwide, of which the EU imported virtually 100%.

These countries are not great garment producers nor was there any indigenous fashion industry. However, 50 years ago, they were part of the French Empire. The French remember their former subjects, just as the British and Belgians remember theirs. These ex-imperialist powers believe—whether rationally or not—that they still possess an ongoing relationship with their former colonies. Where that relationship is reciprocated, there is a concomitant obligation. That obligation has been translated into preferential garment imports.

Political considerations notwithstanding, there are other valid reasons why the EU would import garments from these preferred areas. Eastern Europe has a history of successful textile and garment production. Turkey is the world's seventh largest cotton producer. North Africa offers a vast pool of cheap labor.

Most importantly, most of the work produced in these countries is on a CMT basis. Textiles exported from the EU are processed in Eastern Europe, North Africa and Turkey and returned to the EU as finished garments. For the garments produced on a CMT basis, 60% or more of every dollar paid for imports has, in fact, already been paid to domestic textile producers. Compare this to imports from Asia where 100% of every dollar paid out remains in Asia.

THE FUTURE

Of all the textile and garment-producing areas in the world, the European Union will be best equipped to meet the challenges of the future. Apparel imports into Europe from other regions may rise, but the 43% intra-EU share will be maintained.

Import levels from the preferred export countries will continue to grow at the expense of Asia. How long that trend will continue is difficult to predict. The advantages enjoyed by the Eastern Europe-Turkey-North Africa bloc are macro-cost advantages. As long as the conditions giving rise to their respective preferential status persists, they will enjoy these advantages. However, there is a limit to how far the EU will go. If the choice is between imports from this bloc and imports from Asia, the preferred exporters will prevail. But when EU members themselves are called upon to pay, it will be a different story.

Unemployment in the EU now averages 10%, with the latest figures from France and Italy showing 13% and Germany not much better. Furthermore, each EU country has its own, well-established garment industry to protect. None will give Eastern Europe a totally free ride.

Turkey's future is limited by its historical enmity with Greece, an EU member, and is not expected to accrue any further macro-cost advantages in the short term. Both Eastern European countries and Turkey want full membership in the EU. In the medium term, few, if any, are expected to receive it. Therefore, while both will continue to enjoy advantages over Asia as far as the EU is concerned, they will still be outsiders and subject to some forms of duty and other controls.

North Africa has its own problems. There is a growing consensus that too much aid has already been given to African nations who have dissipated these gifts and done nothing to improve the standard of living of their people. There is also a serious problem of bigotry. The French government may want to do more for their former colonies but to some degree they must take heed of Mr. Le Pen and his fellow right-wing extremists.

At the end of the day, the important lesson to be learned here is the serious impact of political considerations in affecting macro costs. There is no question that Asian countries such as Indonesia, Sri Lanka and Bangladesh are making enormous strides to reduce macro costs. No doubt these efforts will continue. But as far as European buyers and investors are concerned, these same countries must accept their seriously disadvantaged position.

In contrast, the governments of Eastern Europe, Turkey and North Africa have done little to earn their macro-cost advantages. Certainly, their human rights records, the honesty of their civil services, or their levels of infrastructure are nothing to brag about. Buyers do not go to Romania because the government is democratic. They do not go to Turkey because the bureaucracy is efficient or honest. They do not go to Morocco because the communications are excellent. They go because their own governments see political value sufficiently important as to outweigh these other disadvantages. To induce buyers and investors, lower tariffs and other trade benefits are offered.

For European companies, these macro-cost advantages do not exist in Asia. In the final analysis, as the preferred exporters in Eastern Europe, Turkey and North Africa improve quality and raise production capacity, Asian exports to the EU will decline, with only those Asian countries who have unique cost advantages able to compete.

...Americans stagger on as its people keep getting richer...

Chapter 14
The United States and NAFTA

The United States is an extremely difficult country to analyze. By far the world's largest economic power, its overall trading volumes are unsurpassed. American people enjoy both one of the highest standards of living and the lowest unemployment rates in the world. Surely, this is a nation of prosperity.

At the same time, the United States has registered a negative balance of trade for virtually every year since 1952. It is the world's largest debtor nation. It has one of the highest crime rates and, with the possible exception of Russia, enjoys the dubious distinction of having a greater percentage of its population in jail than any other country in the world. Surely, this is also a nation facing disintegration.

In fact, both views are correct depending on your perspective. Like a band of drunken mountain climbers, Americans stagger on as they go yet higher and higher. Despite the violence, the drugs and the chaos, it is probable that the United States and its people will just keep getting richer.

The U.S. domestic garment industry is a microcosm of the American economic and political system. The United States is one of the leading design centers in the world. Its ability to merchandise, promote and retail is unparalleled. In fact, the U.S. garment industry is second to none at everything, except actually making the garments—where it is on a par with Bangladesh.

At one extreme are companies like Levi Strauss, whose annual volume of $6 billion is larger than Indonesia's total textile and garment exports. A closely-held business where the original family owns 100% of all shares, it is arguably the most professionally operated garment company in the world. Yet despite its relative health, Levi's is reducing its domestic production and expanding overseas. At the other end are sweatshops in New York and Los Angeles, where illegal immigrants from Mexico, the Caribbean and Asia are literally held in bondage, forced to sew for below subsistence-level wages and working in conditions far worse than in Indonesia.

How can a country that manufactures the world's finest commercial jet planes and most sophisticated computers be incapable of producing a decent pair of pants without resorting to factories modeled after scenes from the Gulag Archipelago? Why are Germany and Italy able to operate modern garment industries and not the United States?

For the answer, listen to Louie the Lip—the prototypical victim. In 1997, when his real-life counterpart, a Los Angeles sweatshop operator was arrested, he defended his position by pleading: "This is the only way we can compete with imports."

Every year more and more self-proclaimed victims buy into what I call the Great American Garmentmaker's Myth. This is how the story goes.

The Great American Garmentmaker's Myth

American garmentmakers are unable to compete because for 50 years they have been attacked by evil forces beyond their control!

- The domestic garmentmakers were destroyed by rapacious labor unions.
- The domestic garmentmakers were destroyed by the laziness of the American worker.
- The domestic garmentmakers were destroyed by Asian factories paying slave labor wages.

Like most fairy tales, this myth is demonstrably false. It is true that for many years labor unions did make domestic factories less competitive, yet makers did not have to move all the way to China just to escape unions. They could have gone to almost any state in the southern or southwestern part of the United States, just as the textile people did.

It is equally true that the days when Italian, Polish and Jewish immigrants worked 14-hour days, six days a week, are long gone. But to claim that just because the United States no longer tolerates sweatshops that American workers have become lazy is foolish. The U.S. worker has the highest productivity in the world. American workers clock longer hours and more working days than their German counterparts and are more productive than Japanese workers. In fact, nearly every country in the world, both industrialized and developing, is trying to copy the American model to achieve greater worker efficiency.

Finally, it isn't the low-wage, Third World countries which head the list of the world's top ten garment exporters. Half the countries on the list—including France, Germany, Great Britain and Italy, as well as the United States itself—have wages equal to or higher than those paid to American workers. Slave wages have nothing to do with low garment costs.

Put plainly, the American garment industry failed for the same reasons any industry fails—lack of management skills, insufficient investment and poor strategic planning.

European garment factory managers are engineers, many with graduate degrees. Their American counterparts are self-taught. Few have any university education and even fewer U.S. universities have departments teaching factory management skills of any sort, let alone those required to operate a garment factory.

European garment factory owners place a high priority on investment in new capital equipment. To their American counterpart, the choice was first between a new buttonhole machine and a fur coat for the wife, and later between a new fusing machine and a condominium in Florida. The American has comfortably retired to Florida where his wife can wear her mink coat without feeling out of place, but his factory is now out of business.

For years, major U.S. garment manufacturers refused to believe that they were the problem. They lobbied Congress who responded by giving them the highest level of protection of any industry in America. When this failed to stop competition from more efficient factories overseas, they resorted to spurious lawsuits charging unfair competition. Had industry leaders invested only a fraction of the money they threw away on politicians in new equipment, their industry might be cost-effective today. Had they spent more money training managers and engineers and less money hiring lawyers, today the U.S. garment industry could have been in the same strong competitive position as the U.S. textile industry. Instead, even the most supposedly knowledgeable importers are firm subscribers to the myth that cheap wages, no unions and hard-working Asians are the key to their continued success.

To understand how the misconceptions behind the Great American Garmentmaker's Myth took root, it is necessary to briefly review the history of the U.S. textile and garment industries and the rise of garment imports. Today's modern textile industry began in mid-eighteenth century Great Britain. By the end of the century, American mills were already operating in New England with several major U.S. companies such as Deering Milliken still surviving today. Their workers were traditional Americans with very traditional values. Since there was no garment industry to speak of, products were sold to tailors, dressmakers and directly to consumers who sewed at home.

The garment industry began in the second half of the nineteenth century led by menswear which developed shortly after the Civil War. By 1889, a single New York company sold 15,000 men's suits monthly priced at $1.95 (actual costs were $1.125 per suit). Ladieswear began with cloaks and waists. At the time, women's fashion consisted of a long skirt with a bustle and a short jacket. Under the jacket women wore a waist, a long-sleeved blouse ending at the waist. This waist became the first garment to be mass-produced in large scale. Women would still have their skirts and jackets custom-made or sewn at home, but waists were sold over-the-counter by the draper, who also retailed the fabric.

An industry of waistmakers sprang up. Sewers were literally locked into factories and toiled unbelievably long hours. Working conditions were unimaginably poor. The infamous term sweatshop was coined in the New York garment industry. Most of the workers had emigrated from Europe, many for political reasons. Activists in the factories began to form unions, which were ruthlessly opposed by management.

On March 26, 1911, the Triangle Waist Factory—the largest garment factory in New York City—burned to the ground. Of the 850 workers trapped behind locked doors, 146 were burned to death. Some tried to escape by jumping off the roof and were killed. Two labor unions trace their beginnings to this tragedy: the International Ladies' Garment Workers' Union (ILGWU) and the Amalgamated Clothing Union, representing workers in the men's cloak-and-suit industry.

The early perceptions of the U.S. garment industry formed nearly a century ago persist today. Textiles is an industry of gentlemen who trace their roots to the beginning of the country. The people who run these companies are called industrialists. The industry has great political influence. Garments is a business of immigrants. Garment workers are immigrants; their bosses are immigrants. The people who run these companies are called makers.

The end of World War II found the American textile and garment industries in top gear, their factories flush with war profits. After severe clothes rationing for four years, an unprecedented demand for garments of all types was unleashed. With European and Asian industry all but destroyed, the United States was the only country in the world in a position to meet that demand. Doing business and making profit simply became too easy and few U.S. makers bothered about reinvesting their earnings or worried about quality control.

Business boomed over the following decade. Almost anything would sell and at almost any price. Union demands were accepted without fuss and price increases immediately passed on to a docile consumer. But as early as 1955, the first signs of big changes to come were already in place.

At the lowest end of the garment industry where shirts were sold in supermarkets, some companies who had been contracting their production to domestic factories were already experimenting with Japanese production. At the time, 100% cotton gingham was available in Japan for $0.15 a yard; an average garment could be produced for less than FOB $6.00 per dozen and retail for $0.99 a unit. Between 1952 and 1962, thriving industries were created in Japan, Taiwan and Hong Kong. Very quickly, these countries took over large chunks of the U.S. mass-market sector.

In 1962, the United States negotiated its first multilateral quota agreement with Hong Kong, restricting exports of cotton garments and some textiles to 1961 levels. In the next 12 months, similar agreements were negotiated with Japan and Taiwan. Ironically, rather than limiting the growth of the export industries in these countries, quotas actually ensured even greater profits which in turn provided capital for expansion. The manufacturer holding quota realized very quickly that because exports were limited, he could charge a premium for the quota. Simultaneously, manufacturers also began to expand into other fibers which were not yet restricted by quota and trade upwards to higher-value-added garments.

This change did not go smoothly. Indirect costs were high since Asian factories were still inexperienced, nor did they possess the technical expertise required to produce higher quality garments. Furthermore, the existing textile industries in Hong Kong, South Korea and Taiwan were unable to produce materials for anything but the cheapest goods.

Nevertheless, Asian imports did offer real advantages over the goods made in the United States owing primarily to the peculiar methodology used by the ILGWU to calculate labor rates. At the time, American garment workers were paid on a piecework basis—so much to sew a zipper, so much to set a sleeve. The unions recognized, however, that the time, care and experience required to perform each operation changes from style to style. This made it almost impossible to set standardized labor-cost calculations.

The Amalgamated, whose members produced menswear, solved the problem by specifying levels of quality for each type of garment and charging a premium for each increased level of quality. For example, men's jackets were divided into five levels. The cost of setting a sleeve on a No. 5 jacket might be two-and-a-half times more than setting a sleeve on a No.1 jacket. The logic was quite reasonable. Setting a sleeve on a high-quality man's jacket is a four-step operation requiring a considerable degree of skill and a great deal of handwork. The Amalgamated's system worked quite well. As a result, even today, high-quality men's jackets are produced in the United States while no factory in Asia is competent to make a No. 5 jacket.

In contrast the ILGWU, representing ladieswear workers, took a less rational direction. Instead of adding a factor for quality, the ILGWU added a factor for wholesale price. Each manufacturer was categorized by price range—budget, moderate, better, couture. It made no difference what the garment actually looked like or its quality demands. If you classified as a *moderate*, you paid more to get a zipper sewn than your competitor who was classified as a *budget*.

The ILGWU went further, establishing *craft guilds* for technical workers including cutters, patternmakers and graders. Theoretically, the purpose of the guild was to train skilled workers and to maintain standards. In practice, the guilds existed simply to keep their members employed. If you needed a cutter, you went to the guild who supplied a cutter. Once the cutter came to work, you could not fire him, regardless of his limitations. Manufacturers were also prohibited from installing capital equipment in their cutting departments without guild permission. In fact, permission was seldom granted. The level of technology present when you signed your first union contract was the level at which you were kept—forever.

Manufacturers found themselves in a strait-jacket. Fashion was being dictated by the labor union which decided what styles you could afford to make. Even before Asian factories had the necessary ability or experience, U.S. better ladieswear buyers were on their doorsteps pushing them to trade up.

Today, the U.S. apparel market for imports is segmented. At the lowest level, all mass-market retailers in America import garments and also buy domestically. At the higher end, better quality menswear is still produced domestically. However, in ladieswear, the profitable, better market is dominated by imports—a direct result of ILGWU piecework calculations. There is little chance of this market ever returning to the United States.

The U.S. textile industry never had this problem. When labor costs in New England rose and labor unions started to organize, the mills simply closed their doors forever and moved south to warmer climates and to states where unions were forbidden. The textile industry also enjoys heavy political clout. As a result, domestic textile protection includes not only quota but duty rates even higher than those for garments. As already discussed in Case Study XVI, these duty differentials effectively mean that in order to protect its domestic textile industry, the United States government subsidizes overseas garment exporters. It is cheaper for a buyer using non-U.S-made fabric to produce in Asia than in the United States.

On the other hand, for NAFTA and Section 807 garments, the U.S. now subsidizes overseas garment factories who use American fabric. In both cases, normal trade patterns have been distorted to protect the U.S. textile industry—even at the expense of the domestic garment industry. The usual logic would be that politicians should favor the garment industry which, being labor-intensive, employs far more people. However, in the United States, the political influence of the textile *industrialists* far outweighs that of the garment *makers*.

Despite their longstanding advantages, the U.S. textile industry of the 1970s and early 1980s was unprofitable and losing domestic market share. By the early 1980s, however, the industry had woken up and realized that the road to health lay in developing indirect-cost advantages. The three-pronged plan involved:

- Consumer research

- Pure research and development

- Capital investment

The basic concept is deceptively simple: Find out what people want and give it to them. In fact, the reality takes real commitment and substantial resources.

Traditionally, companies develop products and then try to persuade the public that they have a need for these products. Companies often consider their average consumer to be so mentally deficient as to not know what he or she wants. This is true the world over, particularly in Asia, where manufacturers and retailers frequently assume the consumer will buy anything and at any price. The U.S. textile industry also upheld this belief but, faced with falling sales, by the early 1970s they began to change.

...If the United States is, in fact, the consumer society,
it is because the consumer is king...

They became consumer-oriented. Textile companies started spending big money trying to determine what the customer wanted. They realized it would be far more cost-effective to develop products that the public actually wanted than to try to persuade the public that their products were what the public should want. From there, the companies began to invest in pure research, beginning at the furthest upstream point. For cotton, it was seed development—it takes 11 years to develop a new cotton strain. As early as 1973, the U.S. Department of Agriculture together with various specialist research facilities, began primary research into new cotton strains. Today, the high quality of U.S. cotton is to a large degree the result of ongoing work that began over 20 years ago. Similar work has been carried out by the major synthetic producers.

At the same time, mills began to reinvest in capital equipment. From spinning to finishing, the surviving companies totally reorganized themselves.

This system of *product development through consumer research* is unique to the United States, and contributes to the success of U.S. industry in general and the textile industry in particular. If the United States is, in fact, *the consumer society*, it is because the consumer is *king*. Asian industrialists from China to Indonesia would do well to emulate this philosophy before trade is liberalized and the consumer given real choices.

Meanwhile, the U.S. garment industry never underwent reorganization. There are exceptions, but by and large the U.S. garment industry is inflexible, poorly capitalized and badly managed. In a very real sense, NAFTA is the government's own admission that while the U.S. textile industry is worth saving, the garment industry will eventually go entirely offshore. Following world trade liberalization in the coming years, the revived and reorganized U.S. textile industry will remain strong, enjoying cost advantages at all levels.

U.S. TEXTILE INDUSTRY

Direct Costs

All stages of textile manufacturing are capital-intensive by nature. Only material and machinery—not labor—are relevant direct-cost factors. The U.S. textile industry offers low direct costs, combining quality capital equipment with the efficient use of raw materials.

- Raw Materials: The United States is rich in all basic fibers. It is the world's largest exporter of cotton. It has an extensive sheep industry supplying raw greasy wool. It certainly has the world's most advanced producers of synthetic resins. It would be wrong to conclude that the United State's comparative advantage rests only with its ample and relatively inexpensive supply of raw materials. In fact, where the U.S. really compares favorably to other second and third-generation producers is in its efficient use of those materials.

Case Study LXV—Efficient Use of Raw Materials

To ensure the highest quality cotton yarn, spinners must not only buy the most suitable cotton, but they must also ensure that the fiber mix is the best for each type of yarn they produce.

For this purpose, Cotton Incorporated, a nonprofit organization established to promote and increase the use of U.S. cotton, developed a special computerized system called Efficient Fiber Selection (EFS). The system analyzes each bale in the spinner's inventory and automatically computes the best mix to ensure the highest quality product for each yarn type. Today, every major spinner in the United States uses the EFS system.

The system is available to any mill in the world that uses a minimum of 30% U.S. cotton. Cotton Incorporated will go into the mill, set up the system in conjunction with the mill engineers and remain on-site until the system is in full operation. As a nonprofit body, Cotton Inc. will provide the system at below normal commercial rates. Here is an opportunity for Third World producers to bring in cutting-edge technology at minimal cost, but few take advantage of the opportunity. For example, given the high volume of raw cotton that Indonesia imports from the U.S., almost every Indonesian spinner qualifies for the EFS system, yet to date not a single mill has adapted it.

Spinning is a totally capital-intensive industry. It makes little sense for a company to invest heavily in capital equipment, then throw away that comparative advantage by consciously deciding not to use that equipment to its fullest potential.

- Capital Equipment: Twenty-five years ago the American industrial plant consisted of obsolete and worn-out equipment. This was true not only in textiles, but in virtually all areas including steel and chemical production. The United States has learned its lesson. Today, steel production in the U.S. is more efficient than in South Korea. The textile industry has followed course: it is quite competitive and will remain so.

Indirect Costs

The special facilities that allow for indirect-cost advantages also figure prominently in the U.S. textile industry.

- Fast Delivery: As in Europe, American mills and converters produce collections with special fabrics, patterns and colors. Provided customers work within the collection, they enjoy fast, often spot delivery, unmatchable by Asia's contract weavers.

- Small Minimums: Mills and converters that produce their own collections do not ask for any minimums since they do not normally produce fabric against indent orders. Downstream users—again, provided they work within the mill's collection—can choose from a wide variety of product without the need for costly and risky advance greige fabric purchases.

255

- Innovative Product: The U.S. textile industry is constantly working on new fibers, novelty yarns, special weaves and finishes. This is not just fashion—this is technical development. When new products are brought to the market, they often originate from the United States.

Macro Costs

The U.S. government has always taken a sympathetic view towards the textile industry. Whether in the form of high tariffs or specific quota limitations, these biases continue. Other macro-cost factors—education, infrastructure, bureaucracy—remain positive.

Crucial to the American textile revival has been the cooperation at all levels between government, semi-government and nonprofit organizations, universities and the industry. Also, another unique characteristic of U.S. research and development is its practical nature, with many techniques developed by the defense industry, for example, transposed into textiles. This ingenuity and invention is an American specialty.

NAFTA and its astounding early success have further consolidated the U.S. textile industry's strong position. The latest figures would indicate that this trend will continue. Meanwhile, the prognosis for the U.S. garment industry appears to be moving in exactly the opposite direction; U.S. domestic makers, with some important exceptions, will continue to weaken.

U.S. GARMENT INDUSTRY

Direct Costs

The American garment industry today is structured precisely as it was 100 years ago—a labor-intensive immigrant's industry. Each successive wave of immigrants gravitates towards the garment industry and then tries to get out as soon as possible. Today, even as demand for domestic production declines, factories are still unable to attract sufficient workers to fill orders. People would rather work at McDonald's flipping hamburgers than sit in front of a sewing machine.

Indirect Costs

The industry remains inflexible. You buy what the factory produces, or you do not buy at all. With few exceptions, American factories offer the same facilities as factories in the least- developed Third World countries, usually lacking sufficient capital to work on an FOB basis.

Macro Costs

NAFTA and CBI are the straw that broke the U.S. garment industry's back. Why produce in the United States when you can produce in Mexico and Central America using U.S. fabric with cheap labor?

After having supported the U.S. garment industry for almost two generations with high tariffs and quota barriers, the government appears to finally be giving up. The cost to the American economy has simply become too great. Consumers are forced to pay surcharges on imports simply to allow inefficient domestic producers to stay in business. Efficiently run American industries such as telecommunications, electronics and the service sectors are stifled—their ability to expand overseas is held hostage by the U.S. government's demands that other countries liberalize imports of these areas of products and services.

NAFTA

As we have discussed at length, the trading bloc is the single most important factor influencing garment costs. Insiders enjoy a strategic advantage in their geographic areas that no outsider can equal. Each year more garments sold in NAFTA countries will be produced by factories in NAFTA or its preferred Latin American exporters and fewer orders will be placed with the outside world. This trend is here to stay.

From the point of view of the U.S. textile industry, NAFTA is a wonderful institution—an area of free trade which also totally restricts textile imports. To the U.S. garment industry, NAFTA has been an unmitigated disaster. Five years before full quota and duty advantages kick in, Mexico is already the largest exporter of garments to the United States. By 2005, Mexico garment exports to the United States will equal or exceed the entire U.S. domestic production.

NAFTA's Preferred Exporters—CBI

Just as the EU looks upon Eastern Europe-Turkey-North Africa as its exporters of choice, NAFTA has its own list also chosen for political and cultural reasons. These are the members of the Caribbean Basin Initiative (CBI), who also enjoy duty and quota privileges.

The conditions for Section 807 production—duty charges only on additional labor charges for garments made from NAFTA-originated fabric cut in the U.S.—has also produced impressive results. As of 1995, $5.4 billion, or about 15.5% percent of all U.S. garment imports, came from CBI countries. Individually—with the exception of the Dominican Republic whose 1995 exports of $1.7 billion accounted for one-third of all 807 goods—CBI growth has, however, not followed the explosive pattern of Mexico.

Working in CBI countries remains problematic:

• Considerable political instability, in many cases bordering on civil war, especially in El Salvador, Haiti and Nicaragua;

• Little past experience with garments and virtually no textile industries;

• No available trims; all trims must be sent from the U.S.

...NAFTA has forever changed U.S. import priorities. Asian exporters take note...

U.S. companies lack the flexibility of their Asian competitors. As a result, 807 processing, with its extended logistics and underdeveloped operating conditions, is suitable only for large orders of basic garments with very long production schedules. CBI is a classic example of a 0-service industry where low direct costs such as labor and factory overheads are coupled with high indirect costs including high minimums, inability to produce difficult styles and unavailability of trim. In fact, the Caribbean could not have survived as a production center, much less reached a 15% share of the U.S. market, had not political considerations played such an important role.

Despite the obvious inefficiencies, or even because of them, the CBI countries could eventually represent a serious threat to some Asian exporters as the only garments they produce are those currently being produced by second and third-line Asian exporters. Certainly, CBI poses no direct challenge to producers in China, Hong Kong, South Korea or Taiwan who have all opened offshore factories in low-labor-cost countries to produce mass-market merchandise while retaining more complex and sophisticated work in Asia.

For now, Asia seems to be holding its own against CBI exports. However, if current trends continue the situation will change. Trade liberalization notwithstanding, U.S. political policy will always favor Central American countries over Asia. The U.S. textile industry will follow suit. After all, the more goods produced in CBI, the greater the sales of U.S. textiles. Even first-line Asian companies will eventually be forced to invest in the CBI countries in order to participate in the macro-cost advantages.

NAFTA: The Present

NAFTA enjoys all the advantages of CBI, and then some, without most of the drawbacks. Both logistics and division of production are superior. Moving goods to CBI countries requires shipping while the buyer must fly. The U.S., Canada and Mexico are all joined by land: goods and buyers can travel by road to NAFTA countries.

The division of work for CBI is inefficient. Cut fabric comes from the United States and some production must take place there. Garment parts have to be shipped by sea or air to Central America where more production takes place, then reshipped back to the United States. NAFTA is easier. The United States provides material; Mexico provides garment production. NAFTA relationships are fundamentally identical to any domestic textile/garment relationship. The unprecedented 40%-60% increases in Mexican garment exports to the U.S. in recent years would clearly demonstrate that U.S. companies agree.

In fact, the United States and Mexico are moving toward an integrated industry. It is quite possible that the pattern of trade within the EU will be mirrored within NAFTA. From all cost perspectives, the advantages look excellent. In direct costs, the combined strengths of the U.S. textile industry and low Mexican labor rates—20% of those in the U.S.—look unbeatable. An essentially domestic integrated operation would also benefit from maximum indirect-cost advantages. Finally, the macro-cost advantages of U.S./Mexico garment production hardly bear repeating: no quota, no duty, no extended freight times.

NAFTA: The Future

At present working in NAFTA does have some drawbacks: the quality of merchandise is substandard, deliveries are late and the factories have little idea of how to satisfy their customers. Yet, despite these serious problems, exports are exploding. Although some U.S. importers would disagree, the Mexicans will gradually learn to produce a good product and ship on time, just as the Hong Kong, South Korean and Taiwanese makers learned 20 years ago.

Market share for domestic garment production is currently similar for the United States and for countries in the EU—about 50% of garments are produced at home. A further 41% of EU imports originate within the EU, meaning that less than 30% of all garments sold in the EU originate from further afield.

Mexico and Canada each provide only 12.5% of total U.S. textile and garment imports—44% of total garments sold still comes from countries outside the United States. Should NAFTA patterns mirror those of intra-EU trade and reach the same 41%, loss of sales to the United States' current trade partners outside the NAFTA bloc could be as much as $12.5 billion annually. Should CBI grow the same way as the EU's associate exporters in Eastern Europe-North Africa-Turkey, the result—particularly to Asian exporters—would be catastrophic.

In the short term, there is no doubt that NAFTA trade will continue to grow. However, there are limitations, arising primarily from three factors:

- The end of the Multi-Fiber Agreement would make Asia more competitive. Right now both NAFTA and CBI countries have the advantage of no quota. If the MFA goes, this advantage would disappear.

- The requirement to use U.S. fabric limits Mexican production. What the U.S. textile industry produces, it produces well, but the overall industry is still inflexible. Garments requiring fabrics not produced in the United States enjoy no advantage from NAFTA production.

- This inflexibility carries over into the garment sector. The U.S. factory model currently being replicated in Mexico and the CBI is the high-speed shop with little emphasis on worker training or upgrading worker skills.

Excluded Third World producers cannot ignore the threat posed by the NAFTA and CBI trading blocs. Those countries and manufacturers whose exports to the U.S. consist primarily of commodity-type garments will be adversely affected. Those who can successfully compete in the higher quality sector should be able to retain their markets.

Chapter 15
Hong Kong/China

In a truly free-trade environment—a world without tariffs and quota—Hong Kong and China would dominate the international textile and garment industries. With annual sales of $70 billion, Hong Kong/China is the dominant textile and garment exporter in Asia. At $45 billion, it is the largest garment exporter in the world.

Not only unique for its sheer size, this bloc's development is a case study in how to build a successful garment industry. The Hong Kong and Chinese garment industries joined together long before Hong Kong returned to Chinese sovereignty in 1997. For the past twenty-five years, Hong Kong manufacturers have realized that their low indirect costs, coupled with China's low direct costs, would provide a singularly competitive product. The post-World War II history of these once separate industrial giants and the events leading to their amalgamation is well worth looking at.

HONG KONG: UP TO 1976

Prior to 1976, Hong Kong's export industries were totally separate from those of China. Up to that time, the United States prohibited any imports that contained materials of 'Red' Chinese origin. The United States was also Hong Kong's largest export market. Due to customs restrictions, Hong Kong factories dealing with the U.K., another major market, were also cut off from importing materials from China. Because of these conditions, each country's industry evolved separately and in distinct ways.

No superlatives can justly describe Hong Kong's success. Even with the benefit of hindsight, it is almost impossible to imagine how its present industry managed to flourish from its humble beginnings of the late 1950s. Today, Hong Kong is the center of the world's largest export-garment industry. Buyers come to Hong Kong from every importing nation to buy garments. Garments are in fact produced by factories—owned or controlled by Hong Kong companies—located in virtually every corner of the world. In a city of six million people, there are over 6,000 companies actively specializing in garment production and export. More garment orders are placed through companies in Hong Kong than in any other place in the world.

Although Hong Kong still retains its importance as a supplier of upmarket garments, its role as a cutting and sewing center is now diminishing. Yet Hong Kong's success continues due to its unique cost structure:

- Hong Kong offers its customers some of the most attractive indirect-cost advantages available anywhere. If you cannot make the pattern, decide on size specifications, or find the material or the trim, your Hong

Kong supplier will do the work for you. If your designer is inexperienced, never mind, your Hong Kong supplier will help you. Whatever your problem, provided you can open a letter of credit, your Hong Kong supplier stands ready to do the work for you at a cost far less than you would have to pay in your home country. You bring a sketch and the Hong Kong company will do the rest.

- Hong Kong has the lowest macro costs in the world. Do you want to establish a limited company? Your Hong Kong accountant can have the papers ready for your signature in less than an hour. If you can wait another hour, he will have an account opened at the bank of your choice, with temporary checks prepared. Hong Kong's transportation network is among the finest in the world. International communication is both efficient and inexpensive. At 16.5%, its business taxation rate is one of the lowest in the world and yet, nearly every year, the Hong Kong government manages to stay in the black. The bureaucracy is efficient and relatively honest. In short, everything a location, culture or government can provide to make doing business easy and more cost-effective, is available in Hong Kong.

Forty years ago, Hong Kong was just another producer of low-quality cotton garments, existing almost totally on orders that fast-developing Japan was no longer willing to accept. The ex-territory had its own indigenous cotton weaving and dyeing industries. But its customer base was limited to the lowest-priced importers and mass-market retailers in the United States. This situation continued until 1962 when the U.S. government placed non-tariff quota restrictions on the import of cotton garments. Hong Kong's subsequent actions enormously strengthened its position in the region:

- Because Hong Kong was the first to accept quotas, it was able to negotiate the largest quota of any country in Asia—immediately giving the ex-territory a preeminent position among Asian exporters;

- Because quotas restricted increases in existing products, Hong Kong's industry started to expand into other areas. A European export market was developed. Wool double knit suits, sweaters, and synthetics of all types became important industries. When in 1972, the United States extended quotas to include synthetics and woolens, Hong Kong's industry was already in position to benefit.

By 1976, when China began opening its doors, the Hong Kong garment industry was already the leading producer of better-quality garments in Asia, its agents and factories enjoying well-established relationships with better customers in both the United States and Europe.

CHINA: UP TO 1976

China today is the world's largest exporter of garments. For products such as silk or cashmere where China enjoys a natural advantage, it controls the world market. Contrary to a still widely-held misconception,

China's phenomenal success over the past two decades is not only the result of cheap labor. In fact, as we have already pointed out, average wages in Chinese garment-export factories are already several times higher than those in many Third World countries. Certainly, until 1976, no one would have looked twice at China.

From 1955 to 1976, all production in China was carried out by state factories. These large industrial units were totally integrated. Not only did they include weaving or knitting, dyeing and finishing facilities, but also garment production units (plus schools, farms and housing for the workers). In some instances, the in-house process even began with spinning. Because spinning, weaving, finishing and garment production each require differing economies of scale, these massive but inefficient state-controlled factories were incapable of manufacturing a reasonable product at any stage of the production process.

The role of the factory was to produce a specified quantity of output each month. Factory managers spent much of their time looking for materials which were often in short supply. In order to meet production quotas set by the State Economic Planning Commission, a factory which may have stood idle for three weeks awaiting materials delivery would then charge ahead for the final ten days to complete production. In this environment, little care could be taken to ensure reasonable levels of quality and no interest whatsoever was given to the customer's needs.

Just as all production rested with state factories, so all export sales rested with the China National Textile Corporation. China-Tex has branch offices in all China's provincial capitals and major cities. Its role was to work with the customer, negotiate prices, select factories and pass on instructions. When China first opened in 1976, early overseas garment customers quickly realized that any product purchased on indent order from a state-owned company would almost certainly be incorrect, late or of poor quality, and often all three simultaneously.

1976

In 1976 the United States recognized China, setting off a chain of events which would revolutionize Hong Kong and China's respective textile and garment industries. For the first time, Hong Kong companies were allowed to work legally in China and they poured in.

Not everyone understands clearly why Hong Kong industry expanded so rapidly into China. There were two principal reasons:

- Hong Kong factory owners were able to hire unlimited workers who spoke the same language as the Hong Kong managers. The fact that Chinese workers were paid less was an added bonus, not the primary reason for the move. Hong Kong factories moved to China not to attract cheap labor but rather to attract additional labor—regardless of cost. Prior to 1976, the Hong Kong textile and garment industries had suffered serious labor shortages. At one point, the labor shortfall was estimated at over 25%. To find workers, companies went to

263

extraordinary lengths, advertising extensively on billboards and in movie theaters and offering bonuses to employees who could recruit new workers. To retain workers, almost all factories in Hong Kong paid each worker one extra day's pay per half-month. This labor shortage continued well into the 1990s.

- China exerted an enormous cultural draw on Hong Kong. The great majority of Hong Kong people emigrated from Guangdong Province, contiguous to Hong Kong. As the new immigrants became more successful, they would send gifts back to their home villages. In the beginning these were consumer goods—radios, television sets and refrigerators. Later these wealthy emigres sent capital goods such as trucks and electric generators. Eventually, Hong Kong factory owners simply extended this tradition by either helping operating factories to acquire new capital equipment or opening new factories in their hometowns. These charitable early efforts became the forerunners of the Chinese township (or cooperative) factories.

To encourage investment, the central government opened Special Economic Zones (SEZ) directly under central government control. The first SEZs were created in areas adjacent to Hong Kong (Shenzhen); directly across the strait from Taiwan (Xiamen); and near Japan (Dalian). In the SEZs, traditional 'socialist legislation' was voided and bureaucracy was streamlined. Special tax benefits were offered to investors and the Chinese government made exceptional infrastructure investments. Factories built at this time were the early joint-venture and foreign-owned factories. Through their innovative SEZ policy, the Chinese government managed to create little islands of low macro costs in the large still-socialist sea.

Hong Kong investors (and, to a lesser degree, Taiwanese, South Korean and Japanese) very quickly worked out a successful *modus operandi*. For a foreign investor to run a profitable foreign venture, it is not necessary to actually own the factory—particularly if sufficient mutual trust exists. It is only necessary to own the product. Hong Kong and Taiwan investors understood that profits came from two sources: direct-cost advantages and indirect-cost advantages. They also realized that profits from the factory—the result of low direct costs—would be at most 5%-10% of the China factory FOB price. On the other hand, the indirect-cost profit to companies able to offer a risk-free way to capitalize on China's low direct costs would be far greater.

For the Hong Kong and Taiwan investors whose original purpose may have been cultural affinity, the transition from ownership to control was almost invisible. Their initial intention may have been to give their hometown a factory as a gift. Now they would also supply the orders and turn a profit.

Through these joint-venture and township factories, overseas importers also benefitted tremendously. The importer no longer had to contend with the difficulties and high indirect costs of working directly in China.

Sampling, patternmaking facilities, quality control and attaining acceptable minimums were now all in the hands of the Hong Kong or Taiwanese factory who understood the overseas customer's needs and requirements. The importer was able to receive a product close to Hong Kong standards at a much lower cost. Typically, the Hong Kong or Taiwanese investor shared the direct-cost savings with his customer on a 60/40 basis, with 40% going to the customer.

HONG KONG: THE PRESENT

Even before July 1, 1997, when China reestablished sovereignty over Hong Kong, the textile and garment industries of the two countries had already been essentially integrated. It is no longer statistically possible to measure China textile and garment imports separate from Hong Kong. Not only are there considerable listed re-exports of Chinese goods from Hong Kong, there are even greater illegal re-exports as Hong Kong factories use Hong Kong quota to ship China-made goods.[24]

Hong Kong industry is now orientated almost entirely towards marketing, sales, administration and finance. Customers from the world over purchase Chinese-made garments without ever visiting China. But Hong Kong is not depending solely on China. Already, many Hong Kong companies have been expanding away from China to other low direct-cost manufacturing areas—from Saipan and Mauritius to South and Central America and, of course, the rest of Asia. All that remains physically in Hong Kong today of its former woven apparel industry are sampling facilities, very high-quality plants producing small runs, and the remnants of those factories which, having failed to expand offshore, are slowly dying out.

On the other hand, Hong Kong's knit industry has kept a large part of its manufacturing facilities in Hong Kong. Substantial investment in computerized Shimaseiki knitting machines and other advanced equipment has changed production from labor-intensive to capital-intensive, permitting these manufacturers to remain in Hong Kong despite the labor shortage.

Today Hong Kong serves as the management center for a totally offshore industry, with its investment and sourcing tentacles reaching all corners of the globe. Hong Kong offshore garment factories produce garments in all fibers from fabrics purchased all over the world. Most industry professionals, especially those on the technical side, look overseas for employment. Hong Kong's Institute of Textiles and Clothing and Swire School of Design, both part of the Hong Kong Polytechnic University, are training a generation of Hong Kong 'expatriates', who will, while working for Hong Kong companies, probably reside in every country in Asia except Hong Kong.

Hong Kong companies have evolved through two phases and are now entering a third phase which brings them full circle with an added element:

Phase I—1955-76: Reliance on cheap labor and other direct-cost advantages;

Phase II—1976-96: Development of indirect-cost advantages;

Phase III—1997 onwards: Returning to countries with cheap labor and other direct-cost advantages to maximize Hong Kong's own indirect-cost and macro-cost advantages.

THE FUTURE

At the very moment when Hong Kong and China have combined to achieve the greatest level of success, each faces new challenges that they are only beginning to recognize. The future of their combined industry rests in the ability of the Chinese and Hong Kong-Chinese governments to work together with local industry leaders to meet these challenges.

NAFTA and CBI

The spectacular rise of Mexico and the Caribbean nations as major garment exporters to the United States has been far greater than anyone could have anticipated. In the three years from 1994-1996, U.S. garment imports from Mexico tripled from $1.13 billion to $3.63 billion and Mexico is now the largest garment exporter to the United States. The growth rate shows no sign of abating. In the twelve months ending July 1996, garment imports from Mexico to the U.S. increased by 40.9% over the previous year. As already mentioned, most of this growth took place at the expense of China and Hong Kong, where exports shrank by 21.4% and 9.3% respectively between 1995 and 1996. As of 1998, Mexican garment exports to the United States exceeded the combined total of exports from China and Hong Kong. The same growth, albeit from a smaller base, can be seen in U.S. imports from Costa Rica, the Dominican Republic, El Salvador and Honduras.

These changes are entirely the result of macro-cost advantages granted to Mexico as part of NAFTA and the Central American countries as part of the Caribbean Basin Initiative (CBI). Most Mexican garments are no longer under quota and enter the United States duty-free. Garments exported under Section 807 from the CBI countries have a special quota, and duty is paid only on the value of additional processing work. In the short run, these advantages have led to a serious reduction in China exports to the United States.

Trade Disputes

As already discussed at length in an earlier section, trade disputes between the United States and China and the United States and Hong Kong concerning longstanding illegal transshipments of Chinese-made garments through Hong Kong have disrupted normal export activity. The disputes have resulted in severe penalties imposed by the U.S.

266

government and, even more damaging, a loss of confidence among U.S. importers who now fear overdependence on China and who have moved at least part of their production elsewhere. In the short run, the Hong Kong government has acted to reduce the illegal transshipments by stricter enforcement.

However, these crackdowns have seriously affected operations in both China and Hong Kong. Hong Kong has the largest U.S. quota in the world. As long as Hong Kong turned a blind eye to illegal transshipments, this quota was available to Chinese-based factories producing and exporting to the United.States. Once U.S. government pressure forced the Hong Kong government to stop the illegal transshipments, this enormous quota was suddenly no longer available to the Chinese factories and China quota premiums skyrocketed. Not only has demand for Hong Kong/Chinese garments been reduced by competition from Mexico and the Caribbean countries, many Chinese factories holding U.S. orders but no quota, or unwilling to pay excessive quota premiums, could not ship.

The Hong Kong government alone has the power to break this stalemate. The American government cares only that illegal transshipments do not recur. For political reasons, the Chinese government will not interfere in what it perceives to be Hong Kong's internal affairs. Unfortunately, the Hong Kong government appears to be totally controlled by powerful local quota holders who will veto any solution that does not leave the Hong Kong quota firmly in their hands. Various schemes have been proposed, including importing tens of thousands of Chinese sewers into Hong Kong and building an enormous industrial park-cum-concentration camp in Hong Kong's northern New Territory where Chinese workers can be segregated while they produce 'Made-in-Hong Kong' garments. This scheme is totally impractical. In fact, the consensus among Hong Kong quota holders is that if they hold on long enough, the problem will simply disappear as they return to business as usual—the illegal transshipment of garments.

As long as the Hong Kong government remains unwilling to deal with the situation on a long-term basis, they are simply expediting the movement of business away from Hong Kong towards Latin America.

Restructuring China's Industry

The most crucial challenge facing not only the Chinese garment industry but its entire economy is the urgent need to restructure and reorganize China's factory base. China industry now exists in three layers:

- State Factories: This is by far the largest sector of the Chinese economy, employing 70% of total industrial workers. However, state companies account for less than 10% of textile and garment exports. Unfortunately, even by Chinese estimates, half of its state companies lose money each year. A more accurate estimate is that over half of Chinese state companies are bankrupt in the Western sense of the term. These companies stay alive only through massive loans from state banks. The Chinese government has taken steps to modernize and rationalize the state sector but is unable to enact more drastic measures because such measures would result in large masses of unemployed workers and probable social upheaval.

- Township (cooperative) factories: These have grown tremendously in the past twenty years and are often highly profitable. Such factories employ approximately 20% of the industrial workforce but account for 48% of garment exports. Many factories are integrated, encompassing all areas of the textile and garment industries with the exception of spinning, which remains state-controlled due to the virtual government monopoly on raw materials. Some township textile mills are even moving ahead of their state-owned counterparts who previously controlled all textile activities. In recent years, textile and finishing mills have initiated strategic relationships with European mills, who often supply technical expertise to upgrade quality and production in exchange for exclusive selling rights to the mill's output. While some European associates have supplied capital, in many cases the Chinese have paid for the investment themselves.

- Joint Ventures: Despite the rapid increase in township factories, wholly or partly foreign-owned factories still dominate China's garment export market. Today, Hong Kong and Taiwan-owned factories account for 42% of all Chinese garment exports.

China's industrial sector faces an inherently unstable situation. The state industries are for the most part bankrupt yet they remain the sector's dominant employers. If they go under, the result will be massive urban unemployment and possible political instability. As most of the money lent them by state banks is uncollectible debt, these dinosaurs are a tremendous drain on the economy. Strained by sustained stagflation, China's overall economy is fast approaching the point where further loans will simply not be possible. Even now, government cannot open the banking sector to foreign competition because local banks, awash with bad loans, cannot compete. Clearly, this problem must be resolved. Within China, two major schools of thought exist:

- The technocrats believe that as the township and joint-venture factories continue to expand, they will eventually employ sufficient numbers of workers so that the collapse of the state sector will not lead to large-scale unemployment and social unrest. Their solution is to encourage the growth of these sectors and close the ailing state factories.

- The cadres believe that the very existence of township and joint-venture factories poses a threat to the economic, social and political system of the country. Their solution is to loan further sums to the state factories to allow them to modernize, expand and take over the role of the joint-venture and township factories. They look to the South Korean model where giant semi-state conglomerates dominate the industrial sector. Unfortunately, as recent events have shown, the Korean chaebol are unstable for the very reasons that Chinese state factories are unstable—their political influence allows them to implement irrational policies and swamp the national banking system with bad loans.

Shanghai vs. Hong Kong

One last challenge to China's restructuring of its textile and apparel industries is to address the underlying competition between Hong Kong and Shanghai over where China's industries should be centered.

It is impossible to overstate the size of Hong Kong's economy compared to any city in China. Stable government, the rule of law, good infrastructure and an amazingly hardworking population have combined to give Hong Kong one of the highest per capita GDPs in the world. For the past 50 years Hong Kong has powered ahead while Shanghai was pumped as a milk cow by the Beijing-based central Chinese government. However, Shanghai's fortunes are clearly changing.

In recent years, from President Jiang Zemin to Premier Zhu Rongji, Shanghainese people have literally taken over the Chinese government. The Shanghai diaspora has returned seriously intent on rebuilding their birthplace into Asia's premier city. The older generation of influential Shanghainese can still remember when Shanghai was China's leading commercial city while Hong Kong was important only in the south—and they plan to reestablish that position.

As far as the textile and garment industries are concerned, Shanghai is definitely gaining the upper hand. Many Hong Kong companies still believe they are living in 1976 when Hong Kong alone had the capital, the skilled workers and managers, and all the customers. They recall a time when customers worked in Hong Kong just to avoid going to China. They fail to see that time has been and gone. Today, Shanghai, with its four separate textile and garment tertiary institutes, is training skilled technicians and managers. Shanghai managers practice their English while Hong Kong students are being forced into mother-tongue education, back to Cantonese. Shanghai also has the capital and they are about to get the customers. No longer do garment importers cling to Hong Kong's swank Peninsula and Regent Hotels. Today Shanghai has hotels every bit as glitzy as anything in Hong Kong.

Without a major initiative on the part of the Hong Kong government and its industry, Hong Kong will return to its traditional position as a major city for southern China, a place where the major Shanghai companies have branch offices.

CONCLUSIONS

Despite the serious problems listed above, there can be no doubt that Hong Kong/China will retain its preeminent position as the most competitive garment-exporting country outside NAFTA and the EU. Here

269

are some final comments on how garment industry costs will be affected there in the short to mid-term future.

Direct Costs

China is the most populous country in the world with the second largest land mass. It has an inexhaustible supply of labor and unlimited area in which to place it. Wage rates may be high by Third World standards but are sufficiently low and China will continue to be considered a cheap-labor area. China is now upgrading its industrial plant. There exists some duplication because of the competition between state and township factories, a problem that will be addressed only when the government is sufficiently secure to deal with the bankrupt state sector.

Indirect Costs

Hong Kong and Shanghai with their expertise and well-established professional operations are able to supply all the facilities required to benefit from indirect-cost advantages. In the long run, it makes little difference whether Shanghai overtakes Hong Kong as the technological center of China, or if Hong Kong undergoes an industrial renaissance—the combined industry can only benefit from the competition.

Macro Costs

At the present time, the Chinese government is doing its utmost to reduce macro costs. Customs clearance times are being shortened. Considerable investments have been made in electricity and other infrastructure projects. The transportation network, particularly with regard to long-distance road and rail, is being modernized. More than any developing country in Asia, China has tried to present itself as a place where real business can be done. Problems remain, particularly with corruption. However, the government is making real strides towards reducing corruption, and with the exception of quota allocations, the garment industry remains relatively clean.

Chapter 16
Indonesia

At best, Indonesia's future role in the international garment industry will be as a marginal producer. At worst, Indonesia's garment industry has no future at all. This was true even before December 1997 when the entire Indonesian economy collapsed, the Indonesian stock market fell by over 60%, and the Indonesian currency fell by 70%.

In fact, even before the present crisis, Indonesia's garment industry faced almost insurmountable difficulties. In a sense, the future of Indonesia's garment industry is the same future facing almost all second and third-generation garment exporting countries outside the NAFTA and EU blocs.

Indonesia's past performance as a garment exporter gave little hint of its uncertain future. Over the last decade, Indonesia had become a major player in the international textile and garment stage, and in 1994 ranked fourteenth in the world as a garment-and-textile exporting country. At the same time, textiles and garments became the country's largest industrial export sector. In 1995, textile/garment-export volumes exceeded $6 billion and were growing at the rate of 7.15% per annum.[25] In the absence of serious economic, social or political dislocation, we could reasonably have assumed that the industry would continue to grow and prosper. All fundamentals appeared positive.

- There was every indication that domestic demand for garments would continue to increase. For almost a decade, there had been a continuous and marked increase not only in GDP, but in per capita GDP as well. From 1993 to 1995, GDP increased from Rp330 billion to Rp445 billion while per capita GDP rose from Rp1,758,000 to Rp2,299,000 ($824 to $1023).[26]

- Exports, where limited by quota, increased substantially, particularly in the five years up to 1997 due mainly to Indonesia's ability to negotiate substantial annual increases in quota allocations. This contrasted with quota for other major exporters which remained substantially the same, or in some cases was even scaled back.[27]

- The industry had been able to operate relatively freely from outside competition. This closed competitive environment was reflected in both domestic and export sales.

- The Indonesian domestic apparel market was (and for that matter, still is) almost completely closed to imports. Duty rates reach 40%, with most categories levied at between 30%-40%. However, even these relatively high rates of duty would not account for the almost complete absence of imported garments in the local retail market. Certainly the quality of locally produced garments is mediocre at best and prices are often higher than comparable merchandise sold in developed countries. The reason for the local industry's monopoly is that hidden restrictions—for example, unreasonable customs delays or difficulties in obtaining proper import documentation—prevent almost all imported garments from entering the country. In this closed-market environment, local manufacturers are able to sell garments at exorbitant prices, with the knowledge that more competitively priced goods are simply unavailable to the consumer.

- In the export market, quotas were beneficial to the Indonesian industry. Instead of limiting exports, quota became a license ensuring continuous orders. Customers bought from Indonesian factories because they could no longer buy from China—the country of choice—once Chinese quota had been exhausted. Each disruption set off by Sino-American trade disputes brought increased demand for Indonesian production.

However, this trend could not continue. Even before the economic crisis of late 1997, Indonesia began to encounter the same difficulties—falling sales of garments in developed countries and the revival of the Western European garment industry—which has been reducing demand for Chinese-made garments. The growth of export-garment industries in cheap-labor countries such as Bangladesh, El Salvador, Haiti, Vietnam and many African nations, along with the rise of the exclusionary trading blocs, also curbed Indonesia's export expansion.

Increasing trade liberalization and impending tariff reductions likewise dim Indonesia's horizons. The Pacific Rim countries have agreed to progressively reduce tariffs over the next decade. Tariffs will be phased out between 2004 and 2010, with underdeveloped countries following in 2020. Although several countries in the region have recently expressed reservations, there is every expectation that this undertaking will be met.

After decades of import limitations and closed competition, the textile and garment industries will be faced by extreme challenges. Not only will increased competition and decreased demand continue to diminish Indonesia's export markets, reduced tariffs will shrink Indonesia's share of its own domestic market. A generation of Indonesian textile and garment manufacturers has been shielded from real competition. Once APEC trade liberalization goes into effect, Indonesian industry will be forced to compete in their own market against the most efficient producers in the world. Not only will garment manufacturers be seriously affected, many under-financed and ill-prepared Indonesian yarn and greige goods suppliers will also be out of business.

While these same challenges face many garment-exporting countries, they will impact far more on Indonesia than China simply because the fundamental costs of working in Indonesia are so high as to make the entire industry uncompetitive.

DIRECT COSTS

On the surface, Indonesia enjoys one of the lowest direct-cost structures in Asia, due primarily to its very low labor rate. Even before the rupiah collapse, an Indonesian sewer was paid about $0.16 an hour, and many predicted that exports of Indonesian garments would show tremendous increases directly as a result of falling wages in dollar terms. In fact, few buyers shifted production to capitalize on lower labor rates, simply because the actual labor portion of Indonesian production was already so low that any savings would have been negligible. Coupled with the extreme volatility of Indonesia's political and economic conditions at the time, most buyers instead adopted a wait-and-see attitude.

Furthermore, apart from wages, direct costs in Indonesia are far from competitive. High tariffs together with non-tariff barriers effectively keep imported textiles out of the country. Local weavers take advantage of these limitations to keep prices high. For example, Indonesian denim is of lower quality but more expensive than Chinese denim. Similarly, locally available trims are expensive by international standards and of generally indifferent quality.

INDIRECT COSTS

Indonesia has some of the highest indirect-cost structures in Asia and costs continue to rise relative to its Asian competitors. Whatever facility you are looking for, chances are it is unavailable in Indonesia.

- Patternmaking, grading and other specialized skills are either nonexistent or substandard.

- Samplemaking facilities are poor. If a factory cannot provide even a sample to the customer's standard, what possibility is there that stock production will be acceptable?

- Quality control is generally hit-or-miss. Only a minority of factories have good QC departments, and few factory managers have any idea if the production coming out of their machines will meet customers' standards. Buyers complain that in order to save a few pennies off CMT prices, factories will substitute poor quality trims for previously specified items.

- Quality assurance is almost unknown. Factories make little effort to analyze the garment to determine possible difficulties prior to beginning production.

- Most factories lack the ability to source trim and depend on the buyer or his agent. As a result, most factories work on a CM basis similar to operations in the least-developed garment-exporting countries of Burma, Haiti and the nations of Central Africa.

- Minimums remain high. Factories are inflexible about accepting small orders.

- Changes in assortment inevitably result in shipment delays.

- Fast delivery is very difficult even when the production runs smoothly.

- Worker skills are minimal and few factories make any effort to increase skill levels to enable production of higher quality garments.

- Working conditions are seriously below standards acceptable to importers of high-profile branded merchandise. Each time they place an order in Indonesia, importers risk associating their brand with child labor, exploitation of women or unacceptable sanitary conditions in factories.

The Indonesian garment industry is caught in a no-win situation. Unless the industry raises its quality standards and makes an effort to provide the facilities required to lower indirect costs, it cannot work with importers of better quality merchandise. At the same time, any effort to develop these facilities will raise direct costs to the point where factories will no longer be able to work with their present mass-market customers.

The Indonesian export-garment industry is further trapped because it is largely controlled by South Korean and Taiwanese middlemen and mass-market importers whose only interest is to pay the lowest CMT prices. Few factories have any direct relationship with their final customers. Furthermore, given the almost total lack of facilities and the resulting high indirect costs, only the present customers have the necessary means to work reasonably effectively in Indonesia.

Any attempted solution which depends solely on limiting direct costs and fails to address Indonesia's high indirect costs will do little to assist the industry. In the end, importers and middlemen looking for cheap labor can always go elsewhere—there is always a country poorer and less developed where workers are paid even lower wages. Because the vast majority of Indonesia's garment producers rely on low wages to remain competitive, they simply will not survive the coming challenges.

MACRO COSTS

You can sum up the problems of the Indonesian garment industry in two words—nothing works. Since 1997, this situation has only deteriorated, especially in regards to securing letters of credit on international banks. High macro costs are the single most critical problem facing the Indonesian garment industry. Unfortunately, unlike indirect-cost problems, the industry can do nothing to bring about meaningful change. All solutions are in the hands of the Indonesian government whose present leadership appears unable and unwilling to effect the necessary changes. As a result, Indonesia is currently a very expensive place to do business.

To compete effectively in the global economy, Indonesia must adhere to international standards. After the export-garment industry's impressive gains since the 1980s, a carefully outlined and administered medium-term plan to raise industry standards overall was necessary to consolidate the country's position. Instead, the government is pursuing high-tech pipedreams, allocating precious funds for expensive and dubious projects including an attempt to develop a national car (which, in fact, was made in South Korea) and a commercial jet industry ostensibly designed to compete with Western producers. These crazy schemes, along with the country's political and economic turmoil, have left Indonesia with little resources to address its serious macro-cost problems, including:

- Telecommunications: Indonesia's telephone system is poor even by Third World standards. The system seldom works efficiently and the costs are exorbitant.

- Transportation and Logistics: As an island archipelago, Indonesia faces special problems and costs. If the government wants to develop the country, it must create a transportation system to move materials quickly. Instead, Indonesian government policies and procedures exacerbate existing difficulties with customs regulations and bureaucratic procedures tailored to increase under-the-table payments, further slowing goods flow.

- Corruption: Working in Indonesia is synonymous with constant palm greasing. If buyers aren't willing to pay at every step, nothing gets done.

- Education: Following reasonable gains in the 1970s to ensure primary school level education, the Indonesian government has simply failed to sustain efforts in this responsibility. Companies can train workers but they cannot provide in-house tertiary education. The garment industry can no longer survive relying on technicians and managers whose only education is on-the-job experience.

The Indonesian garment industry faces a bleak future. It has nothing to offer but quota and cheap labor. In an increasingly competitive world, this will simply not be enough.

Epilogue:
Some Final Words

In December 1999, foreign ministers, finance ministers and other specialist bureaucrats of the 136 member nations of the World Trade Organization (WTO) met in conference halls in Seattle, Washington, to lay out the ground plan for the next phase of the globalization of world trade. At the same time a loose coalition of representatives from various non-governmental organizations (NGOs) assembled outside those same halls.

Inside, the national delegations struggled to reach an agenda for an impossible consensus: each country wanted to retain their own export subsidies and import barriers while simultaneously reducing export subsidies and import barriers of every other country. Outside, the demonstrators, without the benefit of a formal agenda, had already reached a consensus: they managed to shut down the WTO meeting.

As the bewildered foreign ministers, finance ministers and other specialist bureaucrats returned home, their common lament was that those well-meaning but naive demonstrators simply did not understand the mechanisms and objectives of trade globalization. These so-called educated and informed professionals, living in a state of denial, failed to recognize even the remotest possibility that the demonstrators might actually understand more about globalization than the WTO delegates themselves.

What does all this have to do with FVCA? Simply this:

Both the WTO delegates and a Los Angeles importer sourcing T-shirt blanks from the Ivory Coast have yet to understand that macro costs and indirect costs are far more important than cheap labor. The same selective blindness that made the LA importer schlep his samples and specs to the ends of the earth to find cheap labor paralyzed the WTO delegates whose understanding of world trade remains limited to traditional standards of measuring costs.

Far from being naive, the NGO demonstrators believe that the world already lives in a global society. They understood better than the delegates that globalization is not limited to commercial considerations alone. Globalization is a two-faced beast, one face representing commercial issues and the other equally, if not more important, social ones. Both faces being attached to the same body must inevitably be addressed together.

True globalization is a prerequisite to solving many of the challenges facing the world in the new century. Just as the air we breathe and water we drink are not limited by national boundaries, the problems of pollution, human rights, child labor, malnutrition, disease, and even war, know no borders. The only way to solve the world's problems is at a supranational level. The NGOs outside the Seattle meeting halls were demonstrating for more, not less globalization.

It is painfully evident that globalization's commercial face is often nothing more than a cosmetically retouched mask over an old nemesis: the continuing exploitation of Third World labor forces. Corruption, wages far below local legal minimums, the absence of workers' rights, the use of Third World countries as rubbish heaps for developed world waste, factories without even basic anti-pollution safeguards, and daily human rights violations are conditions endemic to factories in cheap-labor countries. Many consumers will no longer tolerate this situation.

These conditions all raise macro costs yet those involved—the WTO delegates and the transnational importers and exporters behind them-do not understand this fact.

The failure to increase worker skills, to provide better communications and sold infrastructure permanently relegates most Third World suppliers to perpetual 0-service producers whose only asset is cheap labor.

These failures all raise indirect costs and those involved also do not understand this fact.

Everyone—government bureaucrats, suppliers and importers alike—agrees that the goal of successful globalization is to provide better products for world consumption at lower cost. These same people agree that the WTO's purpose is to serve as a framework allowing importing and exporting nations to achieve this goal. Yet how can these objectives be reached when those involved fail to recognize the basic dollars-and-cents reality: that macro and indirect costs weigh far more than cheap labor?

As the demonstrations clearly underscored, if the WTO cannot deal with globalization in all its aspects, including its social macro and indirect-cost aspects, then it is not entitled to a mandate to deal with globalization at all. Until the WTO delegates and the commercial forces behind them understand what is required to actually produce at the lowest cost, they will not grasp the true requirements for a global economy.

Just as Herbie the Mouth, Cousin Phil, Wendell Wasp and Louis the Lip all bankrupted their companies, so too will the foreign ministers, finance ministers and bureaucrats bankrupt the WTO.

DAVID BIRNBAUM
Hong Kong (SAR) - Fiesole (Fi)
March 2000

NOTES

1. See The Economist, July 26, 1997, "Survey Indonesia," p.13.
2. 1997 Index of Economic Freedom, Kim R. Holmes, Bryan T. Johnson, Melanie Kirkpatrick, The Heritage Foundation, and Dow Jones & Co. Inc.
3. See The Economist, February 22, 1997, "India's Economic Survey," pp. 15-19.
4. See The Economist, October 3, 1998, pp. 135-136.
5. See International Herald Tribune, March 3, 1997, p.13.
6. See South China Morning Post, February 28, 1997.
7. Television interview with Mr. Martin Lee, QC, RTHK News Line, March 2, 1997.
8. As of February 18, 1997, China quota premium (for shipment to the U.S.) for T-shirts was $2.25 per piece and for cotton sweaters $4.33 per piece.
9. Under the terms of the NAFTA treaty, quota restrictions for T-shirts Cat. 338/339 are not scheduled to be lifted until 2001.
10. NAFTA schedule of duty and quota elimination

QUOTA PHASE OUT SCHEDULE		
CATEGORY	DESCRIPTION	DATE
218	Yarn-dyed fabric	1994
219	Cotton duck fabric	2001
300/301/607	Yarns	1994
313	Cotton sheeting fabric	2001
314	Cotton poplin and broadcloth	2001
315	Cotton printcloth	2001
317	Cotton twill	2001
326	Cotton sateen	1994
334/634	Jackets and coats (M&B)	1994
	Knit shirts	2001
336/636	Dresses	1994
340/640	Woven shirts (M)	2001
	Trousers	2001
341/641	Woven blouses (W&G)	1994
342/642	Skirts	1994
351/651	Nightwear	1994
352/652	Underwear	1994
359/659-C	Coveralls and overalls	1994
363	Cotton terry towels	1994
410	Wool fabric	2004
433	Suit-type coats wool (M&B)	2004
435	Wool jackets and coats (W&G)	1994
443	Suits MMF (M&B)	2004
611	Artificial fiber fabric	2004
604/607	Yarns MMF	1994
633	Suit-type coats MMF (M&B)	1994
635	Coats and jackets MMF (W&G)	1994
643	Suits wool (M&B)	1994
669-B	Polypropylene bags	1994
670	Handbags, flatgoods and luggage	1994

TARIFF ELIMINATION SCHEDULE	
DESCRIPTION	DATE
Apparel made with U.S. cut and formed fabric	1994
Silk apparel	1994
Underpants (M&W)	1994
Slips	1994
T-shirts	1994
Ski suits	1994
Swimwear	1994
Down apparel	1994
Handloomed and folklore products	1994
Bib and brace overalls	1994
Women's cotton blouses	1994
Brassieres	1994
Jogging Suits MMF	1994
Overalls, jumpsuits, sunsuits, playsuits, tracksuits MMF	1994
Most other apparel products other than wool	2000
Selected wool apparel	2000

11. Source U.S. Census Bureau.

12. The marker is a long, soft paper layout of the garment patterns in different sizes. The width of the paper is the width of the fabric. The length is the total fabric required to cut the number of garments in the marker, exclusive of damages and wasted fabric.

13. The pattern would lay out as follows: two fronts, one back, two sleeves, collar and facings.

14. *BIRNBAUM'S Directory of Garment Factories and Agents, Hong Kong & Southern China 1994-1995*, Third Horizon Press, 1994.

15. *South China Morning Post*, March 24, 1998, p. 19.

Notes

16. Wage comparisons as of 1995

COUNTRY	HOURLY WAGES	U.S.=100	BANGLA DESH=100	S. KOREA=100
Argentina	$ 4.60	38	3,833	60
Australia	$13.91	113	11,592	182
Austria	$15.65	128	13,042	205
Bangladesh	$ 0.12	1	100	2
Bel/Lux	$25.00	204	20,833	327
Brazil	$ 3.84	31	3,200	50
Burma	$ 0.12	1	100	2
Canada	$13.92	114	11,600	182
China (SEZ)	$ 0.48	39	4,030	63
China (Other)	$ 0.14	1	117	2
Colombia	$ 2.14	17	1,783	28
Denmark	$25.65	209	21,375	335
Egypt	$ 0.84	7	700	11
France	$16.45	134	13,708	215
Germany	$21.94	179	18,283	287
Greece	$ 8.92	73	7,433	117
Hong Kong	$ 4.90	40	4,083	64
Hungary	$ 3.18	26	2,650	42
India	$ 0.20	2	167	3
Indonesia	$ 0.18	1	150	2
Israel	$ 7.34	60	6,117	96
Italy	$16.65	136	13,875	218
Japan	$24.31	198	20,258	318
Korea, S.	$ 7.65	62	6,375	100
Mexico	$ 0.75	6	625	10
Pakistan	$ 0.16	1	133	2
Philippines	$ 0.66	5	550	9
Sri Lanka	$ 0.24	20	2,000	31
Taiwan	$ 6.38	52	5,317	83
Thailand	$ 0.72	6	600	9
U.K.	$11.71	96	9,758	153
U.S.	$12.26	100	10,217	160
Vietnam	$ 0.12	2	167	3

17. Comparative value of trained technician to semi-skilled worker

Comparative value of trained technician to semi-skilled worker broken down country.						
Country	Local Sewer/ hr Wage*	Local Sewer Annual Wages	Local Patternmaker Annual Wages	Savings Local vs. U.S. Pattern-maker**	No. Local Sewers per Savings Local vs. U.S. Patternmaker	No. Sewers wages could be increased by 50% per Savings Local vs. U.S. Patternmaker
Korea, S.	$7.65	$19,094	$36,384	$38,616	2.02	4
Taiwan	$6.38	$15,924	$30,344	$44,656	2.80	6
Hong Kong	$4.90	$12,230	$23,305	$51,695	4.23	8
Thailand	$0.72	$ 2,246	$ 4,280	$70,720	31.48	63
Philippines	$0.68	$ 2,122	$ 4,043	$70,957	33.45	67
China SEZ	$0.48	$ 1,498	$ 2,854	$72,146	48.17	96
Sri Lanka	$0.24	$ 749	$ 1,427	$73,573	98.25	197
India	$0.20	$ 624	$ 1,189	$73,811	118.29	237
Indonesia***	$0.18	$ 562	$ 1,070	$73,930	131.64	263
Pakistan	$0.16	$ 499	$ 951	$74,049	148.33	297
China not SEZ	$0.14	$ 437	$ 832	$74,168	169.80	340
Vietnam	$0.12	$ 374	$ 713	$74,287	198.42	397
Burma	$0.12	$ 374	$ 713	$74,287	198.42	397
Bangladesh	$0.12	$ 374	$ 713	$74,287	198.42	397

* HK, S. Korea and Taiwan all work 8-hour days. Others based on 10-hour days.
** Assume $75,000 annual salary for U.S. Patternmaker.   *** Prior to 1997 collapse

18. Top 10 Third World Countries with Garments and Textiles as Percentage of Total Exports (1995)

COUNTRY	TEXTILES		GARMENTS		TOTAL	
	1990	1995	1990	1995	1990	1995
Bangladesh	18.3%	13.6%	35.0%	54.8%	53.3%	68.4%
China	11.6%	9.4%	15.6%	16.2%	27.1%	25.6%
Egypt	21.4%	17.9%	5.6%	6.7%	26.0%	24.6%
India	12.1%	15.3%	14.1%	14.8%	26.2%	30.1%
Mauritius	N/A	N/A	51.9%	55.6%	51.9%	55.6%
Pakistan	47.6%	53.3%	18.1%	20.2%	65.7%	73.5%
Sri Lanka	1.3%	4.1%	32.2%	46.0%	33.5%	50.1%
Thailand	4.0%	3.6%	12.2%	8.2%	16.2%	11.8%
Tunisia	3.2%	3.0%	31.9%	42.4%	35.1%	45.4%
Turkey	11.1%	11.7%	25.7%	28.3%	36.8%	40.0%

WTO Annual Report 1996

Notes

19. World Trade Organization Annual Report Volume II, p. 113.

20. Top 10 Garment Exporters as of 1995

RANK	COUNTRY	VALUE	HOURLY WAGE*	% CHANGE 1990-1995	% CHANGE 1995
1	China	$24.1bn	$ 0.58	20%	1%
2	Hong Kong	$21.3	$ 4.90	7%	-1%
3	Italy	$14.0	$16.65	3%	12%
4	Germany	$ 7.38	$21.94	-1%	11%
5	U.S.	$ 6.65	$12.26	21%	18%
6	Turkey	$ 6.12	$ 2.02	13%	34%
7	France	$ 5.62	$16.45	4%	13%
8	S. Korea	$ 4.96	$ 5.65	-9%	-12%
9	U.K.	$ 4.65	$11.71	9%	13%
10	Thailand	$ 4.62	$ 1.56	10%	2%
WTO Annual Report 1996. * Wage records provided by Textile Intelligence Ltd.					

Top 10 Textile Exporters as of 1995

RANK	COUNTRY	VALUE	HOURLY WAGE*	% CHANGE 1990-1995	% CHANGE 1995
1	Germany	$14.2bn	$21.94	0%	12%
2	China	$13.92	$ 0.58	14%	18%
3	Hong Kong	$13.81	$ 4.90	11%	10%
4	Italy	$12.67	$16.65	6%	17%
5	S. Korea	$12.31	$ 4.96	15%	15%
6	Taiwan	$11.91	$ 6.38	14%	16%
7	Belgium/Lux	$ 7.76	$25.00	4%	14%
8	France	$ 7.47	$16.45	4%	20%
9	U.S.	$ 7.37	$12.26	8%	12%
10	Japan	$ 7.18	$24.31	4%	6%
WTO Annual Report 1996. * Wage records provided by Textile Intelligence Ltd.					

21. EU Textile and Garment Foreign Trade with World 1993-1995

	EXP	IMP	EXP	IMP	EXP	IMP	EXP	IMP	EXP	IMP	EXP	IMP
	World		Intra EU		N. America		C/E Europe		Asia		Africa	
TEXTILES (in US$ billions)												
93	45.98	43.53	29.99	29.99	2.31	1.36	3.39	0.97	2.77	6.53	2.59	0.62
94	51.38	48.82	33.22	33.22	2.57	1.45	4.32	1.4	3.39	7.11	2.72	0.88
95	61.18	57.48	39.36	39.36	2.61	1.75	5.66	1.84	4.21	8.13	3.27	0.95
PERCENT CHANGE												
94	11.7	12.2	10.8		.11.3	6.6	27.4	44.3	22.4	8.9	5.0	41.9
95	19.1	17.7	18.5		1.6	20.7	31.0	31.4	24.2	14.3	20.2	8.0
MARKET SHARE (%)												
93	100	100	65.2	68.9	5.0	3.1	7.4	2.2	6.0	15.0	5.6	1.4
94	100	100	64.7	68.0	5.0	3.0	8.4	2.9	6.6	14.6	5.3	1.8
95	100	100	64.3	68.5	4.3	3.0	9.3	3.2	6.9	14.1	5.3	1.7
GARMENTS (in US$ billions)												
93	39.02	65.19	28.54	28.54	1.79	0.78	1.34	4.54	2.29	19.88	0.63	4.29
94	41.99	68.33	29.63	29.63	1.98	0.78	1.66	5.66	3.24	20.56	0.67	4.72
95	47.8	76.54	33.21	33.21	2.26	0.92	2.1	6.84	3.97	21.81	0.85	5.62
PERCENT CHANGE												
94	7.6	4.8	3.8		10.6	0.0	23.9	24.4	41.5	3.4	6.3	10.0
95	13.8	12.0	12.1		14.1	17.9	26.5	21.1	22.5	6.1	26.9	19.1
MARKET SHARE (%)												
93	100	100	73.1	43.8	4.6	1.2	3.4	7.0	5.9	30.5	1.6	6.6
94	100	100	70.6	43.4	4.7	1.1	4.0	8.3	7.7	30.1	1.6	6.9
95	100	100	69.5	43.4	4.7	1.2	4.4	8.9	8.3	28.5	1.8	7.3
BALANCE OF TRADE (in US$ billions) TEXTILES AND GARMENTS												
93	-23.72		0		1.96		-0.78		-21.4		-1.69	
94	-23.78	0.3%	0		2.32	18.4%	-1.07	37.2%	-21.0	-1.5%	-2.21	30.8%
95	-25.04	5.3%	0		2.20	-5.2%	-0.92	-14.0	-21.8	3.4%	-2.45	10.9%

WTO Annual Report 1995 and 1996

22. Comparison of Textile and Garment Imports into EU from Preferred Exporters and Asia, 1992-1995

Figures in US$ billions

	Total World Imports	E. Eur/ CIS	Africa	Turkey	Total	% Change	Market Share, %	Asia	Market Share, %
TEXTILES									
1992	47.10	0.84	0.65	0.56	2.05		4.35		
1993	43.13	0.97	0.61	0.66	2.26	10.24	5.24	6.53	15.14
1994	48.82	1.40	0.87	0.88	3.15	39.38	6.45	7.11	14.56
1995	57.48	1.84	0.95	0.95	3.74	18.73	6.51	8.13	14.14
GARMENTS									
1992	63.63	3.55	4.29	2.81	10.65		16.74		
1993	65.19	4.54	4.29	2.94	11.77	10.50	18.06	19.98	30.65
1994	68.33	5.65	4.72	3.56	13.93	18.33	20.39	20.56	30.09
1995	76.54	6.84	5.62	3.74	16.20	16.31	21.17	21.81	28.49

WTO Annual Report 1995 and 1996

23. Examples of Tariff Advantages from EU to Eastern Europe, Turkey and N. Africa

EU Tariff Category	Description	EU Base Rate	Preferred Exporters Rate
3921.11.00	Of polymers of styrene	12.5%	6.5%
3921.12.00	Of polymers of vinyl chloride	12.5%	6.5%
3921.13.00	Of polyurethanes	8.4%	6.5%
3921.14.00	Of regenerated cellulose	8.4%	6.5%
3921.19.10	Of epoxide resins	12.5%	6.5%
3921.90.20	Of epoxide resins	8.0%	6.5%
3921.90.30	Of phenolic resins	8.0%	6.5%
4202.19.91	Executive cases, briefcases, school satchels ...	5.1%	3.7%
4202.21.00	With Outer surface of Leather	5.1%	3.0%
4202.22.10	Of Plastic Sheeting	12.0%	9.7%
4202.22.90	Of Other Textile Material	5.1%	3.7%
4202.29.00	Other	5.1%	3.7%

24. Although it is not possible to accurately determine the extent of illegal transshipments from Hong Kong, in 1993 THL surveyed and visited 6000 Hong Kong garment companies. At that time we estimated that local factories retain sewing machinery with capacity to produce less than 30% of annual Hong Kong garment 'production'. See *BIRNBAUM's Directory of Garment Factories and Agents, Hong Kong & Southern China 1994-1995*, Third Horizon Press, 1994.

25. Indonesian Industrial Exports as of 1995 (excluding petroleum)

Rank	Industry	US$ m	+/-1994	Pct Total
1	Garments and Textiles	6,045	7.15%	20.61
2	Wood Processed	5,502	(2.31%)	18.76
3	Electronics	2,523	28.17%	8.6
4	Rubber	2,192	57.15%	7.47
5	Steel, Machinery, Automotive	1,765	29.07%	6.02
6	Vegetable Oils	1,548	3.87%	5.28
7	Pulp & Paper	1,450	98.02%	4.95
8	Leather, Leather goods (including footwear)	1,338	(37.89%)	4.56
9	Food & Beverage	765	2.06%	2.61
10	Non-ferrous metal	645	52.03%	2.20
Top 10	Total	23,744	10.29%	81.06
All Industries	Total	29,328	14.11%	100.00

26. Indonesian National Income Growth 1993-95

Item	1993	1994	1995
GDP (Rp. billions)	330	379	445
GDP pct growth		7.48%	8.07%
GNP (Rp. billions)	317	365	426
GNP pct growth		7.65%	7.27%
GDP per capita (Rp. thousands)	1,758	1,989	2,299
GNP per capita (Rp. thousands)	1,691	1,914	2,198
GDP per capita (USD)	824	920	1,023
GNP per capita (USD)	810	886	978
Population (thousands)	187,589	190,676	193,750

27. Changes in U.S. quota allocations to Indonesia for major categories 1991-1995

CAT	UNIT	1995	1991	CHANGE	PCT	ANNUAL PCT
313	SQM	13616722	8863000	4753722	53.64%	11.25%
314	SQM	47546185	37624000	9922185	26.37%	6.03%
315	SQM	21604102	18768000	2836102	15.11%	3.60%
317/617/326	SQM	20866447	16728000	4138447	24.74%	5.60%
338/339*	DOZ	995657	751000	244657	32.58%	7.30%
340/360	DOZ	1167789	514000	653789	127.20%	22.50%
347/348*	DOZ	1348796	1041000	307796	29.57%	6.66%
613/14/15	SQM	19794028	15906000	3888028	24.44%	5.63%
638/639	SQM	1367464	959000	408464	42.59%	9.30%
625/6/7/8/9	SQM	22154954	17563000	4591954	26.15%	6.00%
641	DOZ	1780531	1579000	201531	12.76%	3.05%
647/648*	DOZ	2673395	2086100	587295	28.15%	6.40%

* Includes regular as well as "H" categories

28. *World Trade Organization Annual Report 1996*, Volume II, P. 111.

INDEX